Living Together

*Tim & Rosemary   New Year's Day 2005
I'm gratitude for our journey together ~ Terry & A.J.*

Living Together
in the Church

Including Our Differences

Greig Dunn & Chris Ambidge
editors

ABC Publishing
ANGLICAN BOOK CENTRE

ABC Publishing
Anglican Book Centre
80 Hayden Street
Toronto, ON M4Y 3G2

Contributions by Michael Ingham, Mario Ribas, and Rowan Q. Smith courtesy of the Lesbian and Gay Christian Movement (LGCM), Oxford House, Derbyshire Street, London E2 6HG, UK. www.lgcm.org.uk

"Now is the Time," copyright 1998, Tom Kendzia. Published by OCP Publications, 5536 NE Hassalo, Portland, OR 97213. All rights reserved. Used with permission.

Text typeset in ITC Legacy Serif Book
Cover and text design by Jane Thornton

National Library of Canada Cataloguing in Publication

Living together in the church : including our differences / Greig Dunn and Christopher Ambidge, editors.

ISBN 1-55126-415-3

1. Homosexuality—Religious aspects—Anglican Church of Canada. I. Dunn, Greig S. II. Ambidge, Christopher

BR115.H6L59 2004   261.8'35766   C2004-900782-3

Table of Contents

Introduction

A Dialogue of Respect

Greig Dunn

—◆—

Again and again the continuing dialogue on the position of gay and lesbian Christians in the church runs into the same baffling frustration: the impasse that results when two opponents can find no way of accommodating each other. This book is offered to the church in the conviction that our disagreements over the place of gay and lesbian Christians in the church are not cause for division.

We have always lived together in the church — gay and lesbian persons and heterosexual persons. We will continue to do so. And it seems likely that we will continue to disagree. Our task at present is to see our disagreement positively, as an engagement to continue the dialogue.

If the disagreement were simply about homosexuality, it would not have assumed its present proportions. But there is more. It seems that God has given us the homosexuality issue as a gift to cause us to reflect on our interaction with scripture and tradition, with one another, and with the world beyond the church.

This issue raises the absolutely fundamental question: How does the church live in and serve God's world as that world now is, while remaining true to its tradition of serving God, especially as recorded in its sacred scriptures? A question that embraces as much as this one does is bound to invite and receive different and contradictory answers.

There is nothing new about the question or about the breadth of our responses. Our whole tradition, including the scriptures, is the story of people who, like Abraham, were called by God to come out, not knowing where they were going. The question posed itself with special force at the time of the Reformation, when the currents running through society — social, political, economic, intellectual, technological — were eroding traditional structures. It is hardly original to suggest that the church at present is undergoing a new reformation and that differences of opinion are inevitable.

In the Reformation of the sixteenth and seventeenth centuries, all parties claimed that they were returning to essentials and affirming tradition. But it is never possible to go back. Ironically, all parties ended by producing something new, the Roman Catholic Church as much as the Protestant churches. The Anglican response was to remodel, in accord with contemporary experience but with close attention to the old structure, both its roots in scripture and its development in tradition. The result was a church that managed to include differences, but that was — and has remained — rather uncomfortable to live in. However, if, as has been said, our Lord's intent is both to comfort the afflicted and to afflict the comfortable, Anglicans can define our discomfort as our way of staying on the Way. As we proceed with dialogue, we will be reminding each other both of the call to go forward with the Spirit in a changing world, and of the voices in our tradition whose following of the same Spirit in their quite different circumstances has brought us to where we are now.

The essays that compose this book begin by assuming that all who engage in the dialogue about the place of gay and lesbian Christians in the church hold their positions sincerely, and that their sincerity deserves respect. They continue by suggesting new avenues along which the dialogue might proceed: wider avenues where roadblocks are harder to build, or at least easier to get around.

The process of the dialogue is all-important. All agree that there will be no quick or easy resolution to it. The dialogue needs to take place at the local level every bit as much as at the level of synods, general synods, and international conferences. It is at the level of the local community, where people meet face to face and week by week (and where gay, lesbian, and straight people are as a matter of fact already living together), that dialogue draws out our willingness to listen with respect and our desire to keep the community together and allow it to grow. As Anglican theologian Frederick Denison Maurice warned over a hundred years ago, different churches and different philosophies are most likely to be right in their affirmations, wrong in negations.[1]

There is no time limit to the dialogue, no certain moment when all will become clear. And the dialogue is bound to include action as well as talk. One Canadian diocese has already authorized the blessing of same-sex unions, and others are likely to do the same. Others may choose not to move on the question — and that too is an action. The assurance we have is that God is present with us now as ever, that God did not stop speaking to us when the last word of the Bible was written. When we speak the truth that is in us, we testify to what God has done. And when we listen to one another speaking that truth, we can discern there the word of God.

The dialogue involves long and deep listening, the courage to be both open and generous, and the willingness to forgive and be forgiven. A name for this process of respectful dialogue is reconciliation. Reconciliation with God and with one another is always personal, not ideological or even theological, because God in Christ loves us not for what we say we think, but for who we are. In Sister Thelma-Anne's words, "In walking our life journey through, with, and in God, each of us becomes, by grace, a living icon through which some aspect of Christ can shine forth."

---

1   Wolf, William J., et al., *The Spirit of Anglicanism: Hooker, Maurice, Temple* (Wilton, CT: Morehouse-Barlow, 1979), 58.

Acknowledgements

The book was conceived by a group of four people. Chris Ambidge, president of Integrity, Toronto, lent his immense knowledge of people and issues to its creation. Eric Beresford, Consultant for Ethics and Interfaith Relations at the national office of the Anglican Church, provided its theme: that the differences among us, though real and unlikely to be argued away, require us to learn ways of respecting each other. Robert Maclennan, manager of ABC Publishing, carried the book through to publication with his gentle expertise. I have had the pleasure — and it was that — of offering the idea of the book, coordinating everyone's effort, and working with the writers to edit their contributions.

Three of the contributions were originally delivered as addresses at the Halfway to Lambeth Conference in Manchester, England, in October 2003. This conference was organized by the Lesbian and Gay Christian Movement of Great Britain (LGCM) to mark the mid-point between the 1998 Lambeth Conference, memorable for its treatment of homosexuality in the Anglican Church, and the next Lambeth Conference, to be held in 2008. Richard Kirker, General Secretary of LGCM, graciously gave permission on behalf of the organization for versions of those addresses to be included here. Each is identified at the beginning of the contribution.

The greatest thanks of all is due to the contributors to this book, who have been moved to give generously of time and knowledge in order to share their conviction that our dialogue is a blessing and that we can live together in the church.

GREIG DUNN, *a retired high school teacher of English, is now a freelance editor and instructor of business writing. He lives with his partner of thirty years in Toronto and worships at St. Thomas's, Huron Street.*

CHRIS AMBIDGE *is a cradle Anglican with an MDiv from Huron College. He has been active with Integrity, a gay/lesbian ministry within the Anglican Church, for twenty years, and currently edits the newsletter of the Toronto chapter. He teaches chemistry at the University of Toronto and worships at the Church of the Redeemer.*

Engaging in Dialogue

Living Together in the Church

How Is It Possible When We Disagree?

TERENCE FINLAY has striven, as Bishop of Toronto since 1989 and Archbishop and Metropolitan of Ontario since 2000, to build communities where people find hope, purpose, and spiritual insight in the life and teachings of Jesus of Nazareth. He initiated a dialogue between those within the diocese who hold opposing views on homosexuality. At the Lambeth Conference in 1998 and as a member of a special commission established by the Archbishop of Canterbury, he has taken this conversation further, engaging with other bishops of the Anglican Communion.

———◆———

In this chapter I would like to offer some of my experiences and observations of the Anglican Church, both worldwide and in my own Canadian diocese, for the light they may shed on the question presently before the church: How can we live together when we disagree so strongly, especially about the place of gay and lesbian Christians in the church?

Establishing Dialogue

In my charge to the synod of the Diocese of Toronto in 1991, I spoke on several issues that were dividing the church. I asked Anglicans in the diocese to start listening to one another, to reach out across the chasms that separate them from each other, and to be involved in bridge building. One of the issues that we particularly needed to address was how we welcome lesbian women and gay men in the church. That synod passed a motion noting that the dismissal of a priest who chose to live openly in a gay relationship, had caused great concern among gay and lesbian Anglicans, both clergy and lay. The synod requested the diocesan executive committee to look into the position of lesbian and gay people within the diocesan family, with a view to making them feel more welcomed by the church. The executive committee commissioned a task force to begin a dialogue and to produce a parish resource. The result was a special insert in the diocesan newspaper called "Bridge building: Welcoming lesbian women and gay men in our church." It contained stories told by gay and lesbian people and suggestions for reference material.

Already in the diocese we had a branch of Integrity, the organization that advocates for gay and lesbian Anglicans, and another organization called Fidelity, which represents a more traditional, conservative perspective. In January 1995 I invited three people from each to engage in dialogue. Our goal was to explore how we could live together in the Anglican Church when our positions differed from each other. We saw ourselves as a kind of clearing house for questions and misunderstandings on both sides of the issue. It was a challenging task to listen actively and sympathetically to each other, rather than interrupting to state one's own particular perspective. My hope was that the group would act as advisors to me, providing ideas and suggestions when questions or issues arose. All of this was to be done in the context of prayer, respect for one another, and a sincere intention to move the conversation forward.

One member of the group said, "Well, you're not going to change my mind, but I want to hear and try to respect your position." That was our purpose: not to convert one another, but to listen to one another, understand one another, and develop a deeper awareness of why people held their positions — and held them so strongly. One much respected member would from time to time get fed up with our endless chatter and force us to go deeper and develop a position that would allow us to live with one another, even though we differed deeply.

Gradually there developed a real respect for one another. Friendships grew, and there were tangible results. One was the statement that we eventually drafted entitled "Emerging Common Ground." (It follows this article.) Another is the fact that at synod meetings, Integrity and Fidelity have chosen to set up their tables side by side. Still another is that when a request comes for speakers on the issue, two people go together, one from each side of the debate. Thus the group has modelled a process for engaging in dialogue, and it continues, though with changing personnel.

In 1996 I asked the members of the synod of the diocese of Toronto and others to write me a letter of no more than one page in length answering the question of whether I should authorize the blessing of same-gender partnerships, and explaining the reasons for their response. There were over eighty replies, marginally more on the conservative than on the liberal side. It was interesting that all those who favoured blessing same-gender partnerships either were gay or lesbian or were closely associated with someone who was gay or lesbian — a child or parent, brother or sister, friend or associate. Those who opposed the blessings almost invariably claimed to be standing by the clear word of Holy Scripture.

The 1998 Lambeth Conference and After

As is well known, the 1998 Lambeth Conference passed a complicated resolution that has been generally understood by both sides to take a conservative position on homosexuality. It would prevent, at least for the present, the blessing of same-gender partnerships and the ordination of persons living in such relationships. Behind the resolution lie the unfortunate politics of the conference.

I was assigned to one of the four sections into which the conference was divided — namely the section that was to consider issues of human sexuality. I have always felt very sorry for Bishop Duncan of Johannesburg, who was asked to chair this section. It was clear from the outset that little attention had been paid to designing a process through which we could engage in a constructive, gracious conversation about human sexuality. Gathered in a tiered classroom at the University of Kent in Canterbury was a mixed group, including some who were strongly in favour of more openness and others who were passionately opposed. The level of balanced conversation, and the process with for it, were both years behind where we had arrived in our diocesan dialogue group — and, in fact, in the Canadian Anglican Church. (Even conservative Canadian bishops said they felt "like raging liberals" in comparison to some commentators.) I dreaded spending three weeks hearing again all the usual quotations from the scriptures accompanied by all the usual arguments. I was most offended by some of the language used, reducing personal relationships to bestiality. Some of the bishops showed little sensitivity to others in the room. At the end of that opening section I was very angry.

Very quickly, the people responsible for guiding the conversation realized that they had to find a more helpful format. For a start, a tiered classroom was the wrong setting. We needed to gather in a large circle similar to the Canadian Aboriginal circle. People would then be able to express their point of view and be heard with the kind of respect that would engender a wholesome conversation. And it happened. It became evident that the participants had very different understandings of human sexuality. Some had trouble even accepting the presence of a person with a gay lifestyle. Others had no difficulty with recognizing that there were gay people in the church, as long as they were not ordained or their relationships were not blessed. Still others of us felt comfortable with the blessing of same-gender commitments and a full acceptance of gay and lesbian people in the life of the church including those ordained.

After two weeks a draft report was produced, summarizing the conclusions and the insights of the participants.[1] The report is a valuable statement that should be required reading for people who are trying to understand the variety of positions in the church's debate about the place of homosexual and lesbian persons in the church. When it was accepted both by John Spong, the well-known liberal former Bishop of Newark, New Jersey, and by the then Suffragan Bishop of North Sydney, Australia, Paul Barnett (now Archbishop of Sydney), a leading conservative evangelical, we felt the presence of God among us. It was a moment of grace, moving some to tears. We left that room feeling that, although we had not answered all the questions, there had been a growth of respect and understanding similar to what I had seen in the dialogue group in Toronto. We felt that we could all live together in such a church.

There are some issues that are best left at the point where people respectfully recognize their differences. Unfortunately the organizers of the Lambeth Conference failed to understand this. They called upon us to draft a resolution that could be dealt with by the plenary session of the conference. Inevitably voting on a resolution would put people into the position of being either winners or losers. Subsequently we have seen how people have used that resolution — or, more usually, parts of the resolution — to forward their own cause. I learned from this. You cannot solve complex issues by resolution or legislation.

This realization has implications for the way we proceed in the church right now. I believe that our consultations and conversations must be directed toward producing outcomes that are broad enough that as many people as possible can find a place for themselves in the outcome. We will still disagree, and few of us will be able to say that the result is exactly what we would have wanted. A few may even find themselves excluded. But most of us will be able to live together with respect for our differences.

At Lambeth, the Anglican Communion showed itself to be deeply divided on the issue of homosexuality, and the reactions in various member churches following the conference emphasized the division. In an attempt to find ways to heal some of the wounds and prevent actual schism, the then Archbishop of Canterbury, George Carey, established the Archbishop's Commission on Human Sexuality, of which I was a member. It consisted of twelve bishops from all over the world, including Nigeria, Tanzania, Hong Kong, Australia, the United States, England, and Canada. We met for three years, usually in a monastery or other place of prayer. Professional facilitators kept us on track. They kept us talking in

"I" sentences, using first-person singular statements instead of third-person pronouncements or second-person commands and judgements. And they kept us to time limits. (These were especially difficult for those who came from cultures that value elaborate oratory.)

The commission allowed for much listening and learning. For instance, I was struck by the position of a Nigerian bishop who helped me to understand the tremendous pressure felt by the Christian church in a country with a strong and rather extreme Islamic presence. Among the Muslims there are those who are looking for anything they can find to offer as evidence that Christianity is not an Indigenous religion and has been tainted by decadent Western culture. They teach that homosexuality is a form of Western corruption, and that in order not to be contaminated, Nigerians should abandon Christianity and become Muslims. The bishop said that for him even to be discussing the issue was enough to mark him as a traitor in the eyes not only of Muslims, but also of many African Anglicans. He personally found it difficult to accept the possibility that gay and lesbian people could be deeply committed Christians, yet over the three-year period of our talks, he came to recognize that in my context, it was possible. That was about as far as our conversation went. Because of this careful process of listening to one another, the report that came out this commission is quite interesting. Differences of opinion were recognized, but there *was* agreement that this should not be a church-dividing issue.[2]

Getting to the Heart of the Issue

I too do not see the question of how we treat gay and lesbian people in the church as a church-dividing issue. It is not an issue of basic doctrine such as the Incarnation, Redemption, Sanctification, or the nature of the Trinity. I do not believe that one's eternal salvation depends on taking the one right position on this issue. I recognize and understand those who see difficulty in welcoming gay and lesbian people into the church. And I believe it is possible to accommodate both their point of view and also the point of view that recognizes the sanctity of Christian gays and lesbians living faithful lives in committed long-term relationships.

The view that even sexuality itself is evil may be the reason why some people are so opposed that they can scarcely articulate their feelings, and resort to very inappropriate and insensitive language.

For many, the issue is not so much the matter of human sexuality as how we understand scripture and tradition. I take seriously the texts that are often quoted to support a conservative position, such as Leviticus 18, Romans 1, and 1 Corinthians 6. However, all of them are condemning forms of promiscuity. None of them presupposes the possibility of committed, long-term, monogamous, same-gender partnerships such as we see today. To me it makes more sense for the church to bless these relationships than it does for the church to bless battleships and pet cats.

What matters most for Christians is that we should look at one another, no matter how much we differ, and see fellow members of the Body of Christ. That we differ does not mean that we cannot work together in proclaiming the gospel and in doing the mission and ministry of the church. Each of us is created in the image of God, but in all of us that image is clouded so that others cannot see it clearly in us, nor we in them. When we listen carefully to others speaking, not just to the words, but to the person and the context from which he or she comes, we can see each more clearly as a child of God. At the same time, we will understand more clearly who we ourselves are as children of God made in God's image. This kind of sensitive, caring listening can build bridges across our divisions.

It is a slow process. Whenever I meet with our diocesan dialogue group, I realize that, even after seven years, we are still uncovering more layers of understanding. When the tension begins to rise, it is often a sign that we are getting close to someone's deeper understanding.

Envisioning the Future in the Church

I believe that the church in Canada will eventually recognize the blessing of lesbians and gays living in faithful relationships and that those who have the necessary requirements will be ordained to the priesthood and episcopate. There will still be difficult times when people who cannot accept this will cause pain to lesbians and gays — and to me and others who have friends and colleagues whom we love and respect.

But overall, Anglicans are an understanding and accepting group and I believe that with a strong emphasis on responsible listening, sensitivity to context, and non-judgemental dialogue there will be a way forward on the issue of homosexuality in the church. Anglicans will be able to live and worship in the same church even while holding differing opinions. To do this will probably require a "local option."

Perhaps that will look something like this. After a process of study and discernment in a diocese, a substantial majority of a synod could decide in favour of the local option and the diocesan bishop could concur. Then a parish vestry could vote to request the bishop for permission to conduct same-gender blessings. Again this would require a substantial support of the vestry and the concurrence of the incumbent. My sense is that only a very limited number of parishes will actually make that request in the beginning. There would be other considerations around this as well. It would be wise to have guidelines in the parish or diocese before proceeding. Postulants for ordination would not be asked to subscribe to a particular position on this issue and priests already ordained would only be expected to act according to their conscience.

Moving now to the international Anglican scene, we find a more difficult picture. Context becomes much more complex here. Deep and important realities for the North American church may be difficult for Africans and Asians to appreciate. Some African Christians feel threatened by fundamentalist Muslims. Many Canadian Christians feel that the treatment of gays and lesbians is both a human rights question and an expression of Christian inclusivity. My international discussions make it clear that a simplistic approach is inadequate.

I wonder, however, what is really fuelling all this anger? I find myself wondering if this is not more of a power struggle than a moral question. It seems so unreasonable to me to break up the Communion over a situation where two people want simply to commit themselves and care for each other throughout their lives. There is so much energy being spent on this issue when there are many important questions needing more attention: children with AIDS, vicious civil wars, ecological disasters, lack of food and water. It seems to me that the church should be rallying around these issues instead of struggling to decide who is more pure.

I always marvel at the vivid stories that Jesus tells the people gathered around him. I was reflecting on the reading about the parable of the pathetic fig tree that was not producing; it was struggling for a full life. One suggestion is to cut it in two, chop it in pieces. But then we hear the caring, wise words of the gardener telling us to be careful, telling us not to destroy something valuable too recklessly, give it a chance. He recommends that we nurture it, let the fresh air get to the roots, allow space for growth, enliven it with cool soothing waters. Give it some options for life, not death.

These prudent words from the Gardener of Life make sense in how we live with each other in these turbulent times. Could we give some space to each other? Could we try to understand our roots, the soil in which we have been formed? Could we nurture and pray for each other and be patient for awhile?

One of the hardest steps in all this is to quietly and honestly tell the truth to ourselves, to one another, and to God; Jesus calls this repentance. With that we may start to see one another as children of the same God, and we may be able to confess our hope for reconciliation, both in our personal lives and in the church.

For a while the Anglican Communion will shudder like a great ship struggling through rough waters, but over time the Communion will find healing and reconciliation. We have been through rough waters before in the great controversies throughout our history. And although we'll be a bit bruised and sore, I believe we will make it.

Notes

1. See *The Official Report of the Lambeth Conference 1998* (Harrisburg: Morehouse Publishing, 1999), 93–95.

2. It is entitled *A Final Report from the International Anglican Conversations on Human Sexuality.*

Emerging Common Ground

The following statement was published in 1997 by the Dialogue Group established in the diocese of Toronto, and reflects some thoughts on the questions around gays and lesbians in the church, from people in the diocese who are on both sides of the question.

> We are on a journey together, and these beginning articulations of emerging common ground are the start of that journey together. As members of the Body of Christ, we are committed to the unity of the church, conscious that some responses to homosexuality have been divisive of this unity. We acknowledge that we all share in a blindness on this subject, in one way or another. We are none of us free of sin and the effects of sin, and we acknowledge that we must repent and be willing to examine our own assumptions and attitudes. Moreover, none have the entire picture because of our own location and our own limited perspective. It is not given to any of us to know the whole truth, and so we need to learn from each other.

> 1. We agree that scripture is not to be used as a "hammer" against those with whom we disagree. We also agree that scripture is not to be mined for "proof texts"; rather, specific passages are to be understood in the larger biblical context. More positively, we agree that in all the diversity and tensions in scripture, there is a fundamental story or direction [that] is embodied in the person and story of Jesus the Christ, [that] cannot be reduced to a simple set of laws or concepts. As we hear the living Word in new situations, we may find that we hear parts of that story in new and different ways.

> 2. We agree that God the Holy Spirit continues to lead and guide the church. As baptized believers we may experience a new insight from the Lord, which must be respected but which must also be tested. The test is the spirit of the

Word rather than the letter of the law. It is our common experience as believers that God's Word is spoken afresh in the situations of our lives.

3. We agree that the tradition of the church is to be respected and listened to, since it represents our conversation partners in many times and places. We affirm that Anglican doctrine establishes the supremacy of scripture, with tradition and reason helping to interpret scripture when it speaks and determine order where it is silent.

4. We agree that homosexuality is only one part of the subject of human sexuality; furthermore we acknowledge that human sexuality is presently a subject of considerable confusion and turmoil. We recognize that dehumanising practices occur across the spectrum of sexual relations. We are united in our opposition to all forms of violence and exploitation.

5. We agree that moral and ethical norms exist in order to nurture healthy human life, within ourselves, with other persons and before the face of God. We also affirm that Christian tradition properly forms our ethical disposition: it helps us by providing a starting point and guidance in difficult situations. However, humans do not exist for the sake of moral and ethical norms. This means that, where we find a large degree of human pain and anguish, we must be willing to re-examine traditional moral norms. We must realize, as the Good Samaritan did, that the suffering is real, and must not use a code for life as an excuse for "passing by." We must also be willing to examine the moral norm and either make a compelling case for it or modify it in certain ways.

6. We agree with the House of Bishops when they said in 1978, "We believe as Christians that homosexual persons,

as children of God, have a full and equal claim, with all other persons, upon the love, acceptance, concern and pastoral care of the Church."

7. We agree that, while God accepts and loves all of us as who we are, we are all in constant need of re-forming ourselves closer to the image of Christ.

8. We agree that heterosexual marriage is commendable because it seeks to provide intimacy for committed partners and a safe place for the raising of children. However, marriage is not a state that is appropriate for all persons and in every situation.

First printed for Toronto Diocesan Synod, November 1997.

The Dialogue
with Scripture
and Tradition

Welcoming in the Gentiles

A Biblical Model for Decision Making

DR. SYLVIA C. KEESMAAT *is Associate Professor of Biblical Studies and Hermeneutics at the Institute for Christian Studies in Toronto. She obtained her DPhil at Oxford University, studying with N. T. Wright, and is the author of* Paul and His Story: (Re)Interpreting the Exodus Tradition, *as well as editor of* The Advent of Justice. *Along with her husband, Brian Walsh, she is the co-author of* Colossians Remixed: Subverting the Empire *[forthcoming, IVP, 2004]. A lecturer for the Creation Care Studies Program in Belize, she also speaks frequently on the implications of living the biblical story in contemporary life. She and her husband have three children and an organic garden in Toronto.*

Biblical Authority and the Making of Decisions in the Church

At the heart of current debates about the place of gay and lesbian Christians in our churches lies the issue of biblical authority. It is right that this is so. Since Christians appeal to the Bible as our normative story, the question of the role that the Bible plays should be front and centre in our deliberations concerning the direction the Christian community takes. To affirm that the Bible is authoritative, however, begs two questions: In what way is it an authority for us? and, What precisely does its authority look like?

Both of these issues are far too large to be addressed at length in this article. However, let me give a brief consideration of both of them, by way of setting a framework for my discussion of a particular New Testament text.

What kind of a book is the Bible? Is it primarily a rule book in which we look up the rules for how to live out our Christian lives? Is it primarily a theological treatise in which we can find handy theological summaries of the nature of reality? Is it primarily a history book, providing a construction of the history of world and the people of God on which we can model our own communities? Or is it a book of heroic examples on which we can model our lives? While these various genres all find their place in the Bible, nonetheless this book comes to us overwhelmingly as a narrative. And as a narrative it has a kind of authority that is unique.

Biblical scholar Tom Wright describes this authority in terms of an unfinished drama. Act 1 is the creation of a good world. Act 2 is the distortion of that world by sin. Act 3 is the calling of Israel to be a blessing to this fallen world. Act 4 is the coming of Jesus, where sin is decisively dealt with. Act 5, scene 1, is the early church, where the life, death, and resurrection of Jesus are grappled with and lived out in the lives of the first Christian communities. Further scenes unfold, from the apostolic era, through the patristic period, and so on to the present. Act 6 is the coming consummation, when Jesus will return and we will join him on the new earth at the resurrection of the dead.[1]

Now, what is significant about this drama is that we are in the middle of it. We are still in Act 5, living as the people of God before Jesus comes again. As Wright emphasizes, in order to live faithfully to the drama, we need two things. On the one hand, we need to be *faithful* to the story that has preceded us. Such fidelity means that we do not abandon the story; rather, we live according to it as it has already unfolded, in faithfulness to the God revealed to us in scripture and in faithfulness to Jesus, who died and was raised. But, on the other hand, we need to be *creative* in our living of the story. It will not do to simply repeat what happened in previous acts. This means that we need to discern what such faithful living looks like here and now, in new cultural situations, and in the light of new workings of the Spirit. Christian integrity is found at the interface of fidelity and creativitiy. Indeed, as we shall see, this is precisely the struggle that engaged the church as recorded in the Book of Acts, chapters 10 to 15.

This means, moreover, that we do not turn to the Bible merely to deal with difficult issues. If the Bible is our story, the script for how we are to live faithfully in the world, we need to be totally immersed in the text, completely absorbed in the story, our imaginations renewed and transformed in every aspect by the vision that the story sets before us. Some inkling of how our imagination would be shaped in this way is given in Deuteronomy 6:6–9. There, every moment of every day is supposed to be filled with Torah, with the story of who God is and what God has done. This story fills your very being, so that you cannot help talking about it to your children at home and to everyone you meet, no matter where you are. When you are awake, you tell the story; when you are asleep, you even dream in its symbols and metaphors. It is on your hand, so that you see it enacted in all that you do, and on your forehead, so that others see it in all that you think and say. Your home and your life in the public square are to be shaped by it. Such an engagement with the story is, alas, foreign to most Christians in our culture, even in most of our church life. However, at the very least, we need intentionally to try to live out the narrative of scripture in our personal and (perhaps more importantly) our communal lives as a precondition of engaging in discussion of any issue.

There is also the question, however, of what authority looks like in the biblical story. What does this story that we try to live out tell us about authority? I take it as true that the authority of the Bible is rooted in our belief that the Bible is the story of our God, and that God demonstrates to us exactly what authority looks like. God's authority creates. It chooses forgiveness over destruction [see, for example, Exodus 32–34]. It works judgement and forgiveness [see Hosea 11]. It is the story of a shepherd-king who redeems by nurturing his flock, seeking the lost, binding up the wounds of the injured, and strengthening the weak [see Isaiah 40:10–11; Ezekiel 34].

The biblical story culminates in the story of Jesus, and its presentation of God's authority culminates in Jesus as well. In Jesus we see the true image of the creator [Colossians 1:15], in whom God's redemptive work comes to its fulfilment. In Jesus we see also the one to whom all authority on heaven and on earth has been given [Matthew 28:18]. So what kind of authority is this that Jesus bears?

In Mark 10:32–45, the disciples are walking to Jerusalem with Jesus. As they continue along the road, they discover that James and John have just asked to be the Lord's right- and left-hand commanders when they conquer the city! The other disciples are outraged until Jesus interrupts with a radical redefinition of authority. Gentiles use authority for violent control and tyranny, but the followers of Jesus are to exercise a servant authority that even lays down its life for others. This kind of authority is antithetical to every authority of the world. Its nature is to serve, even unto death.

This is the way the story comes to its climax. The creative authority of God in creation, the judging and redemptive authority of God in the exodus and the exile, the forgiving authority of God, the nurturing authority of God who gathers the lambs in his arms, and gives strength to the faint and the weary — all of these come together in the life and death of Jesus. On the cross Jesus redeems his people from all the powers that enslave, and works forgiveness even for those who have crucified him. In his resurrection he is the first-born of a new creation, and in the sending of the Spirit he nurtures and strengthens the small Christian community that proclaims his name.

The point is this: God's authority is ultimately exercised over this world, not in a violent power grab, but through the life, death, and resurrection of Jesus, and the sending of the Spirit to empower such a servant community. This is a vision that takes every other story in our culture and turns it on its head, judging it in light of the character of our God, and calling into question every authority that does not submit to the suffering authority of Jesus.

Now, if the Bible is to function as an authority in our life, then its authority must cohere with the authority of the God to whom it bears witness. Therefore, if the Bible is used in ways that deny creation and promote death, then biblical authority is being subverted. If the Bible is used primarily as a text of condemnation rather than a text of forgiveness, then the scriptures become a word of death, not of life. If the Bible is used to enslave and bind up, rather than redeem and save, then the overall thrust and intention of the biblical story is being denied. If the Bible is used in ways that destroy the weak and faint of heart rather than nurture them, then it is being used to justify the kind of brutal authoritarianism that the biblical story itself condemns. The Bible itself — biblical authority itself — stands in judgement over all such misuses and perversions of biblical authority.

The Problem

As the story of the early church unfolds in Acts, we see a picture of a community struggling to find its way in new contexts. One of those struggles is recorded for us in Acts 15, where the apostles and elders are confronted with a problem: Under what conditions do we welcome Gentiles into the fellowship of believers? The question, Whom do we welcome? has been central throughout Luke's gospel and Acts. It begins with Simeon's song of God's salvation for all peoples [Luke 2:29–32], moves to Jesus' clear announcement that God's message of liberation from bondage is for Gentiles, which enraged the people of Nazareth[2] [Luke 4:16–30], and is reinforced in Jesus' command to invite the poor, the crippled, the lame, and the blind into our homes for meals [Luke 14:13]. In the Book of Acts, Luke, the writer picks up the theme once again with the baptism of the Ethiopian eunuch [Acts 8].[3] The theme culminates in the decision to welcome the Gentiles without requiring circumcision [Acts 15].

However, the widening of the gospel to include those who were traditionally excluded does not mean that all are immediately welcomed into the Christian community: the rich man who does not feed the starving Lazarus suffers eternal torment [Luke 16:19–31]; the rich young ruler who is unable to sell all that he has and give it to the poor will have difficulty entering the kingdom [Luke 18:18–25]; and Ananias and Sapphira, who lied about their economic contribution to the community of believers, are cut off in the most dramatic way possible [Acts 5:1–11]. It is clear that some behaviours are *not* permitted in this community.

For the early church, the conversion of the Gentiles was the greatest success and, as it turns out, its biggest problem. For many Jews the turning of the Gentiles to the God of Israel was a good thing only under certain conditions. Gentiles, to put it mildly, did not have a good reputation in Jewish circles. In fact, if the average Jew wanted to describe in a nutshell what the average Gentile lived like, he (or she) might well have used the language of Romans 1. It describes Gentiles as people who by their injustice suppress the truth. They have given up their God-given glory in favour of mere images, and God has given them up to lust and degrading passions. They engage in immoral sexual practices, including temple prostitution, and they are full of covetousness, malice, envy, murder, strife, deceit, and craftiness. They are gossips, slanderers, insolent, haughty, boastful, inventors of evil, rebellious toward parents, foolish, unfaithful, heartless, ruthless. This was standard first-century Jewish diatribe against Gentiles.

Naturally, if this is what Gentiles were like, then permitting them to enter the believing community could cause huge problems for a community that was committed to a very different way of being in the world. The Epistle to the Romans and other Jewish writings trace these kinds of behaviours to their roots in idolatry, in worshipping not the creator but the creature. Furthermore, these vices demonstrate an attitude to community life and sexual relations that is rooted in instant gratification, consumption, and division. These are the results of most of the items on Paul's list in Romans 8:29–30 (covetousness, malice, envy, murder, strife, deceit, craftiness, gossip, slander, insolence, boastfulness, rebellion, ruthlessness), and a sexuality of consumption is demonstrated in Paul's description of a sexuality rooted in lust and degrading passion [v. 24ff.], which is faithless and heartless [v. 32]. In Colossians the link between this sort of sexuality and covetousness is explicitly made [Colossians 3:5]. Throughout the New Testament, idolatry creates divisions in community life, and such divisions are rooted both in the list of social sins summarized by malice, envy, strife, and gossip, *and* in the sexual sins of consumptive passion and sexual immorality. In the eyes of most Jews, therefore, Gentiles were irretrievably rooted in a lifestyle of instant gratification, consumption and division, rather than commitment, nurture, and edification.

You can see the problem here: What guarantee did the leaders of the early church have that the Gentiles were going to leave their idolatrous way of life behind? They knew one way of making sure: by requiring circumcision. What circumcision symbolized was not just a commitment to the God of Israel, but also a commitment to keeping the whole of Torah. And one could not keep Torah and continue to follow the practices of idolatry.

The individuals who came to Paul and Barnabas in Antioch as recorded in Acts 15:1 were on good, solid biblical ground in insisting on circumcision. So were those Pharisees who responded to Paul and Barnabas when they first arrived in Jerusalem, "It is necessary for [the Gentiles] to be circumcised and ordered to keep the law of Moses" [Acts 15:5]. They were right: there was nothing in scripture to suggest that Gentiles could become part of the community without keeping the law and without circumcision. This law had been laid down by Moses and had never been challenged anywhere in any biblical tradition, not even by Jesus. All the texts that speak of the Gentiles joining themselves to the house of Israel also envision that these Gentiles will keep Torah. There was no hint that this requirement would ever be overthrown; there is *absolutely no biblical precedent* for welcoming in Gentiles without being circumcised and following Torah. The Pharisees who opposed Paul had both scripture and tradition on their side.[4]

And so the debate at Jerusalem came down to this central issue: Whom do we welcome into the believing community, and by what criteria do we decide, especially when we don't think the people who want in are morally up to standard?

The Story

Before we look at Acts 15, however, we need to briefly consider the narrative in Acts 10 to 11 that leads up to it, the story of Peter's dream and the baptism of Cornelius.[5] Central to this narrative is the importance of friends and hospitality. When Peter finally reached Cornelius, he knew who Cornelius was from conversing with his friends on the way to the house. In breaking scriptural law in order to eat with Cornelius, Peter established a relationship that then enabled him to testify on behalf of Cornelius to others [Fowl 1998, 117–18]. It is evident from the story that eating with Gentiles was the charge that Peter faced upon his return to Jerusalem [Acts 11:3]. It was also the only means by which he could discern the work of God's Spirit in Gentile lives so as to defend himself against the charge of breaking the law. We need to remember as we read Acts 15 that the whole decision-making process was preceded by the sharing of both stories and meals together.

The Process

And so we come to the discussion of Acts 15. The apostles and elders met to consider the matter, says the text [v. 6]. As we have noted above, the Pharisees argue the theological basis for the necessity of circumcision. There was much debate [v. 7]. Perhaps the Pharisees recounted how this commandment was given to Abraham and is central to Torah; perhaps they discussed the prophetic texts that speak about Gentiles; perhaps they appealed to the tradition of the fathers up until the present day; perhaps they referred to the questionable morality of these Gentiles.

What is striking is that Peter discussed none of these issues. Instead, he witnessed to what God had done with the Gentiles. God had "testified to them by giving them the Holy Spirit," he said, "and in cleansing their hearts by faith" [vv. 8–9]. Peter appealed to his experience of the Gentiles, to the way he saw the Spirit moving in their midst, and to their renewed hearts. Considering contemporary evidence of the Spirit was, for Peter, of central importance in discerning what decision should be made. Luke Johnson describes Peter's story as a narration of God's work in the world: that is, it is the *doing of theology*. "Peter's interpretive narrative of his experience places the issue on properly theological grounds. Can one recognize God's work in the world? Yes, and once the recognition is made, the church's decision should follow" [Johnson 1996, 102].

We should note, however, that Peter's narrative here did echo a scriptural tradition. He began by saying, "And God, who knows the human heart, testified to them..." [v. 8]. This appeal to God who knows the human heart is deeply rooted in the Psalms, where the psalmist appeals to God because of persecution. It is usually part of a plea in which the psalmist asserts that, while others do not consider him to be faithful, God knows the heart. These Old Testament echoes reverberate through Peter's words. The overtones are unmistakable: we might think that we can judge these Gentiles, but God knows their hearts and has testified on their behalf with the Holy Spirit. Who then are we, asks Peter in verse 10, to judge their suitability and insist on a moral code that we have also been unable to bear? Thus, in telling a story that is suffused with the vocabulary of the scriptures, Peter places that story in the larger context of God's work throughout scripture.

Paul and Barnabas then take up the narrative by telling more stories of what God has done among the Gentiles. Given the theological sophistication of Paul's letters, we know that he was as capable as any of theological discussion based on Old Testament texts. We know that he could have drawn on the tradition, talked about Abraham, and made a strong textual argument against circumcision. In fact, he did just this in Galatians. But he didn't do that here. Instead, he and Barnabas appealed to their experience among the Gentiles, to the signs and wonders that God had done.

Only after the stories had been told of God's work in the present did James appeal to a biblical text. Note, however, the unusual introduction he gives to the citation: "The words of the prophets agree with this" [Acts 15:15], *not* "this agrees with the prophets."[6] Scripture is seen to agree with the contemporary working of the Spirit, not the other way around.

James acknowledges that God is doing a new thing, and he reads scripture as if it confirms that new thing, as indeed it does. But let's be clear here. There are many scriptural texts that could be used to make a case *against* admitting the Gentiles who do not follow Torah. Some texts speak not of welcoming Gentiles, but of defeating and crushing them. Others insist on the need for circumcision for those Gentiles who want to join the community of Israel.[7] Conversely, there are no texts that support the position of welcoming the Gentiles without circumcision. So what did James do? He quoted a text that did not address the situation directly, but which could be made to fit the circumstances. James has made the remarkable move of allowing the Old Testament to be illuminated and interpreted by the narrative of God's activity in the present [Johnson 1996, 105]. Moreover, this text still does not assert that circumcision is unnecessary for the Gentiles to be welcomed. That is an interpretive move that James must make himself.

Our contemporary debates about homosexuality are often preoccupied with a very small number of texts that appear to condemn homosexuality. However, if we were to use scripture in the way that James does, we would draw attention away from those texts and ask ourselves whether the experience of the Spirit in the lives of gays and lesbians in our community produces a new reading of the scriptures as a whole. How do we allow scripture to be illuminated by the narratives of God's activity in our present? At the Jerusalem Council, the witness of the Holy Spirit in believers' experience was confirmed by scriptural witness *as the scripture was reinterpreted in light of that experience.* When the Spirit of God is working in people's lives, we don't use the scriptures to inhibit the work of the Spirit. Scripture is for the building up of a Spirit-filled community, not for tearing it apart. Discerning where the Spirit is moving also legitimately influences our interpretation of scripture, as it influenced James who, in light of the Spirit's work, ignored all the texts about the Gentiles that could have led him to a different decision. Scripture here is read through the lens of the Spirit's work, rather than vice versa [Fowl 1998, 114]. We shall return below to what this might look like in our deliberations about homosexuality today.

But there is another important lesson that needs to be learned from how the Jerusalem Council's decision was made. Stories are told about the Spirit's work in the lives of others, *"by* those who are already recognized as people of the Spirit" [Fowl 1998, 115]. In Acts 15 Peter is describing God's work in the lives of others. As Stephen Fowl puts it, "To be able to read the Spirit well, Christians must not only become and learn from people of the Spirit, we must also become practised at testifying about what the Spirit is doing in the lives of others" [116]. As we shall see, this requires a community where such narratives can be nurtured and sustained.

The Parameters

The Gentiles were to be welcomed into the community without circumcision. But that does not mean there were no concerns about their morality. So some stipulations were set. As Gentiles, and especially as Gentiles who did not want to follow Torah and be circumcised, these believers would have been tarred by faithful Jews with the same brush as unbelieving Gentiles. The polemic of the first chapter of Romans was believed to apply to all Gentiles; if they did not worship the living God, they could not be anything but idolatrous and, hence, immoral. And James's decision addressed precisely this question of morality in asking them to abstain from things polluted by or sacrificed to idols, and from sexual immorality, and from whatever has been strangled and from blood [vv. 20–21, 28–29].

All of these stipulations revolve around the issue of idolatry: the Gentile believers are being asked to put off precisely those things that are central to a life of idol worship in the Roman empire. Just as in Romans 1, which sees idolatry as at the root of the depravity of the Gentile life — the sexual immorality, the slander and gossip, the envy and covetousness, the deceit and unfaithfulness — so the Jerusalem Council discerned that idolatry was at the heart of the worship that the Gentiles now had to abandon.

So the Gentile believers were called, first of all, to abandon all that has been sacrificed to idols, or polluted by idols. In the ancient world this would mean no longer going to the theatre, no longer attending any sort of civic celebration, no longer being a part of celebrations in honour of the emperor or his rule. All of these events would have been consecrated by sacrifice to idols and preceded by prayers for the empire. No more of such involvement, says the Jerusalem Council.

Second, they were called to refrain from sexual immorality. The Greek word used here, *porneia*, often translated by the word fornication, actually had a wide variety of overtones: adultery, sex for hire, temple prostitution. All of these ways of behaving betray a sexuality rooted in the idolatrous practices of the empire, a sexuality characterized by promiscuity, instant gratification, and consumption. Instead, the Jerusalem Council called these Gentile believers to a sexuality rooted in commitment and faithfulness, a sexuality that creates and builds up community rather than tearing it apart.

Third, they were called to abstain from meat that had been strangled, and from blood. In the ancient world, the main slaughterhouses were the temples; priests (and this goes for Jewish priests as well) were basically butchers. They spent a large part of their time killing, butchering, and sacrificing meat. Jewish priests were very particular about how meat was butchered; following Levitical law, the animal was slaughtered with a knife and the blood was drained entirely from it. Meat with blood in it would have been slaughtered (probably strangled) by a Gentile priest, and would have been killed as a sacrifice to idols. Since meat was generally consumed only at the time of a festival or as a result of a special sacrifice, the consumption of meat was always linked to the worship of some god, whether the God of Israel or an idol. So calling the Gentiles not to eat meat that was strangled or with the blood in it meant that the eating of idol meat was prohibited.

Even the way meat was eaten was linked to idolatry. In the Roman Empire, such meat was eaten in the service and worship of the emperor. At all imperial meals, where sacrifices were offered in honour of the emperor, the social divisions and hierarchies of the empire were rigidly enforced. Those men at the higher end of the social ladder received the best bits of roasted meat, and women, children, and slaves received much less meat that had been boiled and was likely cold. The Jerusalem Council was calling the early Christian community to put off eating practices that were in the service and worship of the empire.

By contrast, a sign of the early Christian community was that they practised an alternative meal, where all ate together, Jew and Gentile, slave and free, male and female. The Jerusalem Council was calling the Gentiles to become part of a community that worshipped the living God, not idols, and that practised mutual service, not the reinforcement of division.

James summed up the basis of his decision when he wrote the following to the Gentiles in Antioch [v. 28]: "It seemed good to the Holy Spirit and to us to impose on you no further burden than these essentials." And when the believers in Antioch received the letter, they rejoiced.

The Implications

The narrative of Acts 10 to 15 highlights a number of other dynamics involved in making the decision to include the Gentiles in the church. One is the central importance of hospitality. It was enabled by the requirement that Gentiles refrain from meat offered to idols. Fowl describes the importance of this theme in this way:

> Throughout this narrative the offering and receiving of hospitality always seems to be in the background supporting and enabling the sorts of friendships that allow Christians with different convictions to listen together to the voice of the Spirit [Fowl 1998, 118].

Peter is asked in Acts 11:3: "Why did you go to uncircumcised men and eat with them?" (This was an accusation, of course, that echoes the charge made against Jesus in Luke 15:2: "This fellow welcomes sinners and eats with them.") Peter's acceptance of

Cornelius's hospitality makes it possible for him to hear the story of what God has done in Cornelius's life. And, as Fowl points out, "Peter's relationship with the various parties he confronts in Jerusalem affects the way in which his testimony is received" [118]. Those relationships enable him to relate the stories of what God has done in the lives of Cornelius and others. In short, this story describes the type of community that the church must be in order to go about the hard process of making difficult decisions. Such a community is characterized by the sort of friendships that enables the patience necessary for the hard work of discernment. Such friendships are rooted in gracious hospitality.

Such discernment is truly *hard work* for these communities, because *not all* narratives are accepted. The hard work of discernment will involve substantial disagreement, as we saw in Acts 15:2, where it says (dryly) that "there was no small dissension and debate." But what would such discernment look like? What kind of criteria would assist a community in determining whether a narrative is truly the work of the Spirit?

Paul's major emphasis through his letters is to teach and encourage a Christian way that is for the *edification* of the community. The language that Paul uses most often is that of "building up" the community of believers.[8] But what does this building up look like? Johnson describes it this way: "That edifies the church which builds it up in holiness" [Johnson 1996, 122]. Such *holiness*, moreover, is marked by the sign of the cross [129]. The cruciform life is shaped by a lowliness that looks to the service of others, seeks a mind that is in Christ Jesus [1 Corinthians 2:15; Philippians 2:5], and undertakes self-emptying obedience [Philippians 2:5–11]. Such a life bears the burdens of others [Galations 6:2; Romans 15:1–3], forgives others [Colossians 3:13], and walks in self-sacrificial love. Because we follow a crucified saviour, a church marked out by holiness lives out a life of self-sacrifice.

This gives us a criterion by which to discern the work of the Spirit in a narrative: a narrative of faith that reflects the character of Christ has a certain *christological density* [Fowl 1998, 159]. Just as Paul describes his own life story as following the crucified messiah, so the narratives in which the church seeks to discern the work of the Spirit should manifest the Christ-like pattern of self-sacrificing love.

The Christian community is called, therefore, if it follows biblical precedent in struggling with the questions around homosexuality, to listen with welcoming hospitality to the stories that its members tell about gays and lesbians in our midst. At the very least, as Fowl points out, listening to the stories of God's work in the lives of gays and lesbians is necessary before any discernment about such stories can take place. And, following the precedents set in Acts 10 to 15, such stories should take place over a meal. "Christians have no reason to think they understand how the Holy Spirit weighs in on the issue of homosexuality until they welcome homosexuals into their homes and sit down to eat with them" [122]. And once the stories are heard, then the work of discernment begins, for "the Spirit of God, when truly at work, leaves traces in our story. The church does have a way to discern the Spirit's work, but only if the fruits are made available by narrative" [Johnson 1996, 138].

This fruit, the traces of the Spirit's work in the story and the holiness in the lives of believers, is described by Paul in a number of places. The best known of these is Galatians 5. If the lives of gay and lesbian believers display the fruit of the Spirit: love, joy, peace, patience, kindness, goodness, faithfulness, gentleness, self-control [Galations 5:22–23], then the church needs to acknowledge the work of God in their lives, as such work was recognized in the lives of Gentiles in Acts. If, on the other hand, the lives of these believers are filled with sexual immorality, impurity, licentiousness, party spirit, envy, drunkenness, carousing and the like [Galations 5:19–21], then it is clear that the body of Christ is not edified by them. The only way to discern these things, however, is first to hear the stories in our midst.

Another criterion was established in Acts 15 [referred to in Galatians 5:20], when the Jerusalem Council called on Gentile believers to reject idolatry together with the sexual practices and eating practices that followed from it. For the believers in Jerusalem the question of discerning who should be welcomed was answered in the following way: We welcome those in whom we see the Holy Spirit working, those whose hearts have been cleansed by faith. We welcome those who rejoice at the chance to put idolatry behind them and all that idolatry leads to. We welcome those who practise a sexuality that is not rooted in promiscuity and instant gratification and consumption. We welcome those who eat in ways that do not reinforce the hierarchies and prejudices of the world that tear community apart. We welcome those whose long-term commitment, troth, faithfulness, and service to all are rooted in following Jesus. We welcome those who want to be part of a community where the leaders serve the least and all gifts are shared equally with all.

These criteria resonate with those of us trying to live holy lives today. We too live in a culture where sexuality is pimped for consumption and instant gratification. We too live in a culture where an ethos of idolatrous corporate consumption creates ever widening gaps between those who eat at Mövenpick and McDonald's or the soup kitchen. In such a culture, our communities too need to be places where faithful sexual commitment is honoured, and where mutual sharing and service, especially among those who have least, is encouraged. Our communities should be places where *all* who confess that Jesus is Lord are welcomed.

The Stories

It is precisely the contention of many in the church today that the lives of gay and lesbian Christians demonstrate the fruit of the Spirit, commitment, faithfulness, and Christ-shaped service. Ironically, the issue that has caused the most division in Canada around homosexuality, the desire of gay and lesbian Christians for their unions to be recognized as a blessing, is rooted in this desire to practice a sexuality that is committed and covenantally based rather than the promiscuity common in our culture among people of every sexual orientation.

The stories our communities need to hear are stories of what Johnson calls "homosexual holiness" [Johnson 1996, 148] — stories of Christ-shaped lives in which the fruits of the Spirit are evident. The principal burden of telling those stories does not rest on the shoulders of gay and lesbian Christians themselves, but on the shoulders of those in their communities who have witnessed such fruit, who can testify on their behalf, and who believe that the Spirit is truly working in the lives of their gay brothers and lesbian sisters.

To that end I would like to end this chapter by briefly indicating what some of those stories sound like. If I were to relate the working of the Spirit in signs and wonders among the gays and lesbians in my community, as Peter related the signs and wonders he had witnessed among the Gentiles, I would include stories like these: Marj is a nurse who retired early to spend her days binding up the wounds of the many homeless people who come through her church doors each day. Jim and Amy patiently teach young children the stories of the Bible each week in Sunday school. Daniel, a crown attorney, has for five years nurtured the youth group as they attempt to discern what it is to be faithful Christians in the difficult terrain of urban adolescence. Jennifer and Wendy faithfully gave their goddaughter her first Bible and read to her out of it whenever they give a break to her frazzled parents. Michelle and Bonnie opened their home and adopted a child living in foster care. David uses his intellectual gifts for the upbuilding of Christian education in his parish, and his organizational skills to run the fair trade coffee group. Harley personally welcomes newcomers to his parish by cooking most of a special lunch for them. Chris has quietly held many fractious children through many a eucharist. Natasja's quiet work of community building has united the student body in her graduate program. Abigail's academic gifts are exercised consistently in the service of her church. Fred volunteers on the board of his local social justice group, and Jack, a teacher, stuffs envelopes as a volunteer at the same place. Linda gives free reflexology treatments to a man ill with cancer. John's choices of songs that are theologically rich and biblically faithful rival the best sermon on a Sunday morning. These are just a few of the gay and lesbian people I know whose stories are deeply shaped by the cross of Jesus, whose lives bear the fruit of the Spirit, and who with their partners demonstrate a commitment to faithful relationship that challenges the promiscuity and consumption of our culture.

"The gifts he gave were that some would be apostles, some prophets, some evangelists, some pastors and teachers, to equip the saints for the work of ministry, for building up the body of Christ," writes Paul in Ephesians 4:11–12. In my community these gifts have been given to members who are gay and lesbian, for the upbuilding of the body of Christ. Who are we to deny the gifts of God? As I write this, I am astounded by the stories and over-whelmed by the blessing that these people have been in my life and community. Is my experience unusual? For some yes, for others no. It all depends, I suspect, on what kinds of people are welcomed around the table of the Lord.

It is only in the telling of such stories in our communities that we as a people will be able to live out the story of our faith in ways that are both faithful to the witness of scripture and attentive to the new working of the Spirit in our midst. And when we live lives of such creative fidelity, then we will be a people for whom the Bible is not merely a rule book, but a living and authoritative word.

Notes

1. Although I am indebted for the model of the unfinished drama to N. T. Wright, "How Can the Bible be Authoritative?" *Vox Evangelica* 21 (1991), 7–32, my description of that drama in terms of six acts follows J. Richard Middleton and Brian J. Walsh, *Truth is Stranger than it Used to Be: Biblical Faith in a Postmodern World* (Downers Grove: 1995), 182.

2. This is the relevance of his references to the widow of Sidon whom Elijah helped, and to Naaman the Syrian army commander whom Elisha helped (vv. 25–27). Both of these Gentiles were assisted when there were many Israelites in need as well.

3. Although the eunuch was probably Jewish, it is important to note that he was a eunuch and therefore could not be allowed into the community of the holy according to Leviticus. As a result he would have been excluded from table fellowship by both the Pharisees and the Qumran community.

4. Luke Timothy Johnson points out the theological weight and respectability of the Pharisees' position here, in *Scripture and Discernment: Decision Making in the Church* (Nashville: 1996), 101.

5. Unfortunately my treatment here must remain brief. I refer you to the excellent discussions of this passage in Johnson, *Scripture and Discernment*, 61–108, and Stephen E. Fowl, *Engaging Scripture: A Model for Theological Interpretation* (Massachusetts/Oxford: 1998), 101–127.

6. By using the latter translation, the NRSV loses the force of James's introduction, in addition to misreading the Greek.

7. Exodus 12:43–49; cf. Genesis 34. A foundational text for the covenant between God and Israel was, of course, Genesis 17, where circumcision is given as a sign of that covenant. This text was foundational for the importance of circumcision in Judaism.

8. See 1 Thessalonians 5:11; 2 Corinthians 10:8, 13:10; Ephesians 4:12; cf. Romans 15:20; 1 Corinthians 3:6, 9–11; Ephesians 2:2.

Works Cited

Fowl, Stephen E. 1998. *Engaging Scripture: A Model for Theological Interpretation*. Massachusetts/Oxford: Blackwell.

Johnson, Luke Timothy. 1996. *Scripture and Discernment: Decision Making in the Church*. Nashville: Abingdon.

Middleton, J. Richard, and Brian J. Walsh. 1995. *Truth is Stranger Than it Used to Be: Biblical Faith in a Postmodern World*. Downers Grove: InterVarsity Press.

Siker, Jeffrey S. 1994. *Homosexuality in the Church: Both Sides of the Debate*. Louisville, KY: Wesminster John Knox.

Wright, N. T. 1991. "How Can the Bible be Authoritative?" *Vox Evangelica*. 21:7–32.

Reaffirming a History of Christian Sexual Diversity

DAVID TOWNSEND *teaches medieval literature at the University of Toronto, where he also served as the founding director of the University College Program in Sexual Diversity Studies. He and his life partner, Rob Norquay, worship at the Church of the Redeemer.*

———◆———

I am not going to write for you, in the pages that follow, as a credentialed expert in the field of historical theology. I know a fair bit about medieval culture in general and about medieval literature in particular; it's what I'm paid for. I know some theology, but I have no graduate degree in the discipline. I have a lifetime's experience of trying to live mindfully in the presence of the Source of our life — and of often failing to do so well or fully. I have a very great deal of experience of being told by other Christians that I've failed to do so at all, and that my visible presence among them is a scandal to the faithful.

Some of you who read this book would probably tell me, if we were standing face to face, that I'm an unrepentant sinner, or at least terribly deluded. You might go on to tell me that I have no business approaching the Table of the Lord without first amending my life. You might tell me that one of God's greatest gifts to me, my relationship with my lawfully wedded husband (I live in Ontario, where at the time of writing the Queen's courts have ruled on this one in my favour), deserves no recognition within the family of God. You might tell me that the ordination of men and women like me makes a mockery of the gospel.

I might tell you that such words are deeply hurtful to me, that they strike at the root of my dignity as a creature of God, and that they are a scandal to my faith. I might tell you about my struggle to cling to the promises God has made to me, when so many of my fellow Christians keep telling me, with so much energy, that God does not, after all, love me as I am — at least not so unproblematically as God loves them as they are. I might tell you how hard I find it to fathom how you could believe and say such things and yet claim genuinely to love me. I might ask you to search your heart to see whether zeal doesn't sometimes mask simple bigotry and hatred. I might go a step further and ask you whether it's I who am trying to split the church, or you.

Perhaps you would hear me, as clearly as I have heard you for thirty-five years, since I realized to my own initially horrified confusion that I desired other men, body and soul. Perhaps I would be able to set aside my anger toward you, and to hear in your voice a hunger and thirst after righteousness.

And then, without abandoning the concerns and passions that had brought us to this encounter, if God's grace were to illumine both our hearts, we might fall on one another's necks and weep.

As an academic, part of my job is to camouflage my investment in the material I study. This professional convention has a lot to do with models of scientific objectivity that began infiltrating the humanities already in the nineteenth century with the rise of German rationalism. Those conventions gained further momentum with the simple-minded faith in empirical progress that has clear-cut its way through God's creation in our lifetimes. To tell you at the outset that here I make no such pretensions to objectivity is itself like coming out of the closet. I'm exposing myself to easy attack. You can dismiss what I have to say, if you want to, as an unscientific product of wishful thinking.

The academic lust for objectivity has taken some hits in recent years, though, from various quarters. Theorists of historical writing have challenged the baldly "scientific" claims that historians of an earlier generation were wont to make. They have reasserted the fundamentally literary and rhetorical nature of the historical enterprise. Historical fact, they have argued, is not what we find, but what we make of what we find — and even what we find in the first place is a function of what we are capable, given our predispositions, of seeing. Postmodernist philosophers such as Jacques Derrida and Michel Foucault have queried the easy epistemological certainties of thought in the West since the Enlightenment. People of faith have their own reasons for not accepting facile demarcations between the perceiver and the perceived. One of the great insights of twentieth-century religious thought was formulated by Paul Tillich as follows: when we grasp the Ultimate Concern of our lives, we are as much grasped by it, so that we cannot take it as a mere object of scrutiny. To attend to it is to be changed in how we know it and what we are capable of saying about it. It shapes the mode of our knowledge even as we struggle to gain that knowledge.

So in what follows, I'll reflect on the history of how women and men who desire those of their own sex have lived within the church. I won't give you a comprehensive picture, nor will I try to nail down The Way It Really Was. And I invite you to admit that neither can you do so, because ultimately, when we are speaking about the human past, no one can, and no one ever has. We speak of the human past as it is intelligible to us; and the more profoundly we care about that past, the more deeply invested our telling of it is with our own hopes, desires, fears, and aspirations. Nor will I speak narrowly of theology, as though theology as a pronouncement of purer truth can somehow supersede the untidiness of how Christians have experienced lives lived faithfully (and not) in the midst of their own social and cultural moments. I'll speak, rather, of what I choose here to call the culture of the church, of which theological reflection is a deeply interwoven component.

The single best-known scholarly study of homosexuality's history within the Christian tradition almost certainly remains John Boswell's *Christianity, Social Tolerance, and Homosexuality* [1980]. Boswell, at the time an assistant professor of history at Yale, provided a survey of evidence from the rise of Christianity to the fourteenth century. He argued, basically, that received Christian attitudes toward same-sex desire in fact had a history. He demonstrated that those attitudes had not remained constant for nearly two thousand years. Instead, theological rhetoric against homosexuality had shifted markedly, a number of times — and, when it did so, followed rather than led widely-held social attitudes. He pointed to periods and places in Christian history in which sexual diversity had enjoyed relative tolerance and at times perhaps even acceptance. Boswell traced the rich medieval history of deep emotional affect between people of the same sex, though the evidence tends mostly to be about men. He mined the sanctioned traditions of spiritual friendship — whose notable figures include Charlemagne's schoolmaster, Alcuin of York, and Aelred of Rievaulx — to argue that passionate friendship between persons of the same sex had enjoyed safe and culturally sanctioned harbours within the Christian tradition. He combed medieval law codes and documentary evidence for traces of contemporary attitudes; he argued that the defensive tone of many legal pronouncements implied widespread vernacular acceptance of at least some expressions of same-sex desire. In the copious body of homoerotic poetry by twelfth-century churchmen he found evidence for a Christian culture that openly accepted the real and daily possibility that men's desire might be directed toward other men (and less copious evidence that the same was true of love between women). He traced the rise, by the close of the twelfth century, and throughout the thirteenth, of what another historian of the period, R. I. Moore, would several years later term "the formation of a persecuting society." In this latter period, the narrowing dogmatism of high scholastic culture, together with new social pressures of rapidly developing urban economies, swept away the erotic tolerance of a great deal of twelfth-century ecclesiastical culture. (The fortunes of Jews, lepers, and other outsiders similarly deteriorated in Western European Christian society during the same period.)

It still astonishes many scholars in the field to consider the extraordinarily wide readership garnered by a book so laden with long, erudite, multilingual footnotes as was Boswell's. (Mostly, we're jealous.) Many who read it did so not as specialists, but as general readers searching for a past with which they could live. (*Christopher Street*, a gay literary review, carried in the early 1980s a cartoon of two men sitting on bar stools, one of them asking the other, "So how about coming back to my place for a little Christianity, Social Tolerance, and Homosexuality?") Boswell's detractors began appearing very soon after he published his book, and they attacked both from the right and from the left. Conservative Christians objected to his suggestion that the entire Christian tradition might not evince timeless and monolithic consensus on the subject of same-sex desire. Conservative historians and theologians attacked Boswell for his use or misuse of evidence. Adherents of the gay liberation movement's more dogmatically secular wing, at the other end of the scale, sneered at what they viewed as his retrograde attempt to rehabilitate the hopelessly benighted and repressive institution of the Christian church.

Boswell laid himself open to such charges, from both flanks. He was a committed Roman Catholic, and his investment in rehabilitating the openness and inclusivity of his own religious tradition ran deep. He was careful to preserve ostensibly a historian's distance from categories of sexual understanding that obtained in the distant past, and yet he clearly wished to find in that past the reflection of a humanity and breadth of acceptance absent from the present. (Consider that his book was published just three years after Anita Bryant, a born-again former Miss America and commercial promoter of Florida orange juice, led a high-profile campaign to repeal a human rights ordinance outlawing discrimination on grounds of sexual orientation in Miami, Florida.) He tended to assume that literary declarations of passionate, intense love between persons of the same sex reflected lived experience rather than conventions of expression, and further, that such passion was likely to have extended to what we in the present would consider fully sexual behaviour. (Of course, some of his evidence admits little doubt, as for instance when Hilary of Orléans, a follower of Abelard, wrote, "Beautiful boy, flower fair, /Glittering jewel, if only you knew/That the loveliness of your face/Was the torch of my love.") He resolutely refused to read into documents of the patristic and early medieval periods an assumption of antihomosexual bias if the documents did not explicitly state such an attitude; and yet he tended to presume that reference to same-sex affectivity that might well carry sexual connotations for us would do so for contemporaries as well. If an inconsistency tainted his methodology, he showed no more bias than had many scholars, albeit in the opposite direction. The issue was often not so much that he revealed an interpretative prejudice, whereas his detractors did not, but that his bias was diametrically opposed to that which had so long prevailed in the study of the sources.

His book in any case remains foundational to much of what has followed, and few can deny what many attempted to deny before its publication — to wit, that the entire Christian tradition has not been consistently and uniformly at pains to ostracize sexual diversity from the community of the faithful. If Peter Damian's eleventh-century *Book of Gomorrah* is notable as a jeremiad against the evils of "sodomy" (and as late as he comes, Peter Damian is in fact the creator of that term as an abstract noun), it is fundamental to Peter's diatribe that he claims to be speaking of phenomena widespread in the ecclesiastical culture of his day. In this, he in fact lends further support to Boswell's contention that a vibrant homoerotic subculture did exist in the eleventh and twelfth centuries, and that that subculture substantially intersected the culture of the church, in the era of Durham and Chartres Cathedrals, of St. Anselm of Canterbury, Abelard, Peter the Venerable, Bernard of Clairvaux, and Hildegard of Bingen.

Peter Damian's book also illustrates vividly a point that has been made far more forcefully in the wake of Boswell's work: that "sodomy" is, as Michel Foucault put it, "an utterly confused category." It by no means consistently denotes a single act or class of acts; it can mean to the speaker virtually any sort of perceived sexual impropriety and be understood as virtually any other sort of sexual impropriety by the hearer. Later in the history of the term, many such improprieties are fundamentally heterosexual in nature; others at least capable of heterosexual expression. Peter Damian includes masturbation as a target of his invective, although the burden of his obsessions lies clearly with sexual activity between men. Mark D. Jordan has shed particularly clear light on the perplexities of "sodomy" as a category of theological and ethical reflection up to Thomas Aquinas. A number of scholars of the English Renaissance, including Alan Bray and other contributors to Jonathan Goldberg's collection, *Queering the Renaissance*, have shown how foreign its applications are, from Elizabeth I up through the Commonwealth and beyond, to our own categories of sexual understanding. (The very assumption that the essential core of the Sodomites' guilt in Genesis 19 accrues to the homosexual nature of their activity comes late to both Christian and Jewish exegetical traditions. Many interpretations of the passage focus instead on the implication of rape, or on violation of the rigid hospitality laws of traditional societies.)

We can observe another example of Christian culture's variable attitudes to homosexual persons and actions in the *Divine Comedy* of Dante Alighieri. Instead of giving us a single view of homosexuality, his work actually incorporates a range of various views of sexual diversity accessible to late medieval Western Christians. Few literary flowerings of Christian culture surpass Dante's great fourteenth-century myth of the Christian spiritual universe. In case you haven't read Dante in detail or recently, I should start with a quick orientation. The overarching fiction of the *Comedy* is that, at the age of thirty-five, in the year 1300, the author finds himself at an impasse in his own path to salvation that can only be resolved by passing through Hell, Purgatory, and Heaven, in order to witness in its most perfectly observable form God's ordering of the universe. Dante then goes on to people the three realms of the afterlife with identifiable individuals, often his contemporaries, whom he chooses as suitable allegorical representations of moral abstractions. He obviously doesn't intend to suggest that someone consigned to hell in his poem for gluttony, for example, was guilty of that sin and that sin alone; or that in so placing an identifiable individual, he was pronouncing definitively on his or her eternal salvation. What Dante's tour of the afterlife represents is the framework for theologically grounded ethical judgement available to one of the great minds of his generation. Dante represents twice those whom most commentators on his poem call the Sodomites, first in Hell and then again in Purgatory. His portrayal of them is peculiarly shot full of contradictions and inconsistencies.

In the *Inferno*, Dante places the Sodomites in a subdivision of the Seventh Circle, to which are consigned the Violent. He thus in this passage represents homosexual desire not so much as a type of lust as of violence against nature itself. (In this, his imaginative representation recapitulates the received understanding of Thomas Aquinas's moral theology, as first articulated a few decades before Dante wrote.) Dante has already in the Second Circle witnessed the punishment of the Lustful — among them most notably the celebrated Paolo and Francesca. In the *Inferno*, the Sodomites walk forever across an endlessly burning plain of sand while flakes of fire drift down upon them from above. It's a facile, reductive image, the nuanced touches of Dante's genius notwithstanding, and it reinforces the moral prejudices inculcated by the most retrogressive strains of Christian thought.

Dante's concern for symmetry might have led us to expect that he would represent the penitent sinners of the *Purgatorio* according to the same schema of moral theology, but he doesn't. Instead, he shifts gears and speaks of sexual diversity with a tolerance and acceptance of its reality in the lives of Christians for which nothing in the *Inferno* would have prepared us. On his way to the earthly Paradise, the site of Eden itself, at the top of the mount of Purgatory, and just before the final ascent to that place of original blessedness, Dante passes through the last Cornice on which the imperfections of those destined for Paradise are erased from their souls. Here, the sin of lust is purged away, regardless of whether that perversion of the human capacity to love has been directed toward members of one's opposite sex or one's own. Those who have abused their sexuality circle the mountain, enveloped in a ring of purifying fire, but the direction of their circuit depends upon the orientation of their affections.

One might well contend, as Joseph Pequigney, among others, has done, that Dante's take on homosexuality in the *Purgatorio* isn't entirely compatible with the moral framework he'd already espoused in the *Inferno*. Whereas before, his theological justification for denouncing homosexuality suggested that it hardly even bore comparison with heterosexual desire, here he suggests that sexual passion is of a piece. He implies that we are all equally subject to ethical judgement as to whether our sexual behaviour respects our own and one another's dignity as creatures of God, or else whether a disordered use of our ability to love has caused us to fall away from God's will for our lives. In the *Purgatorio* he shows, for a writer so centrally engaged in moral casuistry, remarkably little interest as to whether such failings are heterosexual or homosexual in nature.

Moreover, the souls in Dante's Purgatory aren't stuck eternally on their terrace of the mountain: they move from one level to the next when they've been purified of the sin pertinent to each. And this begs the question: Do those who circle the Cornice of the Lustful in one direction then turn around and circle it in the other, if they've erred in the expression of their sexuality with both men and women? Or does Dante assume that there are fundamentally different orientations inherent in different individuals, and that if you went counterclockwise in life, so to speak, you'll go counterclockwise on Mount Purgatory, and that's the sum of it? Dante seems to be suggesting, in other words, that it is the nature of some people to desire their own sex, which by implication explodes the argument, grounded in Aquinas, that lay behind his treatment in the *Inferno*. There, we saw the Sodomites punished because they had violated human nature; here, homosexual individuals atone for the abuse of what is and remains specific to their nature as homosexually disposed persons. The same may be said of Dante's heterosexual penitents, no more and no less. What Dante of course doesn't offer here is a celebration of sexuality and sexual passion as God's gift, but one could hardly expect such affirmations of a fourteenth-century European, at least not when the overarching conceit of his great work is a summation of contemporary understandings of the vices and virtues. My point here is simply that Dante doesn't know one single thing to make exclusively of homosexual desire. The Christian culture out of which he writes offered him a range of options, some more humane and some less. His work in a sense embodies the implicit contradictions between those options, for rather than choosing between them, he incorporated at least two into the *Comedy*. He thus offers us, in effect, a vivid witness to what it was like for gay people, and those scandalized by them, to live together in the church of the fourteenth century.

The rich tradition of passionate same-sex friendship in Victorian England and America is another well-known locus of toleration for erotic attraction sometimes understated, but sometimes in fact hiding in plain sight. The undergraduate culture of the University of Oxford, as much as any other single institution, provided the wellspring for such sensibilities. Generations of Oxford dons and students alike drew on the prestige of classical Greek literature and philosophy, and above all on the dialogues of Plato, to account for the ennobling effects of love between men. But the culture of passionate affection between Victorian Oxonians owed as much to specifically Anglican sensibilities as to immersion in the Greek Classics. Linda Dowling has examined the traditions of intense emotional and spiritual focus within the Tractarian circle of the 1830s and 1840s, and the close, wholistic bonds between tutor and student first fostered by John Henry Newman at Oriel College, which came to function as a norm for teacher-pupil relations at Oxford for generations. The amalgam of classical learning and fervid spiritual friendship that dominated Oxford (where fellows of the colleges were forbidden to marry until 1884) was often pious — and often charged with intense erotic energy.

Many Oxonians were of course intent upon denying any physical expression of such sensibilities, but the denials often had a peculiar thinness to them. The great Platonist Benjamin Jowett, for example, extolled the philosopher's dialogues as the greatest of human writings save scripture, but he was frequently at pains to insist that Plato's exposition of human love could be accepted only in a heterosexual context, despite Plato's own frank and matter-of-fact assumption of homosexual attraction as an ordinary and daily reality. John Addington Symonds, a pupil of Jowett, broke with his master over just this point, and went on to become a prominent figure in the extensive Victorian movement for the acceptance of homosexual disposition as a natural and morally neutral variation of human personality. (Gregory Woods among many others records that Symonds wrote the American poet Walt Whitman more than once, attempting to elicit from Whitman an admission that the "Calamus" poems from *Leaves of Grass* celebrated sexually consummated love between men. Whitman repeatedly rebuffed the suggestion, but the burden of Whitman scholarship over the last twenty-five years has increasingly assumed the erotic nature of the poet's celebrations of the love of comrades.)

John Boswell turned, in the years before his early death, to another project demonstrating the rich Christian history of same-sex bonds, *Same-Sex Unions in Premodern Europe* [1994]. Here Boswell identified, edited, translated, and interpreted a number of Eastern Orthodox rites (mostly in Greek, but occasionally in Slavonic) that appear to have been in use through much of the later Byzantine period and beyond. The burden of these rites is clearly the establishment of a lasting, ritually recognized bond between two persons of the same sex. Boswell argued carefully and at length that these offices essentially provided rites, parallel to heterosexual marriage, for the church-sanctioned creation of same-sex life partnerships. He spends a lot of time considering alternative interpretations; ongoing objections, though possible, must thus answer his own refutations before they proceed. How convincing such sustained objections are is another matter, and I have to say that I myself find them somewhat tendentious. In any case, Boswell took such pains to recover these rites from their previous obscurity — sometimes in earlier modern editions, but mostly unedited, before his book, in the surviving manuscripts — presicely because he cared passionately about the connection of the Christian past to the Christian present, and so was willing also to risk speculation about the meanings they had for their contemporaries.

I would like to propose a way out of the impasse over interpretation of these latter documents. What if we were all, on both sides of the divide to let go of the question of whether these rites were officially, or universally, or dominantly, understood as same-sex marriage ceremonies? What if instead we asked the more speculative question of the variety of ways in which they might have been interpreted and used in the churches where they enjoyed currency? What if, in doing so, we acknowledged that at least for some Christians, these ceremonies allowed for the integration of their innate affective inclinations with the culture of the church as they had opportunity to live it? (Let's assume, for the sake of argument here, a cross-cultural applicability of the classic Kinsey-derived figure of ten per cent.) We know that these rites were suppressed — but only after they had been in use for centuries. Is it likely that bishops only realized after twenty or twenty-five generations that men might understand themselves to be marrying other men, and women as marrying other women, under cover of rites that were actually intended to allow for adoption as siblings, or as "blood brothers," or simply as singularly close friends (these being the principal alternative interpretations)? If so, the penny dropped with a slowness miraculous even by episcopal standards of response to popular culture. If the rites were eventually suppressed (and in some cases the textual evidence for their very existence mutilated), that suppression may well have reflected rising tides of antihomosexual feeling or thought. But does it undo the obvious possibility that Christians used the cultural materials available to them in order to make social (and spiritual) sense out of the circumstances of their lives?

If you are one of the readers on the other side of the divide whom I addressed at the outset, you may well view such a possibility as merely one more example of the church's ubiquitous fallibility, and as no warrant for an ongoing accommodation of openly gay and lesbian Christians. I only ask you to consider, at this point, that the presence of men and women like me in the church is not a new thing. What is new is that we have a modern language to articulate who we are, and that modern language makes it more likely that you will notice our presence in ways that you cannot easily and comfortably dismiss. We have always worshipped beside you, whether you've been able to pick us out from among your other brothers and sisters or not. We have always found ways to inhabit the culture of the church we share, by what means we can. We will continue to do so. We're not going away, and we will not lightly sell the birthright of our baptism. What has changed is that we are no longer inclined to accept that it's God's will for our lives to wait endlessly on the scraps from the table.

I will suggest here — and this is the point toward which this whole essay has been tending all along — that it is high time for queer Christians (the label is far more succinct than a list of all of us whose sexuality is variously diverse) to appropriate more fully the long history of living together in the church. It is time, that is, to remind ourselves that we've been around, among the followers of Christ our Lord and Liberator, for as long as those who want nothing to do with us. We should ask ourselves how best (and most effectively) to affirm and claim our baptismal dignity as members of the Body of Christ. To argue that we should be accepted openly and fully is of course necessary. But we also need, amidst that struggle for justice (and justice, we keep finding out, is sometimes far more costly than charity) to keep our eyes fixed on the ways in which the culture of the church is already there for us to inhabit. Synods, assemblies, and conferences will doubtless continue to wrangle as to whether we should receive the supports along our path toward God that most Christians assume will be afforded to them. It is up to us, and not only up to bishops and commissions, to find ways of living within the church's culture that make spiritual sense of our lives and that build us up as members of Christ. Throughout much of Christian history, we've flown below the radar to survive spiritually, and sometimes to survive physically. Perhaps we should ask ourselves what lessons we can still learn from such survival strategies of the past — not as a capitulation, but in order to claim for ourselves, in the flawed here and now, our place in the community of the faithful. In doing so, we will not only participate in the culture of the church. We will also inevitably help to shape it. We should do so without apology, and without waiting endlessly for human permission.

What are some of the ways in which we might do this? How, to take just one example, might we discern what Boswell's eleventh-century couples at the altar have to offer us? I'm suggesting that, while we continue to work toward official ecclesiastical recognition of the goodness of our lives, we not focus on such sanction to the exclusion of other strategies to assure our wholeness. I've called attention to the rich tradition of ways in which church culture has over the centuries offered spaces where we have lived as queer followers of Jesus Christ. Boswell's rites of union may or may not have been "marriage," but they were in any case in use, and I'm hard put to see how one can argue that they weren't susceptible of interpretation, by some individuals and by some communities, as "marriage." (You may leave the scare quotes in if you will.) For the time being, should we not consider how we can move forward with the materials that lie to hand? Bishops may not allow same-sex unions; but house blessings are unexceptionable, and in parishes where openly lesbian and gay Christians are fully incorporated into the life of the community, such a liturgy can function as a publicly announced and acknowledged ritual whose meaning is surely as unmistakable as it is officially denied.

Consider the other approved services of the church. Last year, I was present at the baptism of a baby both of whose two moms stood with him at the font. To the *Book of Alternative Services*'s questions to the parents and sponsors, the officiant added one extra: "Do you intend to be known henceforth as the [*your chosen surname here*] family?" With the simple answer, "We do," these women proclaimed the reality of their lives, in front of God and everybody. And their son had a more honest start to his life among the People of God than he might have had otherwise.

Such strategies are anything but anomalous in the history of the church's culture. It's the quintessential genius of Christian ritual language to take old words, ancient words, and make them new. No one argues this point better than the Lutheran liturgical theologian Gordon Lathrop. Christian worship has always begun, he observes, with received language for talking about God, and has proceeded to set it into new contexts that break it open and allow God's light to flow, at least partially and intermittently (with apologies here to Leonard Cohen), through its cracks. We gather weekly and often use Sabbath metaphors for the practice; but we gather not on the last day of the week, but the first day of the new week, which is simultaneously the eighth day of the creation made new in the Risen Lord. We take the Hebrew scriptures and point them, under the guidance of the Spirit, not backwards toward the historical context that gave rise to them, but forwards in ways that sometimes stand their original significance on its head. Thus we worship a God who proclaims that s/he is making all things new, and who announces, "Behold, now it springs forth — do you not perceive it?" Such use of the language and actions of Christian worship is not simply open to us. I would argue further. It is our prophetic calling. As it was the prophetic calling of African-American slaves to sing of the Exodus, to the impotent consternation of their masters and of churchmen who had accommodated the institution of slavery within American society.

Those, on the one hand, who will settle for nothing less than full ecclesiastical recognition of our lives and relationships may balk at such suggestions. Those, on the other, who brook no accommodation within the church of the lives of queer Christians, may protest what they see as disingenuous abuse. To the first group of readers, I'd answer that, given the Anglican tendency to make authority into a fetish (if not indeed sometimes an idol), end-runs around hierarchy are in fact a pretty radical and unsettling act. I'd suggest that claiming the church's cultural vocabulary for ourselves amounts to a practice of ecclesiastical disobedience: we plough the fields, and scatter. Of the second group of readers, I'd ask, What would you have us do? Go on sitting in shadow at the back of the nave so you can pretend we're invisible, while you sit at the front, behaving as though the gospel were proclaimed for you and you alone?

———◦———

I should like to close this chapter by returning to Dante's Purgatory, and to the witness his poem bears to a vision of hope that unites Christians of diverse life experience. The *Purgatorio* is arguably the section of his poem that most directly reflects life as we know it: in Purgatory time and change continue. Things happen; souls progress and move toward God; near the end, there are fabulous, campy, over-the-top allegorical pageants that easily rival the best floats on Pride Day. I've already suggested that in the *Purgatorio* Dante is not at pains to indict human sexuality *per se*: the classification of that desire as "gay" or "straight" (you will pardon the anachronism for its economy of expression) characterizes saints in the making as the individuals they are, but it doesn't serve to establish the rightness or wrongness of one orientation or the other. The penitents simply move about the mountain, on their way to Paradise, in opposite directions. And in the course of every circuit they complete, each in holy charity kisses one from the other group, and then swiftly moves on.

Works Cited

Boswell, John. 1980. *Christianity, Social Tolerance, and Homosexuality*. Chicago: University of Chicago Press.

——. 1994. *Same-Sex Unions in Premodern Europe*. New York: Villard.

Cohen, Leonard. 1993. "Anthem." In *Stranger Music: Selected Poems and Songs*. Toronto: McClelland and Stewart.

Dante. *Inferno*. 1949. Tr. Dorothy L. Sayers. Harmondsworth, UK: Penguin.

——. *Purgatory*. 1955. Tr. Dorothy L. Sayers. Harmondsworth, UK: Penguin.

Dowling, Linda. 1994. *Hellenism and Homosexuality in Victorian Oxford*. Ithaca, NY: Cornell University Press.

Foucault, Michel. 1990. *The History of Sexuality: An Introduction*. Vol. 1. Tr. Robert Hurley. New York: Vintage.

Goldberg, Jonathan, ed. 1994. *Queering the Renaissance*. Durham, NC: Duke University Press.

Jordan, Mark D. 1997. *The Invention of Sodomy in Christian Theology*. Chicago: University of Chicago Press.

Lathrop, Gordon. 1998. *Holy Things*. Minneapolis: Fortress Press.

Moore, R. I. 1987. *The Formation of a Persecuting Society*. Oxford: Blackwell.

Pequigney, Joseph. 1991. "Sodomy in Dante's *Inferno* and *Purgatorio*." *Representations* 36 (Fall): 22–42.

Tillich, Paul. 1951. *Systematic Theology*. Vol. 1. Chicago: University of Chicago Press.

Woods, Gregory. 1998. *A History of Gay Literature: The Male Tradition*. New Haven, CT: Yale University Press.

Icons of Christ

Reflections on Gay and Lesbian Spirituality

SISTER THELMA-ANNE McLEOD, SSJD, *was born in Estevan, Saskatchewan, in 1928 and grew up in Regina. She holds degrees from Queen's University and Bryn Mawr College. She joined the Sisterhood of St. John the Divine in 1957 and has worked in many areas, including music and conducting retreats. She served on the task force that produced the 1998 Canadian Anglican hymn book,* Common Praise. *A member of Integrity/Toronto, she led their annual retreat for over twenty years.*

⸺⸺

In an address given during the annual Long Retreat to the Sisters of St. John the Divine in 2002, the well-known British spiritual writer Margaret Silf observed that, though Jesus was restricted to one particular set of circumstances in his human life — for example, he did not know what it is to be a woman, to be married, to be old and infirm — he wants to experience and redeem all these circumstances through the life of each one of us.

> Each of us walks one pathway through life, and that pathway is unique. If I do not walk it in a way that makes me a channel of grace, no one ever will.... My particular track, traced through my life's events, my relationships, my unique mix of gifts and weaknesses ... is becoming a channel of God's redeeming love, if I am willing to live through, with, and in God [Silf 2002].

In the Eastern Orthodox tradition, an icon is a point of contact with the spiritual reality it depicts, be it a saint or an event in the life of Christ. So it is with us. In walking our life journey through, with, and in God, each of us becomes, by grace, a living icon through which some aspect of Christ can shine forth.

These two themes — life journey as a channel of grace, and being a living icon — will be interwoven in these reflections on lesbian and gay spirituality. But first of all, we need to consider what we mean by spirituality, and how it relates to the sexual aspects of our life.

Spirituality and Sexuality

Spirituality, in general, is grounded in the human search for ultimate reality and value, and finds expression in basic attitudes and in the practices that embody them. For the Christian, the initiative comes from God. Christian spirituality is our response to the work of the Holy Spirit, forming Christ within us. "If anyone is in Christ, there is a new creation." Spirituality embraces the whole of life. It begins with our intimate relationship with the God who made us and loves us. It pervades and transforms all aspects of our being, both mind and body. It embraces all our communal and interpersonal relationships. It reaches out in service to others, and commits us to justice.

If spirituality embraces the whole of life, then it embraces our sexuality. Sexuality is more than "having sex." It includes our self-understanding as male and female, our culturally defined attitudes and characteristics as masculine or feminine, the way we relate to others both physically and spiritually. It grounds our capacity to love and our creativity.

Yet it has been, and still is, widely believed that spirituality and sexuality are at enmity. Flesh wars against spirit. The object of the spiritual life is to control our "animal nature." In fact, much of our spiritual tradition is based on a conflict of "flesh" versus "spirit." This, in turn, arises from a dualism that has dominated our way of experiencing reality for so long that we have come to believe that it presents a complete, accurate, and truthful account of the way things are.

This dualism goes back a long way in our history. Only a sketchy and perhaps oversimplified account can be given here. (For a thorough treatment, I recommend the chapter, "Sexual Aliena-tion: the Dualistic Nemesis" in James B. Nelson's *Embodiment: An Approach to Sexuality and Christian Theology*.) Nelson distinguishes between duality ("two harmonious elements" that "may exist in creative tension") and dualism (" two different elements" that may live together in an uneasy truce but are frequently in conflict") [Nelson 1978, 37]. Thus, a spirituality that celebrates sexuality as an integral part of human life and a potential means of grace could hold together body and spirit in collaboration as a duality. On the other hand, a dualistic approach would see sexuality and spiritu-ality in a conflict that can be resolved only by the victory of spirit over flesh.

Two kinds of dualism have strongly influenced Christian spir-ituality. Spiritualistic, or mind/body, dualism, deriving from late Greek philosophy and reinforced by Stoicism, held that knowl-edge is attained by cutting oneself off as far as possible from the body in order to avoid its infection [Nelson 1978, 46]. Sexist, or patriarchal, dualism is found both in the Hebrew scriptures and in the writings of the early Christian church. The two in combina-tion have had disastrous consequences for women. "Men assumed to themselves superiority in reason and spirit and thus believed themselves destined to lead both civil and religious communities. Contrarily, women were identified with the traits of emotion, body, and sensuality" [46]. Modern secularism has replaced a dualism of body/spirit with one of body/self. The body is seen as a *thing*, an instrument or tool of the mind, a machine or slave owned by the self [41]. Sex is about performance — "*making* love" — rather than ecstasy [43].

From these considerations it would appear that dualism is driven by a need to control and a fear of what is experienced as a threat to control — the body, the irrational, the feminine — what-ever is different, whatever does not fit the system and, by not fitting, calls the system into question. Against this challenge, dualism in-vokes a hierarchy of values to confer power and legitimate its misuse. Worse still, this hierarchy and the abuse of power that stems from it are seen to be the will of God, the order of creation — not only the way things are, but the way they ought to be. Slavery, racism, and the subjection of women have been justified on these grounds. For example, neutral dualities like light/darkness are reinterpreted in terms of value (better/worse, higher/lower, and even good/evil) to justify white supremacy. The language of dualism has been a powerful means of social control: the "lower" classes were supposed to "know their place." Even today, a woman who aspires to equality with a man may be treated to epithets ranging from mildly contemptuous to downright obscene. Dualism, with its built-in emphasis on conflict, on winning or losing, tends toward violence, whether verbal or physical.

In the spiritual realm, dualism, with its mistaken assumption that flesh is necessarily evil and spirit necessarily good, leads to an extreme asceticism, in which the body and its impulses are ruthlessly suppressed. This asceticism is described as "spiritual warfare." The unholy alliance of sexist and spiritualistic dualism is epitomized in words from a well-known hymn: "Fight manfully onward, dark passions subdue." In Catholicism, virginity has been considered to be the highest expression of the spiritual life. Common to both Catholic and Protestant traditions has been the view that marriage exists for the sole purpose of procreation; enjoyment of sex by husband and wife is condemned as mere lust. Sexuality is assigned "not to the good order of creation but to the results of the Fall" [Nelson 1978, 52].

The biblical account of the Fall offers a very different perspective. In the first chapter of Genesis we are told that God created everything and declared it to be good. But we find in the third chapter the story about how we fell from grace and became alienated — not only from God but from each other and from our own bodies. In his book *Jesus, the Liberator of Desire*, the Benedictine theologian Sebastian Moore has some interesting things to say about this alienation and how it created the chasm in our nature that makes dualistic thinking so attractive. He writes that "failure of the 'higher' to befriend the 'lower' is the key to the whole thing.... Ironically, the would-be god whom the serpent has duped finds the evidences of his/her own animality embarrassing" [Moore 1989,

98]. Before the act of disobedience, the couple were naked together and knew no shame. In the act itself, they knew themselves to be naked. Afterwards, they hid from God because they were ashamed of their nakedness. Shame is "how sexuality looks to the human pretending to be God; it is the looking down on sexuality that is the immediate effect of claiming divinity as one's own." Sin, Moore suggests, consists "in contempt for the flesh" [99]. Alienated flesh gets its revenge by "behaving like the outlaw it now is — and this is lust" [98]. No wonder that so much of our spiritual tradition is profoundly suspicious of sex.

From this account, it would appear that value-laden dualism is not part of the original order of creation but rather, the result and symptom of the original act of disobedience. When God tells the couple that the wife's desire will be for her husband, and that he will be her master, God is describing how the relation between man and woman has been perverted. Instead of a companion, the woman becomes a despised slave, and the man becomes a tyrant whose right to dominate the woman is divinely ordained. Society is built around this primal domination.

By his life and teaching, Jesus challenges the dualistic model in many ways. In his teaching about marriage, for example, he allows the possibility that a woman, as well as a man, might initiate divorce. He challenges the very premises on which dualistic society rests by modelling non-defensiveness as an alternative to that of domination/submission. This is what he means when he says to Pilate, "My kingdom is not from this world — [otherwise] my followers would be fighting to keep me from being handed over" [John 18:36]. Jesus' mission is to heal the dualistic split and to restore wholeness. Against this, by their very nature, the powers and principalities brought into being by the original alienation ("becoming like gods") mobilize their strength, and will continue to crucify Christ until the end of time.

Side by side with the prevailing either/or dualism, there have always existed integrative (both/and) spiritualities, based on a model of human wholeness, of harmony rather than conflict. In these spiritualities, mind, body, sexuality, are seen as reflecting the goodness of creation. That celebration of erotic love, the Song of

Solomon, has been interpreted in Christian spirituality as an expression of the love between human and divine partners. To give a few examples, the language of erotic love has been used by mystics to express our relationship with God. Ignatian spirituality is based on the question, "What is my deepest desire?" Desire is central in the writings of Sebastian Moore. In a famous essay, "The Body's Grace," Rowan Williams states that "the whole story of creation, incarnation, and our incorporation into the fellowship of Christ's body tells us that God desires us, *as if we were God*" and that the rationale of the Christian community is to teach us so to order our relations (including our sexual relations) that "human beings may see themselves as desired, as the occasion of joy" [in Hefling 1996, 59].

Psychology has underlined the importance of an integrated sexuality for human wholeness and well-being. In the words of James B. Nelson, "Sexuality thus expresses God's intention that we find our authentic humanness in relationships. But such humanizing relationship cannot occur on the human dimension alone. Sexuality, we must also say, is intrinsic to our relationship with God" [Nelson 1978, 18]. This is not surprising. Our spirituality and our sexuality flow from the same source, the deep wellspring of God's creative love, and to that love we must respond with our whole being.

Unlike the dualistic model, the integrative view of sexuality recognizes that masculine and feminine are not mutually exclusive. The mature person incorporates and celebrates the positive characteristics of the opposite sex. The integrative model also recognizes that we are neither exclusively heterosexual nor exclusively homosexual, but rather that we are on a continuum. "All normal mature people are 'bisexual' in the sense of having an ability to relate to persons of either sex in ways that are tender, warm and deep" [Rees et al. 1980, 182].

The Gay Challenge to Dualism

In his book *Spiritual Direction and the Gay Person*, the Jesuit spiritual director and theologian James L. Empereur writes:

Homosexuality is one of God's most significant gifts to humanity. To be gay or lesbian is to have received a special blessing from God.... God has given to gay men or lesbian women a special sexual gift which shows forth the diversity and beauty of God in our world in a public way. All creatures show forth God's handiwork, but the world also needs variation so that the richness of this handiwork is unmistakably evident. God gives gays and lesbians the rather startling variation of their sexuality to help their brothers and sisters have greater insights into the reality of their God" [Empereur 1998, 1–3].

Empereur goes on to describe this gift as a "sexual charism." (A charism is "a gift given to someone to be shared because the world needs the presence of that gift.... All charisms converge in the task of raising up the God hidden in our world and in our lives" [3].)

How can this be? First of all, the presence and increased visibility of lesbians and gays challenges the whole dualistic system. By their built-in deviance from the "world" with its pattern of domination/submission, gays and lesbians (and all other "misfits") relativize and subvert it. (Although I do not specifically address the contribution of bisexual and transgendered persons, they too challenge the claims of male/female dualism to tell the whole story about human sexuality.) Because gay men are perceived as having feminine characteristics and lesbians, masculine, people with a same-sex orientation threaten to dissolve the neat, either/or categories. They do this by calling into question the roles and the defining characteristics assigned to male and female. Some of this, to be sure, is stereotypical. The flighty, emotional, "feminine" gay man affronts the masculine self-image, while the tough, "macho" lesbian who can live quite happily without a man insults the fantasy that a woman is incomplete and a failure without a male sexual partner. Being gay or lesbian can only threaten those who operate according to fixed stereotypes of what it means to be masculine or feminine. The presence of persons with a same-sex orientation calls into question our understanding not only of sexual roles but also of such social institutions as the family.

Same-sex relations, Rowan Williams suggests, "oblige us to

think directly about bodiliness and sexuality in a way that socially and religiously sanctioned heterosexual unions do not." Same-sex love "annoyingly poses the question of what the meaning of desire is — in itself, not considered as instrumental to some other process, such as the peopling of the world. We are brought up against the possibility not only of pain and humiliation without any clear payoff, but just as worryingly, of nonfunctional joy — of joy, to put it less starkly, whose material 'production' is an embodied person aware of grace" [in Hefling 1996, 66].

Moreover, by living exemplary Christian lives that manifest the fruit of the Spirit, lesbians and gays invite the churches to see grace at work where they thought it impossible. We are in a situation similar to that of first-century Jewish Christians in their struggle to accept and welcome Gentiles, who were regarded as unclean and beyond redemption. What convinced Jewish Christians that Gentiles could be included was that they too had received the Holy Spirit. Canon Gray Temple, a charismatic Episcopal priest, discovered that lesbian and gay Christians not only lead exemplary lives, but receive the same gifts of the Spirit, including tongues, as straight Christians — and remain homoerotically oriented. He found that the gay and lesbian Christians he came to know "spoke of Jesus as we ourselves know him; that these folks lead lives as orderly as our own; that their deepest relationships manifest the same grace as our own marriages" [para. 17].

Gays and Lesbians as Icons of Christ

Gay and lesbian Christians present Jesus as marginalized and outcast, an exile in the dominant culture, the suffering servant, despised and rejected, yet bringing healing through his very wounds; as the stranger, whose presence calls us to remember our own strangerhood. In so doing, they become for other Christians, icons of Christ.

Before considering these themes in more detail, we need to be clear about what it means for any Christian, gay or straight, to be an icon of Christ. We distinguish between being an icon of Christ (a sign to the church) and being Christ-like in our own lives. Every baptized person is called to be an icon of Christ. This does not automatically confer a likeness to Christ. What it does confer is a call to follow him and by grace grow into that particular aspect of Christ-likeness to which each one of us is called.

The theme of exile as a metaphor for the experience of gays and lesbians is developed by therapist John E. Fortunato in his book *Embracing the Exile*. To live authentically as gay and Christian is to place oneself on the outskirts of both society and the church. Rejection by family, harassment at work, verbal abuse, and physical violence are ever present realities. Those suffering from HIV/AIDS are treated as lepers. Protection against hate crimes is only now being guaranteed by legislation in our own country. It is hardly necessary to point out the rejection which gays and lesbians experience in the church. Precisely because of this rejection, it is often remarked that it is harder to come out as Christians in the gay community than to come out as gay in the church.

"Exile is simply where we find ourselves when we are who we are.... Banished. We come bearing gifts that aren't welcome. We come with love to give that's rejected" [Fortunato 1982, 17]. The acceptance of being rejected and marginalized calls lesbians and gays to find meaning and worth at a deeper level. "What matters is that you love and are loved by love. And nobody can take it away from you. Nobody. That's solid. That's real" [91]. This knowledge brings with it the freedom to love and to forgive. "Loving anyway, sharing anyway. Giving gifts even when no one wants them. Embracing the exile" [17]. This way of living is based on a profound belief that not only can life on the fringes be endured by gay Christians, but that "being banished can be viewed as an incredible spiritual opportunity.... Loving in the face of utter rejection means following in some of the most painful footsteps of Jesus, the Christ" [18].

To respond to the call to walk in the footsteps of Jesus is to find meaning and purpose in what would otherwise be undeserved, unwarranted pain. The person who finds himself in this place is able, through grace, to align his sufferings with those of Christ, offering to God himself and all that befalls him. The fruit of this is union with Christ, and a growing confidence that, by having embraced the reality of her situation as vocation, the person's life becomes a channel of God's redeeming love. Christ lives in her and she in Christ. Little by little she grows into the likeness of Christ, manifested in love, forgiveness, empathy, and compassion.

I am not suggesting that suffering is good in itself. Jesus came that we might have life and have it abundantly. He came to live, and to show us how to live, in God's love. He chose to keep on living in the truth and fullness of God's love, even though it cost him his life. He calls us to be wholly who we are, and to live that to the full, even though it may bring suffering and, all too often in our present world, even death. In being called to live fully the life they are given, gays and lesbians do indeed become icons of Christ, the suffering servant.

Lesbian and gay spirituality, shaped by experiences of marginality and suffering, holds before the church this image of Jesus. It challenges the church to be like him in accepting the marginality and suffering which are inevitable for those who ally themselves with the outcasts, and in so doing, to call into question the power structures ("principalities") of the world. This calling is not unique to gays and lesbians. Members of any group which is perceived as deviant from the dominant norm — be it women, people of other races, the elderly, the ill, the cognitively challenged — can bear the image of the Christ who was despised and rejected. At this point in the history of church and society, we are beginning to recognize sexism, racism, and other forms of discrimination as the evils they are. Nevertheless, there are many people who consider gays and lesbians fair game.

This is certainly not intended to suggest that the vulnerable and disenfranchised should simply be content to be victims. To work toward a just society is the duty of all and integral to Christian spirituality. Indeed, we have seen incredible changes in the last thirty years in the acceptance of gays and lesbians in society (and even in the church). In becoming more mainstream, however, lesbians and gays need to recognize the danger of total assimilation to the values of the dominant society. Remembering that as they were once "strangers in the land of Egypt," they must continue to welcome the stranger and stand beside those still marginalized.

Journey toward Wholeness, Journey in God

We are now in a position to consider the journey of faith by which lesbians and gays move toward the likeness of Christ. This is a journey that all Christians take, in one form or another. Various developmental models from psychology speak to us about growth toward maturity through the different stages of life. Similar models have been developed to describe the maturing of faith over a lifetime.

The biblical theme of Exodus has been crucial in shaping the imagination of both the Jewish and the Christian faith communities. Likewise, "coming out of the closet" is central to the life and spirituality of lesbian and gay persons. An essay by Roman Catholic therapists Evelyn Eaton Whitehead and James D. Whitehead, "Passages of Homosexual Holiness" not only charts the journey of gays and lesbians toward healing and integration; it also has implications for all human maturing.

The starting point of the journey is the widespread rejection already described. Lesbians and gays absorb this negativity and internalize it as self-hatred. The growing sense that one actually *deserves* the contempt and persecution so evidently sanctioned by society is reinforced by personal experience. Demeaning jokes, stereotyping, and even well-intended condescension confirm the sense of worthlessness. For faithful Christians, the ponderous pronouncements of the churches, or simply the discrepancy between statements of support and the knowledge that acceptance depends on hiding one's true identity, weigh heavily.

How does the lesbian or gay Christian move from self-hatred and dread to the secure knowledge of being loved and affirmed by God? The short answer is, by grace. A gay man on the brink of suicide experiences an epiphany, an assurance that he is loved and created in the divine image. Another, while at prayer, receives the message, "I will make of your gayness something creative." A lesbian wakes up one morning to discover that the self-loathing and fear of her sexuality with which she has struggled lifelong is simply there no longer, and recognizes this as sheer gift. Such glimpses of grace undergird and sustain the long and arduous journey from bondage to freedom which each is called to undertake.

The Whiteheads speak of journey, or passage, as a major metaphor of the Christian life. The central paradox of passage is loss and gain. It begins in disorientation and the threat of loss, and matures as one allows oneself to fully experience and name this loss. But this time of vulnerability and loss is also a time of potential grace, an opportunity for extraordinary growth. Amid the chaos and turmoil there come new strengths, an unexpected ability to risk and to trust. To negotiate such a passage brings new confidence and a new direction in life.

The closet is an "image of perilous transition" [Whitehead and Whitehead 1986, 133] for lesbians and gays, a developmental haven meant to be outgrown. To venture out of such secure confinement is to initiate a dangerous and exciting lifelong journey. The Whiteheads identify three closets and three passages in the process of coming out: an interior passage (coming out to oneself); a passage of intimacy (coming out to trusted others), and a public passage (being generally known as a lesbian or gay person). The first two are indispensable for emotional and spiritual growth; the third is seen as a special call, not feasible for everyone.

Coming out to oneself is the passage from the closet of ignorance or denial to the light of self-acceptance. It may come early or it may be long delayed. "This is a passage of identity and vocation — coming to admit and love who I am and who I am called to be" [Whitehead and Whitehead 1986, 134]. Fears will be powerfully reinforced by family, church, and culture, but the passage must be made. It is "foundational and nonnegotiable" [134]:

> All of our adult love and work hinge on the self-knowledge and self-intimacy released in this passage. Those Christians who over many years find themselves to be predominantly and enduringly homosexual must come to accept and love this

important part of themselves. To refuse this passage, to turn back because of the terror of this transition, is to choose a self-denial of a most unchristian form.... In the closet of self-rejection we can be obedient children, fulfilling every church law, but we cannot become adult believers [134–5].

Coming out to trusted others means being led into a way of presence with others in which one is known for who one is. One experiences a tension between the need and desire to share oneself and the fear of rejection and humiliation. But the growing comfort with oneself, gained in the first passage, opens the way to enter the risk and excitement of being known. The experience of being accepted and loved by family, friends, and colleagues still further affirms ability to love oneself. This passage is necessary "because it is so difficult to continually come up close in friendship and in work while keeping closeted an important part of oneself" [139]. Whether choosing a celibate or a sexually active lifestyle, the lesbian or gay person must face this passage. In the deepest sense of the word, intimacy is not optional. As in the exodus story, one does not make the journey alone, but as part of a community.

The third passage, being publicly known as both lesbian/gay and Christian, seems to be a special vocation. It *is* possible to grow in maturity without coming out publicly. But there are some for whom this third passage comes as a distinct call. The motive is generativity, the impulse to care for and to contribute to the good of humankind, and particularly to the good of those coming after us. The public witness of homosexual maturing in a community of faith becomes a gift to the next generation. It provides role models to young people who are still closeted or struggling to decide whether there is a place for them in church or synagogue, mosque or temple. It educates the faith community to accept and welcome lesbian and gay believers in their midst. Exodus means being entrusted with a mission.

Welcoming the Stranger, Healing the Church

What has all this to do with living together in the church? Another biblical theme, welcoming the stranger, provides a clue. Jesus himself welcomed strangers. It was integral to who he was. He did not keep to his own kind, but was willing to encounter and include lepers, women, tax collectors, and other outcasts. In so doing, he himself became identified as an outcast, and was treated accordingly.

If we could see those with whom we disagree so profoundly as strangers to be welcomed as Christ, our dialogue could be transformed. The present crisis has made us realize the extent to which we *are* strangers to one another in the church. We have long taken for granted our inclusivity, our tolerance of diversity, but we are coming to recognize that we have maintained this by keeping out of each other's way. We can no longer ignore each other. We are faced with a choice. We can remain strangers who, at best, confront one another in fear and hostility and, at worst, go our separate ways. On the other hand, we can become friends who can converse with respect and perhaps even affection, despite profoundly differing convictions. We might even come to see one another as icons of Christ.

To become open to this possibility demands from us a willingness to meet the stranger within ourselves. Only so are we able to relate to others in a non-defensive way. As Elisabeth Koenig suggests, "knowledge of one's own subjective structures, with all their painful and unflattering truths, is the necessary prerequisite for a discernment that is clear and objective, whether one is deciding personal matters, or those that concern theology, society, and politics" [Koenig 1991, 114]. Real dialogue is impossible from a "defensive or controlling position, that is, one where the speaker somehow holds her/himself aloof from complicity with sin" [115].

Seen in this light, dialogue, if it is to be fruitful, must be grounded in a spirituality that goes very deep, a prayer that is transformative. Such a spirituality commits us to being open to be taught and healed by God in Christ. It commits us to contemplating Jesus in scripture and consenting, by grace, to learn and live by the values he lived and taught. It commits us to the kind of silent waiting on God that allows us to be both judged and healed. Such prayer allows old hurts and fears to surface so that the defences we have built up to shield ourselves are broken open. This enables us, little by little, to withdraw projections, let down our defences, acknowledge the complicity with sin that is our human condition, and leave to God the prerogative of passing judgement.

Such prayer brings us face to face with the stranger within, and in this encounter we may find, to our surprise, an unexpected wholeness. In encountering the stranger within, we find out who and what we are meant to be — and in so doing, we encounter Jesus. Rowan Williams writes:

> In order to find the pivot of our identity as human beings, there is one inescapable encounter, one all-important conversation into which we must be drawn. This is not just the encounter with God, in a general sense, but the encounter with God made vulnerable, God confronting the systems and exclusions of the human world *within* that world — so that, among other things, we can connect the encounter with God to those human encounters where we are challenged to listen to the outsider and the victim [Williams 2003, 138].

In responding to Christ's call to live non-defensively, we transcend the dualistic, "we/they" attitude that makes us enemies. We live as Jesus did — rather, we invite Jesus to live in and through us, in order to break down the barriers that divide us. It is this dimension of spirituality that is so often overlooked in our debates over the place of gays and lesbians in the church. Yet it is precisely in our spirituality, this intimate relationship with Christ that recreates us and grounds our lives as faithful followers, that we find the common ground on which we must stand as we seek to live together in the church.

Works Cited

Empereur, James L. 1998. *Spiritual Direction and the Gay Person*. London: Geoffrey Chapman.

Fortunato, John E. 1982. *Embracing the Exile*. New York: The Seabury Press.

Koenig, Elisabeth. 1991. "Review Symposium of Jesus, the Liberator of Desire." *Horizons* 20, no. 1:112–118.

Moore, Sebastian. 1989. *Jesus, the Liberator of Desire*. New York: Crossroads.

Nelson, James B. 1978. *Embodiment: An Approach to Sexuality and Christian Theology*. Minneapolis: Augsburg Publishing House.

Rees, Daniel, and others. 1980. *Consider Your Call: A Theology of Monastic Life Today*. London: SPCK.

Silf, Margaret. Unpublished notes from a retreat given to the Sisters of St. John the Divine, 2002.

Temple, Gray, Jr. "The Gay Challenge and Charismatic Episcopalians." *Online:* http://andromeda.rutgers.edu˜lcrew/temple 01./html

Whitehead, James D., and Evelyn Eaton Whitehead. 1986. *Seasons of Strength: New Visions of Adult Christian Maturing*. New York: Image Books.

Williams, Rowan D. 1996. "The Body's Grace." In *Our Selves, Our Souls and Bodies: Sexuality and the Household of God*, edited by Charles Hefling. Cambridge, MA: Cowley Press.

Williams, Rowan D. 2003. *Christ on Trial: How the Gospel Unsettles Our Judgment*. Toronto: ABC Publishing.

Reclaiming Christian Orthodoxy *

MICHAEL INGHAM *graduated in theology from the University of Edinburgh, and studied at the Hebrew University in Jerusalem and the Center for the Study of World Religions at Harvard. He was ordained in 1974, has served in parish ministry, and was principal secretary to the primate of the Anglican Church of Canada. He is currently the Bishop of New Westminster in Vancouver, BC.*

———

In the Sermon on the Mount in Matthew's gospel Jesus asks, "Is there any one among you who, if your child asks for bread, will give them a stone? Or if your child asks for a fish, will give them a snake?" [Matthew 7:9–10]. Jesus was speaking of the love of God for the whole human family. He was in particular challenging the notion that God's love is reserved for the pious and the pure, the ritually kosher and the institutionally orthodox. Just as human parents will not refuse their own children food — or love — he says, so the Lord God will not refuse those who ask for bread in the name of Jesus Christ.

This, simply put, is the reason why the church in many parts of the world is rethinking its traditional stance on homosexuality. We have become aware in the last several years that gay and lesbian

---

*   A version of this chapter was first presented as an address to the Halfway to Lambeth Conference in Manchester, England, in October 2003.

Christians have been starved and denied the spiritual food of acceptance and love they have a right to expect as baptized members of the Body of Christ. We have become aware of the suffering, hardship, and rejection experienced by many gay and lesbian Christians throughout the world. Some are denied admission to the Holy Communion. Most are refused permission to serve in lay and ordained office. Many are persecuted by civil and ecclesiastical laws. Some are forced to become refugees. Some are tortured and murdered.[1]

In the summer of 2003 at least two dioceses in the Anglican Communion — whose names both begin with the word "new" — decided to do something to promote change in the direction of justice. The dioceses of New Hampshire, where Gene Robinson, a partnered gay man, was consecrated bishop, and New Westminster, where the blessing of same-sex unions has been officially authorized, believe that God is calling the church to end discrimination and prejudice based on sexual orientation. With many Christians around the globe, they believe that the continued exclusion of people through the misuse of scripture, and the repetition of inherited and unexamined prejudices against minority groups such as homosexuals, is a sin against the love of God.

Our actions in Canada and in the United States have been guided by the Holy Spirit, who is the Spirit of freedom and of truth. They were taken in response to changes in the sciences and social sciences that affect our understanding of human sexuality. They were taken after a careful, lengthy, and detailed process of study and dialogue unparalleled in any other diocese of the Anglican Communion. They were taken not in rebellion against scripture, but in faithfulness to its constant and greater witness that God does not deny his own children the bread of compassion and justice.

Still, our actions have been denounced in some quarters as "unilateralist" and "unorthodox." My own reading of the history of Anglicanism suggests that the first criticism is rather weak. The Anglican tradition, as a distinctive branch within the Christian family, came into existence through the unilateral actions of the church in England in the sixteenth century.

Some of the proposals being made today by proponents of so-called "orthodoxy" — proposals that would impose on the church for the first time the necessity of a universal consensus in moral and pastoral matters — are the same arguments that were made by the opponents of the very English Reformation that these defenders of orthodoxy claim to represent. Anglicanism began when the church in England acted independently of the church of Rome — significantly, on the issue of marriage (that of King Henry VIII). Far from being foreign to our ethos and tradition, "local option" is a defining Anglican characteristic.

Just as the English church in the sixteenth century declared its faithfulness to tradition while claiming the right to oversee its own affairs with a degree of local autonomy, so provinces and dioceses in the Anglican Communion today are declaring their faithfulness to tradition while claiming that same right to make pastoral provision for the People of God within their boundaries. This is entirely within the history and traditions of Anglicanism.

The reaction this has provoked in many parts of the world is to be expected, and it must also be respected. Most of us acknowledge that it is culturally and theologically difficult for some people to come to terms with changes in our understanding of human sexuality, especially homosexuality. Those of us who argue for a new respect for gay and lesbian Christians must ourselves show respect for those of a traditional conscience in these questions. In New Westminster no one seeking the full inclusion of gays and lesbians in the life of the church is trying to drive anyone else out of the church. That strategy, however, seems to be the position of some of our critics who describe themselves as "orthodox."

Those of us who take the inclusive position must challenge the claim that Christian orthodoxy is the sole property of one segment of the church. We must examine the assumption that orthodoxy is dogmatically uniform and unambiguous on the matters in question. We are bold to say before God and the church that we too participate in the orthodox Christian faith, and that our witness is to the Triune God, in whose image we have all been created.

The proponents of a narrow orthodoxy claim that God condemns homosexuality, that the witness of scripture is unambiguously contrary to same-sex relationships, that the authority of scripture itself is at stake in this debate, and that the church cannot permit different moral standards in different parts of the world.

But we, from a broader orthodoxy, reply that God condemns no one who has been made in God's image, that Jesus Christ has taken upon himself the condemnation of us all, homosexual and heterosexual alike, that homophobia[2] is one of the unexamined sins of the church today, and that no doctrine of creation that ignores homosexual persons is an adequate doctrine of creation. We say that moral standards do in fact vary in different parts of the Christian world, and that this is cause for deeper discussion, not institutional separation.

A recent conference in New Westminster brought together people interested in social justice in our diocese with other people interested in evangelism. I had come back from Lambeth in 1998 deeply impressed by the way African bishops hold firmly together the twin imperatives of evangelizing and social transformation, and I knew that we in the Western world tend too often to separate them into different activities. Our conference speaker was an American Baptist, and he began by saying this — and here I paraphrase his remarks:

> You Anglicans are a mystery to us Baptists. You have bishops in your church who deny the resurrection of Jesus, and you say, "Hey, we're a broad church. There's room for everybody here." And you have theologians who question the virgin birth and the gospel miracles, and you say, "Hey, we're a broad church. Everybody can have their say." And then along come gay and lesbian people asking for a blessing and you say, "Hey, we gotta draw the line somewhere!" At least if you're going to break up your church, do it over something important.

This raises the question of how we distinguish primary and secondary issues in the church. To gay and lesbian Christians, of course, the experience of exclusion is a primary issue. But theologically we must treat the question more dispassionately. What are first-order issues in the church? And what are second-order issues?

The best and most enduring effort int Anglicanism to answer these questions is the Chicago-Lambeth Quadrilateral of 1888. It defines four first-order issues for the Anglican Church: the scriptures of the Old and New Testaments, the ecumenical creeds, the divinely ordained sacraments, and the historic episcopate.

It is important to understand that these four pillars were originally conceived within the Anglican Communion *as a framework to define membership*. They were proposed and adopted in the late nineteenth century in response to the growth of the church throughout the world and the requests by regional churches for recognition as autonomous Anglican churches. They remain the only defining criteria for membership in the Communion. And they have recently been re-affirmed. As the primates said at their meeting in Portugal in 2000, only "formal repudiation of the Lambeth Quadrilateral" could count as a cause for the departure of a province from the Communion. And no part of the church has yet done this.

No particular doctrine of human nature is contained in the Quadrilateral, neither expressly or implied. No fixed and immutable conception of human sexuality or Christian sexual ethics is named there. This is not to say that Christian ethics and behaviour are not central to Christian belief, for clearly they are. But it is to say that first order issues for Anglicans are higher order issues, and nothing in our tradition prevents ethical or doctrinal development when the gospel itself comes into contact with new social conditions or changing human knowledge.

To say that one believes in God, in the divinity of Jesus Christ, and in his sacrifice on the cross for our salvation, is to make a statement of a different order than to say that one believes in restricting sexual activity to heterosexual marriage or in blessing same-sex unions. Faith in God is foundational; Christian social ethics is derivative. While we must not separate them — and we should never claim that moral law is merely a human construct independent of the will of God — neither should we confuse the eternal and timeless truths of the Christian faith with the historic and temporal working out of those truths in the changing conditions of human life. To do so is a fundamental category mistake.

Yet some among those today who claim a narrow orthodoxy wish to dissolve the distinction altogether. They hold that the question of same-sex relationships is a first order issue on the same level as the very existence of God. Some bishops meeting in Kuala Lumpur announced they would be in communion only with those who subscribe to their understanding of human sexuality. Other bishops have deviated from the very definition of the historic episcopate by asserting powers they do not have, and by attempting to plant churches and to license clergy in dioceses where they have neither authority nor jurisdiction. In the name of "orthodoxy" they create disorder and anarchy. When asked how these actions are consistent with the church's tradition and understanding of the episcopate, they blame homosexual Christians and their supporters, arguing that the rejection of homosexuality and the rigorous prosecution of a strict heterosexuality for everyone without exception is the litmus test for the entire edifice of Christian and biblical truth. They present us with an "orthodoxy" that is not merely contingently homophobic but necessarily homophobic, with a gospel that has become law, and with a newly structured church that is more committed to expulsion than inclusion.

The intellectual theft of the word "orthodoxy" by conservative modernists is a tragic development in the church today. In reality, historic Christian orthodoxy has accommodated a variety of spiritualities, theological schools, doctrinal convictions, and pastoral practices. Genuine orthodoxy includes people like Julian of Norwich, who called God "mother"; Francis of Assisi, who protested the church's submission to money; and Desmond Tutu, who defied the Christian fundamentalist-backed system of apartheid. Historic orthodoxy has seen centuries when marriages were never performed in the church and, if Boswell is right, periods when same-sex relationships were joyfully and publicly celebrated [Boswell 1994].

What remains unchanged is the church's universal moral commitment to love and compassion for the despised and the rejected, to justice for the suffering and the poor, to bread for the hungry. This is the reason why we have seen the demise — admittedly slow and often painful — of cherished and fiercely held doctrines like the divine right of kings, the institution of slavery, the prohibition against usury, and the strictures against divorce. Still, in our own times the church must continue to challenge the principalities and powers of this world that corrupt and destroy the creatures of God, for the imperatives of justice and compassion are not subject to time and decay.

Orthodoxy is a broad river, not a narrow stream. Every river has its banks, of course, but river banks also change over time (every river dweller knows this). Authentic Christian faith is anchored in the Holy Spirit who leads us into all truth, and the living tradition of faith under the guidance of the Spirit is always open to a new word from God and to the changes such a word implies.

There was a time, for example, when Christian orthodoxy seemed necessarily anti-Semitic. The frequent New Testament passages that appear to condemn Jews were taken as evidence that Jews were to be openly held in contempt. The English Missal, following the Roman Catholic Missal, prayed for the conversion of what it called "the faithless Jews, that our Lord and God would take away the veil from their hearts ... graciously hear our prayers which we offer for the blindness of this people, that they, acknowledging the light of thy truth, may be delivered from their darkness" [English Missal: Good Friday Collects].[3]

In a post-Holocaust world these sentiments are now understood not only to have been a misreading of scripture, but to have led to a human catastrophe of obscene proportions. Yet in this same world, homophobia has replaced anti-Semitism as the last acceptable prejudice in some parts of the church. Now, as then, ecclesiastical authorities remain silent or actively justify discrimination and oppression in the name of their religious beliefs. Official statements and declarations — even the ones making an attempt at balance and fairness — go to great lengths to reassure self-described traditionalists, while offering at most a sentence or two of acknowledgment to homosexual people.[4]

Gregory Baum, a Roman Catholic theologian, draws a parallel between anti-homosexual prejudice and anti-semitism. He cites the rejection of anti-semitism by the modern church as an example of authentic development of Christian tradition in the direction of deep renewal and change. He writes:

When tens of thousands of homosexuals were put into concentration camps in Nazi Germany, the world did not cry out against this brutality. As the Christian church remained silent in regard to the elimination of the Jews, so it uttered no word to protect homosexuals from a similar fate. Why this indifference to murder? What is it in our culture that makes us so hardhearted in the face of the suffering of certain groups? In this case, it is undoubtedly due to the church's teaching that homosexuality is a perversion, a sin against nature, a manifestation of evil. Even though Jesus summons us to be in solidarity with the despised, the vulnerable and the "least of them," we are ashamed to be seen in public as friends and supporters of gays and lesbians and to defend their dignity and human rights. The murders of homosexuals on our streets accuse us of a certain complicity, just as the violent manifestations of anti-semitism do. An increasing number of Christians see here a contradiction between doctrine and love [Baum 1997, 140–141].

Baum says that when the church perceives a contradiction between doctrine and love, a contradiction it cannot discern until certain conditions are present in history, then it is plunged into a re-examination of truth. This process has five steps, he argues. The first is the sense of contradiction that arises when something in the tradition strikes us as incompatible with what we know of God's love and justice through Jesus Christ. The second step is a search for the root of the contradiction in scripture. Third is a re-reading of scripture and tradition to find hints for resolving the contradiction. Fourth is turning to Christian experience — in this case, the experience of gay and lesbian Christians in their life in Christ — as verification of a new perspective. And fifth is the development of a systematic theology capable of overcoming the contradiction.

Over the years, the church has done this with respect to usury, monarchy, slavery, capital punishment, the equality of women, and the termination of marriage. In each case, the Holy Spirit has guided the church through a period of difficult change and brought us to a fresh appreciation of Christian responsibility and freedom. In each case, orthodoxy has proven itself both durable and flexible, both unchanging and yet ever self-renewing in its power and faithfulness.

None of this involves rejection of the authority of scripture. On the contrary, the same Spirit that inspired the writers of the Bible inspires the church in its reading of the Bible. The Holy Spirit that breathes through the text, breathes through the church. Charles Hefling writes:

> To perceive the Spirit's work, the work of the Spirit is needed; and while every biblical word *may* become a sacrament of the Word, no biblical word always or automatically *does* convey the Word to every reader or every worshipping community. Prayer and study, the exercise of discernment and reason, play their part as interpreters, in weighing the scripture, are themselves weighed. The process is reciprocal, unavoidable, and unending [Hefling 1993, 28].

To place ourselves under the authority of scripture, therefore, is to enter a dialogical circle in which both church and text encounter each other with new questions and new insights in a continuous and never-ending round of interrogation and revelation. In this process we learn new things both about ourselves and about the sacred text.

So, for example, we have learned from liberation theologians and base communities of the poor that God speaks a particular word of freedom and empowerment in scripture to the marginalized and oppressed peoples of the earth. And we have learned from women that certain texts in scripture have been used by men to control and dominate, to justify male superiority and give it the appearance of divine sanction. Phyllis Trible has called these "texts of terror" [Trible 1984] in which humiliation, subjugation, rape, and murder seem to be justified by biblical authority. These texts of terror, these oppressive texts, have been used against gay and lesbian people too, and we must confidently say to the church and to the world today that they are *not* the word of God.

In a statement of interpretive principles prepared for the diocese of New York recently a group of biblical scholars said this:

> Faithful interpretation requires the Church to use the gifts of "memory, reason, and skill" to find the sense of the scriptural text and to locate it in its time and place. The Church must then seek the text's present significance in light of the whole economy of salvation. Chief among the guiding principles by which the Church interprets the sacred texts is the congruence of its interpretation with Christ's Summary of the Law and the New Commandment, and the creeds.[5]

The New Commandment is that text in John's gospel: "A new commandment I give you, that you love one another. Just as I have loved you, so you also should love one another" [John 13:34]. Love, according to these scholars, is to be the guiding principle by which we interpret scripture. Not the sentimental love of modern society, not the "if-it-feels-good-do-it" philosophy of today's intellectual and moral relativists, but the costly love of Jesus, the sacrificial love that is lifted up on the cross for the life of the whole world.

The authority of scripture lies in Christ himself. This is the orthodox position, for he is the love of God made flesh. "He is the reflection of God's glory and imprint of God's very being" [Hebrews 1:3]. Whatever reveals Christ in scripture is authoritative for the church. Whatever is not of Christ, not consistent with the love of God shown in the crucified and risen Lord, is not authoritative and cannot be made into doctrine necessary for salvation.

The hatred, contempt, and vilification of God's gay and lesbian children that claims the name of orthodoxy today is not condoned nor blessed by Jesus Christ. It has more to do with those forces of religious fearfulness that crucified Jesus than with the love for which he gave up his life. The problem faced by gay and lesbian Christians, and those who stand with them, is not that we are victims of tradition, but rather casualties of those who have not grasped tradition deeply enough.

One of the elements of our tradition, of course, is sexual abstinence. There has always been recognition in Christianity of those specially called to the single or celibate life. The voluntary renunciation of sexual activity is a particular gift of self-offering and service that some individuals are called to make, and it can be a deep expression of love and faithfulness. There is also a place for periods of voluntary sexual abstention in marriage itself. These things are rightly honoured in Christian tradition.

Unfortunately, celibacy has not always been voluntary. It has been imposed on people who have no calling to it, and required of people who cannot bear it. Far from being a blessing, in these situations it becomes a curse that denies normal, healthy human intimacy to people who are in every other way faithful servants of God. When people fail in it, as they often do, the response of the church has been to blame the individual, when it would have been better to question the teaching. Imposed celibacy is a contradiction in terms.[6]

Anglicanism, to its credit, has never imposed celibacy on its clergy. Our clergy are free to marry and enjoy all the freedoms and responsibilities of human intimacy. This is enshrined in the 39 Articles, no less! [Article 32], as if we have recognized from our beginning as a distinct church that ordination does not require renunciation of sexual life. Some individuals may have such a calling, it is true, but they are few in number. Anglicans have instinctively recognized that human beings are sexual beings, and so we have accorded the clergy the same marital privileges as the laity.

Except, that is, for gay and lesbian clergy. Here we meet a cruel double standard. Homosexual people alone must accept imposed celibacy. Homosexual Christians alone are denied the full expression of intimacy with their partners because only for them does the church still insist on the procreative theory of sex. Only for them does the church continue to require renunciation of the sexual life.

This double standard denies and diminishes the humanity of gay and lesbian people. It is an aspect of homophobia. The fact is, both homosexuals and heterosexuals alike are people with the same legitimate yearnings, desires, hopes, and dreams for stable, faithful, and lifelong intimacy. We are different only in the object of our attraction. We share the same fundamental humanity, the same sinfulness, the same image of God given to us all in creation. We have the same Saviour and Lord who accepts us and loves us unconditionally. Archbishop Desmond Tutu asks:

> Why should we not want homosexual persons to give expression to their sexuality in loving acts? Why don't we use the same criteria to judge same-sex relationships that we use to judge whether heterosexual relationships are wholesome or not? I am left deeply disturbed by these inconsistencies, and I know the Lord of the Church would not be where his Church is in this matter.[7]

Where, then, is the courage of the church? Where is our tradition of reasoned faithfulness, our ancient compassion mandated by Christ himself and bequeathed to the church by the Spirit? Will the church continue to call for costly sacrifice by its gay and lesbian members through the renunciation of their full humanity, but not take upon itself the costly sacrifice of witnessing to God's love for them in homophobic societies or to other world religions?

Why are Christians willing to live or die for the uniqueness of Jesus Christ but unwilling to proclaim the true depth of his uniquely unconditional love for the despised and marginalized of the earth to people of other faiths? Why are we accused of conformity with secular trends in Western society, while conformity with inherited prejudice and the standards of other religions goes unchallenged? It is time, as the Bishop of Oxford so forcefully argued after the pitiful and sordid affair in which Jeffrey John was prevented from accepting appointment as assistant bishop of the diocese, to turn the argument back on those who are raising the voices of panic.

In their book *We Were Baptized Too,* Marilyn Alexander and James Preston speak words of encouragement to the church. Three words, first to gay and lesbian Christians, second to the faithful, hardworking clergy of the church, and third to the ordinary members:

Gay and lesbian Christians, we can walk through the storm. Though the walk may be long and rocky, and our burdens heavy, we can walk together. We can be a sign to the Church that has forgotten what it means to trust, what it means to love, and what it means to do justice.

Pastor, you may think that the storms of homophobia brewing out there in your congregation may be too threatening to enter. You hear the thunder and you see the lightning, but can you stand in the doorway and watch the opportunity to walk with the liberating Christ pass you by? Yes, your walk will not be easy nor your burden light, but you are not alone. Come out into the rain; remember your trust in God; remember Christ's embodied stand for justice.

Church member, have you been silent about your loved one who has been turned away, rejected, despised in the name of Christ? Forget your umbrella, it won't do you any good in this storm, but come on out where you can see the rainbow in the distance. The winds are blowing, the hail is beating, and it is a long way to the car, but can you do any less than to go to the House of Unconditional Love? Tell the stories, cast out the shame, love God's children, and seek justice [Alexander and Preston 1996, 88–89].

We in New Westminster have joined our voices with those millions of gay and lesbian people throughout the church who are asking for bread, not for a stone. We with them are asking to be heard as a voice of hope and a voice of love. Let us give thanks that the Lord Jesus Christ in his mercy has accepted us, and pray that one day we may be accepted by the church that bears his name.

Notes

1. See, for example, the experience of Ugandan Christians, forced to flee rape and imprisonment as documented by Amnesty International. Look on
    /www.changingattitude.org
    news_i_c_uganda_vancouver_refugees.html.

2. The Lambeth Conference of 1998 spoke of homophobia as "an irrational fear of homosexuals." No one explained what a rational fear of homosexuals would be. I use the term to denote prejudice against and denial of the dignity of homosexual people.

3. They were revoked by Pope John XXIII in 1959.

4. Recent statements on these matters by the primates of the Anglican Communion are uniformly unbalanced and one-sided, even when efforts are clearly being made to recognize the existence of a genuine debate.

5. See *Let The Reader Understand: A Statement of Interpretative Principles By Which We Understand the Holy Scriptures* (Diocese of New York, 2002).

6. As one speaker put it, in a recent debate in the General Synod of the Anglican Church of England, "forced celibacy is as abhorrent as forced marriage." See the *Church Times* (London, UK), 13 February 2004.

7. See his Foreword in Marilyn Bennett Alexander and James Preston, *We Were Baptized Too: Claiming God's Grace For Lesbians And Gays* (Westminster John Knox Press, 1996).

Works Cited

Alexander, Marilyn Bennett, and James Preston. 1996. *We Were Baptized Too: Claiming God's Grace For Lesbians And Gays*. Louisville, KY: Westminster John Knox Press.

Baum, Gregory. 1997. "Faithfulness And Change: Moments of Discontinuity in the Church's Teaching." In John Simons, ed., *The Challenge of Tradition*. Toronto: Anglican Book Centre.

Boswell, John. 1994. *Same-Sex Unions In Premodern Europe.* New York: Villard Books.

Hefling, Charles. 1993. "Summaries of the Four Papers." In Frederick Borsch, ed. 1993. *The Bible's Authority in Today's Church.* Pennsylvania: Trinity Press International.

Trible, Phyllis. 1984. *Texts of Terror.* Philadelphia: Fortress.

The Dialogue of
Church and Culture

Christ, Culture, and the Blessing of Homosexual Relationships

Born in Uganda, East Africa, KAWUKI MUKASA *is a specialist in congregational development for the Anglican Diocese of Toronto. He studied Political Science, Religious Studies and Theology in Africa and is currently a PhD candidate at the Toronto School of Theology. He has published numerous articles in popular and academic books and journals including* The Power of Community; Touchstone; The Minister's Annual Manual; *and* The Toronto Journal of Theology and Studies in Religion. *His books include* In God's Presence and Sojourner: Finding Faith Beyond Hope. *Mukasa lives in Mississauga, Ontario, with his partner, Margaret, and daughter Irene.*

——◆——

I do not know if he is a sinner or not....
One thing I do know: I was blind and now I see
[John 9:25].

O ne of the most frustrating aspects of the debate on the blessing of gay and lesbian relationships is the difficulty of finding a middle ground where the two sides can engage in productive dialogue. Both are stuck in zero-sum positions. Any form of concession on either side feels like total capitulation.

Since the positions people take on this issue are inspired by strongly held values, they will be vigorously defended with little room for compromise. If, for example, I approach the issue as a moral problem that violates everything I have come to accept and believe in, it is impossible for me to compromise, even for the sake of engaging in dialogue, without jeopardizing my personal integrity. On the other hand, if I approach the problem as a basic human rights issue, then I stand in a long tradition of people whose unwavering commitment to justice is vindicated by history and has made all the difference in many people's lives. Caving in to pressure from the conservative side would seem too costly in the long run.

What we have then is a debate with no prospect of resolution. Attempts from either side to win over the other are all but futile. The dispute represents a conflict not only of strongly held values but also of mutually exclusive positions. How can I, approaching this as a justice issue, accept claims of moral standards that for some people are in fact an oppressive reality? For how long must these people wait? As a person of African descent, I understand what it is like to live in a world that insists on keeping you closeted, out of sight. But I am also in awe of the brave men and women before me who risked everything so that I too may stand tall and say: "I am who I am." How do I live with myself knowing that I am a silent party to the continuing oppression of a certain group of people?

This is my position. I have no doubt that those on the other side can be just as passionate in articulating the rationale for standing firm and defending their position. Compromise is unlikely.

In view of this, we may want to pay less attention to the positions we have taken and look at some of the larger dimensions of the problem that frame and explain our choices. In other words, we need to shift our focus from the emotionally charged battles over diverging values to the broader, more generalized questions about values in general. Where do values come from? What do they point to in society? How are they formed in a given community? Are values handed down from above or a product of developments in society? Do values change in space and time? Is it possible to make a distinction between superior and inferior values? Where values are in conflict, how do we know what is true and what is not? On what basis or criteria do we construct such knowledge? These questions point to the ground of our knowledge about human values, the basis on which our assumptions about right and wrong are formed.

The substantive question in the debate on the issue of homosexual relationships focuses on determining who is right and who is wrong. However, before we can make that determination we need to examine the assumptions we bring to the issue and how our knowledge of truth is structured. An exploration into how assumptions about the values we hold are formed and the approaches we take to arrive at our understanding of truth, is bound to invite a more fruitful conversation than any attempts to determine upfront who is right and who is wrong. Then we move beyond the two mutually exclusive positions to a place where a more productive dialogue on the issue can happen.

The question I am posing here is whether our search for truth on this issue arises from correct assumptions about the relationship between Faith and culture. I am using Faith with a capital "F" to indicate the Faith that is confessed and handed down in the church, as opposed to faith with a small "f," which is a reference to the trust a person places in God. Do our assumptions about Faith and culture serve us well in attempting to resolve the issue of gay and lesbian relationships in the church?

Before I attempt to answer this question, let me share a brief testimony on how I have wrestled with the issue in my own journey. Sexuality was never openly discussed when I was growing up. Any public conversation about sex was considered highly inappropriate. Mere curiosity could get one into a lot of trouble. Only bad boys and girls showed interest in the subject.

Nevertheless, sex was a hot underground topic. There were secret conversations with peers, conversations fraught with mystery, wild stories about other people's experience. There was the occasional *Playboy* magazine smuggled in by a daring brother and the titillating stories about what went on in those secret meetings between our sisters and their aunts.

It was primarily through this underground forum that my assumptions on sexuality were formed. Within this framework the issue of homosexuality occasionally emerged. It was remote from my experience or that of anyone I knew. My assumptions on the issue were therefore of mythical proportions. Like the character in one of my short stories, "I heard many stories but they were always about people I didn't know, often middle-aged European men living alone in Africa, men who already had a cloud of mystery about them. Stories right up there with three-legged creatures and humans with three heads" [Mukasa 2001, 19–20].

For a long time in my life the issue of homosexuality fell under the category of sexual morality and was related to the problem of temptation. From where I stood "fornication" was perhaps the most difficult temptation to resist. "Adultery" happened, but only with married people who had an insatiable appetite for sexual intercourse. "Homosexuality" I would never have to worry about. The likelihood that I might be tempted to go down that path simply didn't exist.

It was not until I met and got to know people who openly identified themselves as gay or lesbian that my assumptions about homosexuality changed. I began to understand that this is not an issue of morality but one of personal identity and integrity. I learned that homosexuality is not so much about what people do as about who people are, a dimension of certain individuals' identity. Once all this became clear, I realized that my knowledge about homosexuality rested on questionable assumptions. I would have to trust those who live out of this experience to provide an authentic representation of what it is like. The significance of this observation will become clear.

The Christ and Culture Schema

The debate on homosexuality in the church has to do with the problem of reconciling Faith with culture. If homosexual relationships are part of culture, how does this element of culture relate to the confession of the Christian Faith? A model developed by Richard

Niebuhr more than half a century ago is often employed to respond to this question. It consists of a spectrum of possible answers by means of which the problem may be resolved.

One end of the spectrum emphasizes the opposition between Faith and culture. Biblical revelation and elements of church tradition that are deemed to be essential to the Faith stand entirely outside culture and in opposition to it. Proponents of this position will argue that homosexuality is a product of fallen human nature, in opposition to the redemptive work of God in Christ. From this position, however, even heterosexual relationships will be admissible only for procreation, as some readings of the Bible and tradition suggest. The elaborate social practices and institutions that human beings develop around heterosexual relationships will likewise be rejected by this extreme position.

Modified versions accept certain products of human culture while maintaining the qualitative distinction between Christ and culture. All culture is under Christ's judgement and may be deemed either in accordance with or against God's will. In this regard, heterosexual relationships and the elaborate practices and institutions around them may be deemed in accordance with God's will. On the other hand, homosexual relationships will be rejected as a product of human nature in opposition to God's will. What is acceptable and what is not is determined by an understanding of God's will through the confession of Christ.

At the other end of the spectrum Christ is presented as a "great hero of human culture…"; Christian Faith is "the fulfiller … of the hopes and aspirations [of human culture], the perfecter of its true faith, the source of its holiest spirit" [Niebuhr 1951, 41 and 83]. Inasmuch as God accepts human beings through Christ, so will the products of human culture be acceptable to God in Christ. To distinguish aspects of human culture that are acceptable to God from those that are not, other categories are employed. Any product of culture that promotes justice and love among people, any work of human beings that improves the quality of life for people, would be considered Christ-like and therefore acceptable to God. Anything in human culture that negates life, justice, and love reflects that human sinfulness for which Christ died to deliver us.

From this position homosexuality is a product of culture that is acceptable to God insofar as it promotes love and a better life for some people. Conversely, the practice of denying rights on the basis of people's sexual orientation is unjust and oppressive and, as such, part of culture that is not acceptable to God.

While these two positions stand in opposition to each other, they both recognize the ambiguity of culture, that is to say, that culture is not all bad or all good. Since it lies with Christ's authority to judge what is good and what is bad in culture, Niebuhr proposed another position: Christ's authority transforms culture and makes it new. Both sides in the debate over homosexual relationships can claim this position to justify their argument. On the one hand, Christ may be presented as one who will transform and redeem a culture that accepts homosexuality. The church as an instrument of God's redemptive work must therefore resist sanctioning same-gender relationships. On the other hand, Christ may be understood as the transformer of an oppressive culture in which gay and lesbian people are treated unjustly because of their sexual orientation. The church must therefore resist such oppression and seek justice for gays and lesbians. We are back where we started: a debate with no prospect of resolution.

Limits of the Christ and Culture Schema

The Christ and Culture models are employed quite extensively in the debate on homosexual relationships. These models are designed to respond to what I have called substantive questions. Their objective is to determine who is right, what is true, and which position the church should take. I have observed that these are mutually exclusive questions but, nevertheless, legitimate. The assumptions behind these models, however, are not always fully examined. I will raise at least two concerns.

First, the position that assumes Christ to be outside of culture as something in itself is misguided. The doctrine of Christ is itself a product of culture. It originates from and reflects the human experience and expression of faith from the New Testament church to the present. Its meaning depends on its appropriation in particular cultural contexts.

As a child, I was exposed to images of Jesus as a tall, Caucasian man with long, blond hair. I was told that this man had died for my sins so that I may be forgiven and that, if I believed in him, I would go to heaven. As I grew older, this Christ and the Faith he embodied sounded increasingly fictitious and irrelevant to my life. It is not surprising that, as I became more reflective about my experience as a person, I jettisoned this Christ. What brought me back to the Faith was the culture of violence and suffering that gripped my country throughout my teens and beyond. The brutality of Idi Amin's regime and the civil war that followed his ouster provided the context in which the story of Jesus and the symbol of Christ spoke meaningfully to my life. Christ as an abstract teaching was meaningless and irrelevant until it became fully embodied in my culture and experience.

When the debate on homosexuality assumes the doctrine of Christ to be a thing in itself apart from culture and yet in judgement of the latter, it begins on the wrong premise. To interrogate a particular human experience with doctrine is in fact to impose on that experience the values of another culture, that is to say the culture from which the doctrine in question was constructed. Since doctrine is meaningful only in dialogue with human experience, the meanings employed in judgement of culture are themselves imported from prior human experience. The images of Jesus and doctrine of Christ introduced to me as a child were constructs of another culture. As universal absolutes standing in judgement of culture, they simply could not integrate well with my experience.

This leads to my second reservation about the Christ and Culture models, namely the assumptions on how Faith and culture relate. When faith is conceived as something that contains absolute truth apart from culture, the assumption follows that it is to be consumed as a package from above that will transform our lives or impose judgement on our values. In other words, it is a one-way relationship. Faith (in the form of doctrinal propositions) feeds culture. This view of the relationship ignores much of what we are beginning to understand about the way our knowledge of truth and reality is structured.

More than two hundred years ago, the German philosopher Emmanuel Kant proposed that truth or reality in itself is unknowable. Knowledge of what is real is possible only in conjunction with the structure of our minds. Human consciousness is not just a passive recipient of objective truth. It is actively engaged in processing and structuring our knowledge of perceived objects and therefore engaged in the production of reality itself, or (more precisely) reality as we know it. This observation should remind us that we cannot speak of reality or truth as existing apart from the person who claims knowledge of it. Thus, Faith as truth is realized only in conjunction with the confessing subject.

These two limitations have significant implications for the debate on homosexuality. There is no pure doctrine of Christ "untainted" by culture. From the original formulations in the New Testament, through the ages to the present, Christ is always and already an enculturated reality. It is therefore not on the basis of Christ that culture will be valued, judged, or transformed. Rather it is on the basis of culture (including subjective experience) that Christ is confessed meaningfully.

Alternative Approach to the Issue

When we engage the issue of homosexuality in the context of Faith, there are no absolute doctrinal or moral precepts outside human experience for us to appeal to. The place to begin is with the real life experience of human beings. Thus, to understand the Faith of the New Testament church, we begin by listening to how those communities attempted to articulate their experience of Jesus and how they formulated their confession of Christ. To understand the Faith of the church in Africa, Asia, or South America, we have to listen to how particular communities in those places appropriate the gospel story in the context of their particular experience. The meaning of Christ is not to be imposed on us. It must come from within upon listening to the gospel in our particular circumstances. Christ is real only when encountered through lived experience.

God is revealed by testimony, not dogma. The story of the blind man in the gospel of John illustrates this observation very well. Confronted with a challenge to prove that Jesus was indeed God's messenger, the man disavows any knowledge of the truth on the basis of religious doctrine. "I do not *know* if he is a sinner or not," he says. How does he then *know* for sure that this is a righteous man? How does he *know* that he has been touched by God's grace in Jesus? He has nothing but his own testimony to stand on. "One thing I *know*," he says, "I was blind and now I see."

Whether or not a given community's behaviour is in concert with our view of correct doctrine is not the issue. It is that community's testimony and what it reveals about the nature of God for the rest of us that we should be looking for. Only they can tell us what Christ means to them, just as only we know what Christ means to us.

Honouring the discovery arising from one another's experience is vital for a more complete understanding of the Faith. It is impossible for any one of us to have all the answers because our experience of God is limited. As an individual my experience extends across an infinite number of identities rooted in distinct communities. I am Black, African, Canadian, male, heterosexual, husband, father, Anglican, clergyman, middle-aged, Ugandan. I am also among the small percentage of the population that is prone to gout attacks. I am a beef-lover, a commuter on public transportation, a licensed driver, and so on. Who I am, then, is this set of intersecting identities linked to groups of people or communities of infinite diversity.

Two levels of consideration arise. First, as an individual, my experience is unique and particular. No other living individual will have the exact replica of my experience. Secondly, the experiences of all those groups and communities that touch my life are also unique and particular. No living community or group will have the exact replica of another group's experience. It follows that I know God in ways that no other living individual does. My encounter with Christ and God's revelation to me are unique and particular gifts. Likewise, every group and community that my life intersects experiences God in unique and particular ways. It is in listening to and in sharing with one another what God is doing in our very complex and diverse experiences that a more complete representation of the divine will emerge.

Because God is revealed to all of us in particular ways, we have all been entrusted with God's gifts. We are stewards of God's revelation. But we are not just separate entities. Rather, in listening to one another and in sharing testimony, we come to a more complete understanding of God. We do not have to agree on doctrine (although doctrine has its place as I will soon show). Nor do we need to support one another's positions or strongly held values. Yet, rather than defending our positions and attempting to prove others wrong, we should instead be sharing what God is doing in our lives. Then the issue of homosexual relationship becomes, for some, an opportunity to listen and learn about a dimension of God's grace and an intervention into human life that we otherwise have no access to. For others, it becomes an opportunity to share testimony about God's grace that is uniquely revealed to us.

Practical and Theological Implications

There's a saying in my language: *"Bakuuma lubugo, lubaale mubbe."* A direct translation would be: "They're protecting an empty piece of cloth; the gods are stolen." The saying relates to the legend of a people baffled by the silence of the gods. Day after day they go to the sacred place and call the holy ones by name as loud as they can, hoping to catch their attention and get them to respond. Sadly, the people cry out in vain because the gods have already been stolen. The silence of the holy ones is permanent.

We hear a lot, these days, about the need to return to our traditional values. Every time I hear that plea, my heart goes out to those who are genuinely invested in this hope. They do not seem to have come to grips with the realities of our time. There will be no returning to "our traditional values." This is not because of stubbornness on anybody's part. Nor is it because the true believers have not cried out loud enough. It is because the landscape has changed permanently. Those "traditional values" are no longer adequate to deal with the practical realities of today. We have to learn new ways of living in this radically transformed landscape.

God has created a world of infinitely diverse and even conflicting subjectivities, each with the potential to claim recognition or validation. When hitherto silenced voices erupt like a volcano, they permanently change the landscape. Now when a group or community says, "We're here and will not be silenced," that is more than simply a statement of defiance. It is a statement of fact that we have to integrate into our collective experience. In the past it was possible to silence all but the most dominant voices. The values emerging then were those that reflected the dominant experience. The experience of minor subjectivities in their infinite diversity was simply ignored, rejected, or glossed over. Determining what was acceptable or unacceptable was then a considerably simpler exercise. It was easier to name universal values because only the dominant voices could be heard. We can no longer count on silencing minor voices for the sake of one clear dominant voice. The new reality is one of multiple subjectivities, multiple voices, multiple sensibilities.

So there is a practical imperative demanding new rules of engagement. How do we live together in the context of diverse views and competing values, all claiming to be heard? One option could be to try even harder to silence minor voices in the hope of re-establishing the dominant experience as the universal voice. This, I am arguing, is no longer desirable. The other option might be learning to listen to one another and to recognize one another's experience as unique and given by God. This requires us to adopt new rules and a new set of practical tools for living together.

The changing landscape likewise calls us to take another look at how we do theology. The traditional approach begins with dogma or doctrinal principles, with an interest in applying these to particular situations or contexts. As I have shown above with respect to the

Christ and Culture models, the theological dimension of the debate on homosexuality tends to follow this approach.

In the last three or four decades we have witnessed a proliferation of alternative models of theology which have drawn attention to the inadequacy of the traditional approach. What these new theologies have in common is a commitment on our part as the confessing subject to articulate for ourselves the questions that are of the greatest significance to us from our unique experience. This development has shifted the starting point of theology from dogma to the circumstances of the confessing subject.

Segundo has conceptualized this approach in terms of a hermeneutic circle. We begin from the concrete circumstances of our existence. The questions arising from there lead to a critical examination and reinterpretation of the dominant ideological and philosophical structures that explain the prevailing realities of our time. The critique provides us a tentative explanation of our particular set of circumstances as well as some options for action. At this point, we are ready to engage in dialogue with doctrine, the biblical witness, and church tradition. The purpose of this exercise is not simply to apply doctrine to our circumstances. It is rather to reinterpret the Faith in light of those circumstances.

Segundo employs the term "hermeneutics of suspicion" to describe this process. According to him, it is "the suspicion that the prevailing interpretation of the Bible has not taken important pieces of data into account" [Segundo 1976, 9] because it emerges from a set of circumstance different from our own. The reinterpretation of doctrine from our own unique set of circumstance provides us a "new hermeneutic" that allows us to live out the Faith with authenticity.

Segundo's model of doing theology is an intensely self-reflective exercise. Theology is something that we must do for ourselves, from our particular circumstances, in order to understand God's special gift of revelation for us. Since I am not living my neighbours' experience I cannot theologize for them. I must trust them to develop their own understanding of the Faith and what it means in their special circumstances. It follows that there will be different forms of engagement with God, different conceptualizations of Faith, different meanings and different theologies, because we all come with different experiences.

Summary and Conclusion

The debate over the issue of Faith and homosexual relationships continues with little prospect of resolution. The rift between the two positions widens and threatens the unity of the church. I have argued that at least part of the difficulty may lie in presenting the issue as a mutually exclusive problem. Determining who is right and who is wrong seems to be the focus of attention in this regard. This view of the problem encourages a protracted defence of the positions that appeals to a flawed concept of the relationship between Faith and culture.

I believe the time has come for the parties to step back and consider a more productive approach to this problem. My suggestion is to shift our focus from the need to observe correct doctrine at any cost to the need to celebrate the real life experience of human beings. I have argued that there are both practical and theological imperatives for this change. On the one hand, we simply must be able to live with one another as brothers and sisters. We are all here to stay. If necessary we must learn new ways of relating and living together. On the other hand, we must consider the theological observation that God is revealed to all of us in particular ways and that we are all in some way stewards of God's revelation. In light of this, we should focus our energy on sharing testimony about what God is doing in our lives rather than arguing about doctrinal positions.

Works Cited

Niebuhr, Richard H. 1951. *Christ and Culture.* New York: Harper Colophon Books.

Kant, Immanuel. 1998. *Critique of Pure Reason.* Cambridge: Cambridge University Press.

Segundo, Juan Luis. 1976. *Liberation of Theology.* Maryknoll, NY: Orbis Books.

Mukasa, Kawuki. 2001. *Sojourner: Finding Faith Beyond Hope.* Toronto: Kamu Kamu Publishing.

Our Humanity is God's Glory*

The Many Faces of Our Communion

Born in 1943, ROWAN Q. SMITH *was educated in Cape Town and then read theology at King's College, London. After working as a priest in the Cape Town diocese from 1967 till 1977, he became a member of the Community of the Resurrection until 1989. From 1990 to 1995 he was on the staff of Archbishop Desmond Tutu, and since 1996 has been Dean of Cape Town.*

⊰•⊱

The Church in the Province of Southern Africa (CPSA) includes the Republic of South Africa, Lesotho, Swaziland, Namibia, Mozambique, St. Helena, and since very recently, Angola. The whole CPSA has been much affected by events taking place in the Republic of South Africa, where the majority of its members live.

Forty years experience of legalized apartheid has influenced our response to a great many social issues. During the apartheid years, we as a church had to deal with issues that could have torn us apart. Our church was striving for justice, but during the 1970s and 1980s some Anglicans were known to be serving in the Security Forces and in the Security Police, by whom a number of activists had been tortured and killed, among them Steve Biko. There was a

---

* A version of this chapter was first presented as an address to the Halfway to Lambeth Conference in Manchester, England, in October 2003.

strong move to have these persons excommunicated and expelled from the CPSA. In the end the synods agreed that dialogue and sharing our concerns was the best way forward, not excommunication. In a strange way God used even apartheid to teach us about unconditional love and grace.

Huge changes have taken place in the Republic of South Africa since the release in 1990 of Nelson Mandela after twenty-seven years of imprisonment under the apartheid regime, and the church has responded to them as well. The new constitution of South Africa includes a section that prohibits discrimination on the basis of categories listed there, including both gender and sexual orientation.

It was against this background of the beginning of the political transformation of South Africa that the provincial synod of the CPSA, meeting in Swaziland in 1992, voted in favour of women being ordained to the priesthood. This vote took place against the background of a synod that respected the integrity of individual bishops and dioceses, so that no bishop would be compelled to ordain a woman if they had voted against the resolution. I was present at the synod as provincial executive officer.

Arguments were presented against the ordination of women based on culture: for example, since tribal custom prevents women from becoming chiefs, logically it must also prevent them from becoming bishops. Other arguments were adduced from scripture: for example, St. Paul says that a woman owes obedience to her husband as head of the family. Still other arguments were based on ecumenical concerns: ordaining women would deepen the divide between the Anglican churches and the Roman Catholics and Orthodox. However, in the end it came down to a question of justice and to deciding what was right for the Anglican Church in southern Africa. Sexual identity is a given, and just as we could no longer discriminate on the basis of colour, so we must no longer discriminate on the basis of gender. As for the matter of ecumenical unity, it was pointed out that Rome already denies the validity of Anglican orders, and refraining from ordaining women would not by itself alter that situation. In any case, even the question of unity must be weighed against the question of justice. After the motion to ordain women had been passed, one of the comments I heard was, "The next major debate will be on homosexuality."

In March 1997, three years after our first democratic elections, the synod of bishops endorsed the report "Anglicans and Sexual Orientation," produced by the Southern Africa Anglican Theological Commission. Although the statement of the synod of bishops on receiving the report acknowledged that there was no consensus among the bishops, it went on to say, "Where we do agree, however, is that as a church we have been responsible over the centuries for rejecting people on the basis of their sexual orientation." It went on to say, "As bishops we are unhappy at the tendency in some quarters to attack homosexuals on the basis of simplistic interpretations of certain scriptural texts."[1]

Recent challenges to existing laws in the statute books, based on the new constitution of South Africa, have resulted in the constitutional court upholding the right of gay and lesbian partners to adopt children and to receive spousal benefits such as medical insurance, and a 2003 report of the Law Commission on the Marriage Act has proposed recognizing same-gender unions. Our own CPSA commission, under Professor Joan Church, made an interim report in September 2003 to the synod of bishops, and our provincial standing committee (the executive body of the provincial synod) passed Resolution 9: *Same-Sex Unions*. It said:

> We are called to discuss same-sex unions, particularly where this issue affects our communities. We are talking about people in our families, in our churches, and in the Body of Christ. We ask Christians and parish communities to recognize this debate as a pastoral reality.

Of course, not everyone in our church accepts that there is a need for change as regards gay and lesbian members. Not everyone agrees that God calls us *as we are* through baptism to bear witness to Christ.

Some African church leaders claim that homosexuality is the result of decadent Western influence in Africa. By contrast, in a recent BBC publication [*Focus on Africa Magazine*] Dr. Sylvia Tamale, a senior lecturer in law at Makerere University in Kampala, Uganda, writes:

> Anthropological research shows that same sex eroticism existed in a variety of forms in at least fifty-five African cultures. Moreover, such practices are ancient and entirely indigenous to this continent. It is a time for Africans to bury the myth that homosexuality has no roots in Africa.[2]

She further suggests that the colonial influences of Islam and Christianity lie behind the present homophobic pronouncements.

There are those who argue that sexual orientation is a matter of choice, though they would seemingly confine that choice to people of homosexual orientation choosing to be something else. We cannot be accepted in the church, they say, be ordained, or have our unions blessed unless we convert and become heterosexual. Others argue in response that our situation now concerning the place of gay and lesbian Christians in the church is analogous to that of the church in the Acts of the Apostles, when the church in Jerusalem argued against St. Paul and others that before Gentiles could become Christians, they had first to become Jews.

Africa stands in a special relationship to the diversity of humanity, which is God's glory. Because of her history of exploitation, she should be in the forefront of those who struggle against prejudice, seek liberation from exploitation, and celebrate diversity. Slaves were taken from West Africa and exported to Europe and the Americas, where their God-given dignity as human persons was denied. In South Africa, slave owners prevented slaves from being baptized in case baptism was seen as raising them to the status of equals with their owners in the sight of God and the church. (The growth of Islam in the western Cape, which did not discriminate against people in this way, was due in no small measure to this discrimination.) It is sad when African church leaders discriminate against homosexual persons and deny their full inclusion in the Body of Christ. By contrast, Archbishop Ndungane of Cape Town has found that experiencing discrimination on the basis of colour has made him aware of discrimination against people on the basis of sexual orientation. He was imprisoned for three years on Robben Island for being a member of the Pan African Congress, and discovered his vocation to the priesthood there.

The enormous problems facing our continent leave us no room for hatred and scapegoating. For example, the church has not emerged clean even from the genocide in Rwanda, where allegations of complicity in the slaughter have been made against some of our own bishops. We gay and lesbian Anglicans, especially those of us in positions of leadership, have much to contribute to the healing of the continent. We understand the pain of discrimination and we understand being frustrated of our desire to love.

In my personal experience as a black South African, I have had to confront my own prejudices and come to terms with my own brokenness. Both are the result of my social context and also of my own failure to realize that my humanity is God's glory. Despite my baptism and despite my largely supportive family — we are nine children altogether — for a great part of my life I believed that I was defined by the colour of my skin and that, because of my colour, I was a lesser being. It was my involvement in student politics from 1960 till 1962, just before I went to study at King's College, London, England, that first made me aware of my own worth as a person. Then when, in my second year at college, I became aware of my sexual orientation, I wondered what God was up to: had God really made me both black and gay? But when I returned to South Africa and was ordained, my continuing journey in the church led me to see the truth that we are all God's children by adoption and grace. God's grace alone allows and enables us to be God's children.

At rallies during the apartheid era, Archbishop Tutu used to say that the nationalist government should have banned the Bible because it affirmed, "Herein is love, not that we loved God, but that God loved us and gave his Son to be the propitiation for our sins." When we look into one another's faces, we should see God because we are all made in God's image; we are icons of God. As Rowan Williams said in the sermon he preached at his enthronement as Archbishop of Canterbury [27 February 2003]:

No one can be written off: no group, no nation, no minority can just be a scapegoat to resolve our fears and uncertainties. We cannot assume that any human face we see has no divine secrets to disclose.

—⋄—

Notes

1. Letter sent out by the synod of bishops in March 1997 with reference to *Anglicans and Sexual Orientation,* a report prepared by the Southern African Anglican Theological Commission.

2. BBC *Focus on Africa Magazine*: October to December 2003. Vol. 14, no. 4. Online: http://www.bbcworldsrvice.com/focus

Works Cited

Most of the church documents referred to or quoted in the text of this paper are held in the Archives of the Church in the Province of Southern Africa, University of the Witwatersrand, Johannesburg, South Africa.

A Note on Lambeth Conferences and Homosexuality: 1988, 1998, 2008

When Archbishop Ndungane of Cape Town raised the concern in 1998 that the church must listen to the voices of its gay and lesbian members, he was following the precedent established during the apartheid years when the church, led especially by Archbishop Desmond Tutu, sought to be the voice of the voiceless.

Plans are now afoot to explore the feasibility of holding the 2008 Lambeth Conference here in South Africa. It will inevitably return to the issue of gay and lesbian believers in the church that received such spectacular attention at the 1998 conference. If we look further back to the 1988 Lambeth Conference, we find a more enlightened consideration of the question. Its Resolution 64, *Human Rights for those of Homosexual Orientation,* urged that the church's study and reflection on the subject should "take account of biological, genetic, and psychological research being undertaken by other agencies, and the socio-cultural factors that lead to different attitudes in the provinces of our Communion" [Coleman 1992, 226].

This approach of avoiding prescription acknowledged that we live in a fast-changing world and that our responses to it as Christians do not rely solely on our own ecclesiastical context. We apply to "other agencies" to help our understanding and are influenced by "socio-political factors." The 1998 conference took a step backward. The report, drafted by Section 1 of the conference after two full weeks of discussion on questions of human sexuality, entitled *Called to Full Humanity,* was brought forward with the recommendation that no resolution on human sexuality be presented to the plenary session of the conference because there was no clear consensus on some of the issues. But at the insistence of the conference organizers, Resolution I.10 was cobbled together, and in such a way as to undermine the intentions and hard labour of the working session. This resolution was such an affront to so many people that it has produced a counter response that seeks to give expression to the more pastoral approach envisioned in 1988.

When the next Lambeth Conference meets in 2008, it would be a sad and retograde step if discussion of the place of homosexuals in the church simply proceeded from Lambeth 1998. But much will have changed between 1998 and 2008 that the bishops will have to ponder. They will be helped by taking cognizance of the 1988 Lambeth resolution. Looking back over the resolutions of previous Lambeth Conferences, we can see how the bishops struggled with issues around polygamy and the ordination of women to the priesthood before they eventually arrived at positions that almost everyone could support. Let us commit ourselves, then, to pray for grace to be truly open to the Holy Spirit and to one another, allowing the Spirit to blow where it wills.

Work Cited

Coleman, Roger, ed. 1992. *Resolutions of the Twelve Lambeth Conferences 1867–1988*. Toronto: Anglican Book Centre.

The Church
in the Closet *

MARIO RIBAS *is a priest in the Anglican Church in Brazil. For the last four years he has worked as parish priest at All Saints' Church, Santos, in the Diocese of São Paulo, as well as lecturing at the Anglican Theological Institute of São Paulo. He holds a BA in theological studies from Trinity College, University of Bristol, England, and a Master of Sciences of Religion from the Methodist University of São Paulo.*

⟶•◆•⟵

I want to share some thoughts about the church and its resistance to including those who are outside the dominant cultural system. The title is a claim that the church itself is "in the closet" in a way that parallels the experience of many gay and lesbian people. Those very people can help the church in the "outing" process.

For gay or lesbian[1] people to be "in the closet" means to be secretive about our sexual orientation. It means disguising ourselves by conforming to the demands and expectations of the *hetero-patriarchal* dominant system. This makes life easier, but the cost of inner dishonesty is internal conflict — the sense that truth is being denied and that one is not whole.

---

*   A version of this chapter was first presented as an address to the Halfway to Lambeth Conference in Manchester, England, in October 2003. A version of the address was also published in the journal *Theology and Sexuality* (London: Continuum, March 2004).

Yet the cultural and religious situations in which we find ourselves greatly influence our decisions about whether to be "in" or "out of the closet." In Latin America, including Brazil, coming out of the closet means facing life threats, loss of jobs, and social rejection. It means facing the stigma and rejection imposed by a macho dominant society. It can mean being thrown out of one's home and family — a very dire punishment in a strongly family-oriented culture. According to the gay group in Bahia [online: Grupo Gay de Bahia], three hundred gay and lesbian people have been killed in Brazil through homophobic attacks over a period of three years — an average of a hundred deaths a year [online: Grupo Gay de Bahia]. Although Brazilian society is slowly changing in ways that have made life easier for gays and lesbians, we still have a long way to go before we find acceptance.

The stigma that attaches to gay and lesbian people in Brazil is deeply rooted in our Roman Catholic heritage and reinforced by the work of fundamentalist evangelical movements. They are part of the dominant system. On the other hand, the Anglican Church and also the Lutherans have been more open to discussing the issue and to welcoming people who are gay, lesbian, bisexual, or transgendered.

Coming out of the closet, according to Richard Cleaver,[2] is the act of naming oneself as somebody outside of the dominant system that defines social roles, including those based on biological gender. It is the act or process of untying secrets, breaking silence, and feeling free. In order to challenge the dominant assumptions of both church and society and to bring about a change in attitudes, those of us who are gay and lesbian must face our own orientation and recognize the reality in which we find ourselves even though the cost is martyrdom, which is almost inevitable, at least in the beginning. Changes do not happen until persons come out of the closet.

What does it mean, then, to claim that the church itself is in the closet? It means that the church is afraid to exercise its prophetic role. Instead, it conforms to the socio-political situation while denying its vocation to be a counter-cultural movement. For example, one of the excuses advanced for not accepting gay and lesbian people in the church is that it would create problems for the church in countries where there are many Muslims or members of other religious groups whose cultural values are strongly patriarchal. In other words, human justice is to be sacrificed so that the church and its members can maintain a relatively comfortable place in the society. This is not being faithful to the teaching of Christ, who was always out of the closet in his refusal to conform to the dominant system.

By contrast, and in contrast to what its detractors claim, the Episcopal Church in the USA has begun to break with the culture of intolerance that still prevails widely in North America. An FBI report [online: Civilrights] shows that in 2002 the number of anti-male homosexual hate crimes reported was 825, representing 11.1 per cent of all hate crimes [online: Civilrights]. One such crime was the murder of a gay couple by a white supremacist who claimed that it was not a crime because he was doing what the Bible told him to do [online: News]. In this way, to accuse the Episcopal Church in the USA of following a culture of sexual permissiveness, as many conservatives in the southern hemisphere have done, does no justice to all those who have died as victims of intolerance.

A church in the closet maintains the Western, negative attitude toward the body and sexuality. It maintains a heterosexual[3] moralist paradigm that gives legitimacy to a structure of power through the religious moralist discourse that has prevailed through the centuries. The roots of this paradigm lie mostly in the dualist concepts adopted by theologians after the fifth century of the Christian era. According to this paradigm, corporeity is a state inferior to pure spirit. Corporeity is associated with the earth, with the feminine, with carnal pleasure, and ultimately with evil. This paradigm condemns as immoral the role of pleasure in sexual relations, which are reduced to a merely procreative function. It imposes silence on women because they represent a danger both to male dominance and to the established mentality that demonizes pleasure and fragments our lives. It imposes silence on gay people because they represent one way of overcoming the gender dualism, male/female. When pleasure becomes a sign of evil, suffering becomes the only path to holiness. Having adopted this way of thinking, the church has required that people withdraw into a kind of "monastery of the mind." As a result, this denial of body in order to make spirit alive is deeply embedded in our mentality.

The gospel brought by the Portuguese and Spanish colonizers to Latin America did not mean entirely good news to the native inhabitants of this part of the world [Pérez 2000], by insisting that the native people should cover their nakedness with clothes like Europeans, they taught shame about the body and sexuality. Worse still, they brought with them the Inquisition, with its holy hatred of heretics, infidels, and others deemed to be sinners. Many accused of "sodomy," including especially those supposed to be gay, were imprisoned, tortured, and killed. By and large, the church supported and legitimized the colonial governments and the whole socio-political order that they represented. Too often it failed to speak out against the abuses perpetrated by those who held power. It was a church in the closet.

In Brazil the church lost its official connection with government when a new constitution was adopted in 1891, two years after the abolition of the monarchy, although for several decades the Roman Catholic clergy and laity resisted the changes and tried to maintain the social and cultural order of the old imperial church. The military juntas and other governments that followed tended to reaffirm the dominant system of male heterosexual thought and practices. Their support, and that of the church, were intensified in the mid-twentieth century in opposition to the perceived threat of communism. Additional support was given to the dominant system by the fast growth of pentecostalism and charismatic groups among the poor.[4]

Eventually after 1960, the church's silence and conformity were broken through liberation theology. In challenging oppression, the church came out of the closet and played an important role in the effort to demolish the system that the church itself had previously supported. However, the success was incomplete: liberation theology did not go far enough in undermining the power structures, and in any case the papacy intervened to suppress it. At the same time the church, like the society, kept women and gay people silenced. It never really gave up its power and never really ceased to maintain the structure of power. What had seemed to be a permanent "outing" proved to be just another way of the church seeking popularity in a country that could no longer support so much oppression.

Gays and lesbians have become a test for the church. For the church to accept people who are outside the dominant system means that the church itself is stepping out of the closet. It is time for the silence to be broken for the sake of those who are suffering. This includes not just gays and lesbians and not just women (who are half the human race!), but all who suffer under the dominant system of oppression in which all forms of injustice are rooted: poverty, denial of human rights, wars, and so on. The Anglican Church has mobilized itself worldwide in favour of or against the new developments on homosexuality because this is the testing issue. If power structures can begin to be broken by facing this issue, which the church is now actually facing, then maybe the repercussions will be felt in all forms of oppression against which the church has not yet mobilized itself, at least to the same extent.

Therefore gays and lesbians have an important part to play in the process of helping the church to "out" itself, exercise its prophetic calling, and address the real issues in society. We can show the church how to break down the "monastery of the mind" that it has built, a state of affairs in which our corporeity is regarded with such holy hatred that the result is a culture of death and destruction to which we are expected to conform. We can deconstruct the construction of hetero-patriarchal power. For this to be possible we need first to create an "outing" theology, a theology born of our own reality and our own struggle that questions deeply the old paradigms that have proven to be merely a way to legitimize the dominant system.

Again, things do not change unless silence is broken. It is necessary for an "outing" to occur in order for people to build their own history and recover their own dignity. Those who have been oppressed, including women and gays and lesbians, need to break silence, tell their own stories, hear others' stories, and win their own liberation. We must challenge the dominant forces that have domesticated God and the Bible to defend and increase their own power and position. We must re-read the Bible from the vantage point of our own reality to build a theology of "outing" that might help the church to get itself out of the closet and face the true problems of the world today.

Outing is a difficult process. Not everybody can successfully fight their own feelings of inadequacy and challenge the models offered by society. Even if they make a beginning, they may not reach the point where they are fully conscious of the extent to which their reality is different from the socially defined standards — the point at which they can begin to develop a new identity [Musskopf 2002, 68].

When the sense of inadequacy is the result of a religious system that marginalizes or condemns us, it may be more difficult to deal with, since we have been taught to look to the church for moral guidance. It is hard to realize that the church, in regarding sexuality apart from procreation as itself sinful, is not proclaiming the truth of the gospel. As we feel our own inadequacy, it is necessary to focus on the grace of God as the source of all things. All things are conceived in "original blessing" rather than "original sin." The theology based on original sin has created a society and a church based on shame and guilt, and has locked not only gays and lesbians, but also straight people, in the closet. It maintains oppression. By contrast, a theology of grace can liberate us from oppression.

André Musskopf, a young Brazilian theologian from a Lutheran background, points out [Musskopf 2002, 59–61] that one of the difficulties of the established theology is that it normally dissociates spirituality from corporeity, mainly because the body is regarded as weak and dominated by pleasure. And pleasure, in the traditional understanding, does not allow for spiritual development. Consequently Jesus is also stripped of his corporeity (which denies the theology of incarnation), and also of his sexuality. Jesus becomes a bodiless and asexual person, instead of the one who through his acts denounces those values and beliefs that prevent our humanity from being entirely fulfilled. Musskopf says that the awareness of their corporeity, which is common amongst gay people, is perceived as a contradiction to spirituality, since sexual expression is regarded as sinful except within traditional marriage and for procreation. Consequently those who are alienated because they cannot conform to traditional marriage need a new way of doing theology that addresses their reality.

> The consciousness present among gay men reveals the sins present in the patriarchal ideology, heterosexist and exclusive, because it questions those models and proposes new ways of relationship based on self-giving, mutuality, and caring for each other, and on seeking a corporal and healthy expression that is based on liberty, inclusiveness, and justice. These were the intention of Jesus for everybody [Musskopf 2002, 59-61].

This might be the way forward to re-create a theology that challenges oppression wherever it may be found.

Following the methodology established by the Latin American proponents of liberation theology, we begin by re-reading the Bible from the point of view of our own reality. The intent is not to find scriptural verses that support our way of life, but to find healing for the trauma caused by oppression and exclusion. In the process we come to recognize the inadequacy of established models of living and thinking to tackle oppression and reflect the contemporary situation, and we construct new models of living and thinking for ourselves to follow. By naming oppression wherever we find it, we define ourselves — gays, lesbians, and many others — as those who, standing outside the dominant system, are oppressed. We recognize that we lack a legitimate identity within the established order. But the doctrine of salvation by the grace of God reminds us that God accepts us regardless of our identity. When we arrive at that realization, we have created a rupture with socially institutionalized homophobia. The doctrine of salvation by God's grace is fundamental to an outing theology

In her book *Indecent Theology*, Argentinian theologian Marcella Althaus-Reid presents the dominant systematic theology as an arbitrary sexual theory with divine implications. Of the two ways of talking about sex — either as gender identity or as sexual activity — the feminist liberation theologian prefers the first. However, as she says, the dominant way of talking about sex in official theology throughout the centuries has been to describe sex as desire or concupiscence. The intention has been to condemn it. When theology addressed questions of sin and grace with sex in mind, its eyes were turned toward bedrooms. Established moralism, which is a way to define the narrowing of morality to matters of sex, became a priority in theological development along the centuries, while real moral issues, such as peace and human rights, were completely ignored.

To return to the central theme: as gay and lesbian people develop a theology based on their own experience of coming out of the closet, the whole church will be served. It too can come out of the closet of the dominant system, regain its prophetic voice, name oppression where it finds it, and help the oppressed to liberate themselves. Matthew Fox has this to say:

> The gay who wants to make a spiritual contribution to society will do it the way all others do: by non-repressive sublimation of working for others' pleasure and service. In other words, prophecy will play just as important a role in the gay's lifestyle and consciousness as will the sensual. Because gays are so often excluded from society's institutions [like women are], we can hopefully depend on them to offer alternative institutions — ones that are more sensual, more alive and quickening than the ones we have inherited [Fox 1981, 236–237].

He goes on to say that gays and lesbians have a responsibility to get out of the closet, not only for their own personal pride and sense of self-worth, but also for the sake of society's (and the church's).[5] We can break the domination of the senseless, a-sensual, and sadistic, and develop a theology that recovers pleasure in and thankfulness for our embodied state, including our sexuality. This outing would be the first step in undermining the current theological establishment, which creates anxious and narrow minds that deny the humanity of Christ, as well as the humanity of everybody else, including women, Native people, the poor, and anyone alienated from society. An outing theology is a way to place the church back on the margins where Jesus was, and away from conforming itself with the present reality of dominance and oppression.

Gay people — and anyone on the margins — cannot wait for the good will of political and religious authorities to recognize their rights to exist and belong. They cannot work toward finding a way to fit themselves into the current systematic theology. Rather, they must work for their own liberation and re-create a theology out of the closet that is not ashamed and does not fear facing the reality of our world and our church.

Notes

1. Although I often use "gay" and "lesbian" as definitions of sexual mi-
    norities that are excluded, that does not mean I want to be limited to
    this North American binary definition, but rather also refer to bi-
    sexual, transgender, intersex, and queer categories.

2. Cf. André Musskopf, *Uma brecha no armário — Proposta para uma Teologia
    Gay* (São Leopoldo: 2002), 69, citing Richard Cleaver, *Know My Name
    — A Gay Liberation Theology* (Louisville, KY: Westminster John Knox,
    1995).

3. I employ the terminology "heterosexual" instead of patriarchalism,
    following Adrienne Rich's classical definition of heterosexuality as a
    compulsory political institution. (See A. Rich, "Compulsory Hetero-
    sexuality and Lesbian Existence," in Marcella Althaus-Reid, *Indecent
    Theology* [London/NY: 2000], 176.) This concept is also applied by M.
    Althaus-Reid, who argues that it "has the advantage of challenging
    us at the level of current theological praxis including action and re-
    flection on justice and development."

4. The fast growth of the Protestant missionary movement in Latin
    America, especially of pentecostalism, was seen by some scholars as a
    conspiracy to stop the expansion throughout Latin America of lib-
    eration theology, which was seen as advocating communism. The
    Protestant influx has been described as "an expression of North
    American capitalism, an element of conquest, friend of capitalism,
    and enemy of the labour force. [Their] program was the
    americanization of the people through their schools, churches, and
    sports" (José Miguez Bonino, *Rostros Del Protestantismo Latinoamericano*
    [Buenos Aires: 1995], 11–15).

5. Matthew Fox, *Whee, We, Wee All the Way Home* (Sante Fé, 1981), 236–
    237. The words between brackets are my additions.

Works Cited

Althaus-Reid, Marcella. 2000. *Indecent Theology: Theological Perversions in Sex, Gender, and Politics*. London/New York: Routledge.

Bonino, José Migues. 1995. *Rostros Del Protestantismo Latinoamericano*. Buenos Aires: Nueva Creacíon. 11–15.

Fox, Matthew. 1981. *Whee, We, Wee All the Way Home: A Guide to a Sensual, Prophetic Theology*. Santa Fé, NM: Bear and Company.

Musskopf, André. 2002. *Uma brecha no Armário*, São Leopoldo, EST: Brasil.

Pérez, Iván Hernández. 2000. *Teologias de la Liberación y Minorias Sexuales en América Latina y el Caribe. Consideraciones Preliminares*. Essay presented in the Congresso da Sociedade de Teologia e Ciências da Religião: SOTER, Belo Horizonte, Brazil. July.

Online

Civilrights
  http://www.civilrights.org/issues/hate/details.cfm?id=17044

Grupo Gay de Bahia
  See http://www.ggb.org.br/welcome.html

News
  Gary Delsohn and Sam Stanton; text available at: http://www.salon.com/news/feature/1999/11/08/hate/print.html

The Dialogue with
Other Disciplines

Good Psychology
is Good Theology;
Good Theology
is Good Psychology

DONALD MEEN, *a son of the Canadian prairies and a lifelong Anglican, is a clinical psychologist in hospital and private practice. He also teaches psychology at Douglas College and is an Adjunct Professor of Psychology at Simon Fraser University. He lives with his partner of 27 years, Kevin Simpson, in Vancouver. He served on the Anglican Church of Canada task force that developed the study program* Hearing Diverse Voices, Seeking Common Ground, *and was co-chair of the Gay and Lesbian Voices Commission for the dialogue on homosexuality in his home diocese of New Westminster.*

W hatever is good psychology is good theology and vice versa," says theologian and psychotherapist John McNeill [1988]. Both our psychology and our theology, to be good, must lead to the good health and flourishing of both individuals and communities. Our Lord called it "life abundant." On the other hand, "if living out our understanding of the scriptures and God's law leads to our human destruction, if in attempting to live that life we become neurotic, depressed, addicted to drugs or alcohol, irritable or unhappy, then something is wrong with our theological understanding, and something is especially wrong in our personal relationship with God. The great heresy of pathological religion is that we can only give glory to God when we are frustrated, unhappy, or suffering" [McNeill 1988, 29]. Rather, as St. Irenaeus said, "The glory of God is humankind fully alive."

A scientifically correct understanding of the created world is not inconsequential to Christian faith. In a recent *Catholic New Times* article Episcopal theologian Matthew Fox paralleled the Vatican's disagreement with Galileo over which celestial orb circled which, with its current pronouncements about the characters and lives of gay and lesbian people. He quotes St. Thomas Aquinas: "A mistake about creation is a mistake about God." Furthermore, Christians need to be as accurate as we can when describing people, so that we do not bear false witness against our neighbour. To be ethical persons requires educating ourselves sufficiently to be able to discern the truth, and then telling it.

Psychology helps us to avoid making mistakes about creation by offering facts on which to ground our current conversations about homosexuality. Perhaps even more importantly, psychology offers a way of thinking critically, which equips us to sort the fact from the fiction, the true from the false. The requirement for thinking scientifically is an open-minded skepticism that says, "I will allow that what you claim may be true, but I need to see the evidence." Psychology can help us evaluate that evidence rigorously and systematically.

What Does Psychology Tell Us So Far about Gay and Lesbian People?

How Many Are There?
Counting, much less describing gay and lesbian people, poses a challenge because we're an invisible minority. Social scientists must rely on us to identify ourselves, but even today in Canada, many lesbian and gay people would decline to do so because of the potential risks.

The most rigorously-designed recent surveys estimate that

between 2% and 4% of men and 1% and 2% of women self-identify as gay or lesbian. The 10% figure one often hears points to another truth: not everyone who has homosexual feelings or even acts on them self-identifies as gay or lesbian. People report varying degrees of homosexual and heterosexual feelings and behaviour, with those patterns sometimes varying across individuals' lifespans. For example, a study by Janus and Janus in 1993 found that 9% of men and 5% of women in their survey, which they claim to be representative of the American population, had frequent or ongoing homosexual experiences, but only 4% of men and 2% of women said they were homosexual. Another 5% of men and 3% of women said they were bisexual; 91% of men and 95% of women described themselves as heterosexual, despite the fact that 22% of men and 17% of women also reported homosexual experiences. This variability among people has led social scientists to posit continua of homo- and hetero-erotic attraction, with some people exclusively homosexual or heterosexual over their lives, and others experiencing bisexual attraction from the incidental to the significant.

What Are They Like?
On the TV show *Queer Eye for the Straight Guy*, five gay guys take a straight guy in hand and shape him up to be more attractive to his girlfriend. But is there really a "queer eye" for things decorative and aesthetically pleasing? Do all gay men have it? Maybe not all, but most? What about gay women?

How do we evaluate such notions or gather other information about what lesbian and gay people are like? Psychologists survey a sample of people from the population of interest — gays and lesbians, in this case — but the sample must be representative, not biased. Do you see the problem? If we can't even identify with certainty who belongs to the population, how can we select an unbiased sample of it? Conclusions and theories based on biased samples of gay and lesbian people have plagued social science. For years, theories about homosexuality were based on homosexually-oriented people *in therapy*. That is like drawing conclusions about alcohol use among Anglicans by surveying the ones you find at a bar. So what does social science tell us about those characteristics of lesbian or gay people that in all cases distinguish them from non-gay people? Nothing except the gender of the person with whom they fall in love!

Let me introduce another key concept from social science: a group's "central tendency" (such as an average score for the group on some variable) does not allow us to conclude anything about a "tendency" in any single member of the group. Let's use the stereotype underlying *Queer Eye for the Straight Guy* as an example. Suppose you study two hundred gay men and find that 60% score high on aesthetic judgement. That is a group tendency, but any individual in the study could score above, below, or right at the group's average. It is quite incorrect to say that he has a 60% tendency within himself to have good aesthetic judgement.

Intellectual rigour compels psychologists to seek out evidence that *disconfirms* cherished notions. So, if you are looking for what is "typical" of gay men, of course you would want to be sure it is not also typical of straight men. So you measure aesthetic judgement in a group of two hundred straight men matched with the gay sample you have just tested on as many relevant characteristics as possible. If there is no significant difference between the two groups' averages, you may just have learned something about men in general. Even if there is a difference, you would also find that some gay men in the study have better aesthetic judgement than some straight men; some straight men have better aesthetic judgement than some gay men; and some straight and gay men have about the same level of aesthetic judgement. Again, comparing group tendencies tells us nothing about any individual in either of the groups.

Despite the difficulty of finding representative samples, social science research does point to some conclusions. Importantly, no differences are found between heterosexual and homosexual people on standard measures of mental health. Concerning relationships, Peplau's [1993] review of the research found consistently that enduring close relationships are desired by gay and lesbian people and that, indeed, 40% to 60% of men and 45% to 80% of women were in couples at the time studies were conducted. It has been estimated that 20% of gay men have been heterosexually married, in contrast to about a third of lesbians. Gay and straight men, when compared to lesbians and straight women, are more permissive in their attitude toward casual sex, more concerned about good looks, and more easily aroused visually. Some studies report that gay men give less importance to monogamy than heterosexual men, and that a substantial and roughly equal majority of lesbian and straight women regard monogamy as important. Studies suggest that gay men are about ten times more likely to live in urban centres than rural. Myers [2003] cites a study by Ludvig [1995], who examined biographies of over a thousand eminent people and found gay and bisexual people over-represented (relative to what is estimated to be their percentage in the general population) especially among poets, fiction writers, artists, and musicians. Myers [1999] cites research evidence that, when one compares persons who attend church only rarely with those who attend regularly, the regular attenders are less likely to have cohabited before marriage, had fewer sexual partners, were less likely to abuse drugs and alcohol, to divorce, or be juvenile delinquents, "yet they are virtually as likely to be homosexual." He concludes, "Unlike sexual behaviour and other moral tendencies, sexual orientation appears unaffected by an active faith" [see htpp://www.davidmyers.org/sexorient/accepting.html].

Statistics show that men earn more than women on average, and a smaller number of gay men than others have children; it is extrapolated, therefore, that gay male individuals and couples have more disposable income than average.

There is no evidence of a set of characteristics or lifestyle that differentiates all gay and lesbian people from all straight people. For example, there is no way of knowing to what extent the stereotypical "gay bar scene" characterizes the lives of lesbian or gay people as a whole. A meaningful comparison would be the proportion of straight people of similar age for whom a "bar scene" figures prominently in their lifestyle. Generally lesbian and gay people describe their concerns as similar to those of heterosexual people: making a living; looking after physical, emotional, social, and spiritual needs; building and maintaining relationships; paying rent or mortgages; planning holidays or retirement; contributing to community and church; and so on. Some are in couples, some are single; some have children, others do not.

Testing Out What People Think They Know

Psychologists began evaluating ideas about gay and lesbian people when the social climate still condemned homosexuality, and many of the ideas were far from innocuous.

Are They Psychologically Disordered?
Changing Our Minds: The Story of Dr. Evelyn Hooker is a film documentary about the psychologist who is credited with beginning, in the early 1950s, the systematic scientific evaluation of the prevailing idea of the time, that homosexual people were psychologically disordered. Studying matched samples of gay and straight men who were not receiving mental health treatment, expert clinicians, kept blind to the sexual orientation of the men they were studying, were unable to differentiate gay from straight men. Subsequent scientific study has been consistent in its findings that "on standardized measures of personal adjustment and psychological well-being, gay and lesbian individuals, couples, and parents are comparable to their heterosexual counterparts" [Garnets and Kimmel 2003, 647]. Homosexuality no longer appears in the major diagnostic classification systems of mental disorders, including that of the World Health Organization, because the research evidence simply does not support its inclusion.

This is not to say that gay and lesbian people are never psychologically troubled or mentally ill, but that this is not intrinsic to homosexual orientation. However, lesbian and gay people report some special psychological and social pressures that can lead to distress: internalized homophobia, social stigma, and acts of discrimination and violence. Internalized homophobia refers to anti-gay attitudes and feelings that lesbian or gay people may absorb from their social context and apply to their own homosexuality. It has been found to be associated with depression, low self-esteem, substance abuse, and relationship instability [Garnets and Kimmel, 2003]. Meyers [2003] in his sample of gay men found internalized homophobia, perceived anti-gay stigma, and actual "prejudice events" predictive of demoralization, guilt, suicidal ideation and behaviour, and inhibition of sexual intimacy.

Remafedi, Farrow, and Deisher [1993] summarized a US government report on youth suicide that estimated gay youth were more likely than their peers to attempt suicide, accounting perhaps for as many as 30% of successful suicide attempts. Those researchers found among their sample of gay youth who had attempted suicide that anguish over their homosexuality was the second most common reason reported, after family problems, for their suicide attempt.

How Do They Get "That Way"?
Psychologists have also tested the several theories expounded as to what "causes" homosexuality. Since the social climate has been largely hostile, theories of causation have reflected the idea that homosexuality is pathological.

Some theorists have suggested that homosexuality is caused by such conditions as "homo-seductive" mothers or fathers, distant and/or hostile mothers or fathers, weak or unhappy marriages between mothers and fathers, or domination of fathers by mothers. Siegelman [1974] believed that the theories were being generated from non-representative samples, primarily of neurotic individuals in therapy. To control for this bias, he studied homosexual and heterosexual men low in neuroticism and found no significant differences in their parental background. Bell, Weinberg, and Hammersmith [1981] tested the major environmental theories at the time to see if homosexual and heterosexual people's autobiographies conformed to those theories. They concluded, "No particular phenomenon of family life can be singled out as especially consequential for either homosexual or heterosexual development" [191].

Other theories contended that homosexuality was the result of dysfunctional peer relations, childhood and adolescent sexual experiences of various sorts, or social sex-role non-conformity. Once again, these researchers found the life experiences of their homosexual and heterosexual groups simply did not differ significantly, with the exception that more homosexual than heterosexual people were disinclined as children to enjoy gender-stereotypical activities and saw themselves as not conforming to social sex-role stereotypes for their gender. It is important to note that descriptive or correlational research such as this may identify associated characteristics but can tell us nothing about cause and effect relationships. A misunderstanding of this may underlie the advice of a self-described pro-family writer in a recent book, where he urges parents to insist that their sons act like "typical boys" and their daughters like "typical girls" in order to prevent their becoming gay or lesbian.

In recent years, the focus of scientific study has shifted to possible biological contributors. As yet unreplicated studies have identified differences in some brain structures and genetic material between heterosexual and homosexual people. Twin studies point to genetic influence, given a higher concordance (if one twin is gay, the other is) found among identical than fraternal twins. Pre-natal hormonal influences could explain the higher-than-expected concordance for homosexuality among fraternal twins as well as the observation that men with several older brothers are more likely to be gay. As Myers [2003] summarizes, "Consistency of the genetic, pre-natal, and brain findings has swung the pendulum toward a biological explanation. Nature more than nurture, most psychologists now believe, predisposes sexual orientation" [480]. What might facilitate or inhibit any predisposition becoming someone's reality is not yet known.

Healing and Homophobia

The study program *Hearing Diverse Voices, Seeking Common Ground,* produced by the national office of the Anglican Church of Canada, offers an overview of the various ways people use the word "healing" in our conversations about homosexuality. When homosexuality is seen as willful sin, healing means repentance — choosing another direction. When it is seen as pathological, healing means changing orientation or sexual abstinence, with the aid of therapy, "addiction" recovery programs, or resolution of the dysfunctional relationships held to be at the root of homosexuality. Evidence from social science does not support the premises from which these ideas of healing are derived. Another view conceives healing as establishing the most responsible and healthy intimate relationships possible given an unchangeable, flawed condition.

But when homosexuality, like heterosexuality, is seen as intrinsically ordered toward the good of intimate loving, then healing means "coming out" to self-affirmation, sexual wholeness, and integrity, and to self-giving in relationships of mutuality, care, and respect.

Can People be "Reoriented"?

John is forty-eight and a recent grandfather. He was married for over a dozen years and says that he cared for his wife and that they enjoyed sexual intimacy. A few years ago he found himself unable to continue in the marriage. In his words, he couldn't continue to live a lie. "I've always been gay," he says. Now he lives with his life-partner, another man in his forties, who appreciates the presence of John's children and grandchild in their life. John has never felt happier or more complete.

Susan is a new Christian and happily married for the first time at thirty-eight. She describes having a profound religious experience a couple of years ago. Throughout her adult life till then, she described herself as homosexual and she had been in a couple of lesbian relationships. Now she says she has no homosexual feelings whatsoever, only heterosexual feelings.

Is John "ex-straight"? Susan "ex-gay"? Were they deceived or confused but now have found their "true identities"? Or are they now deceived or confused, having been right before? Are they "really" bisexual people who have always had a capacity to respond with sexual love to both genders? Or did their sexual orientation actually change?

Science can draw no certain conclusions from people's self-reports. Anecdotes don't give us the objective and independently verifiable facts we need. The same applies to the contention that sexual orientation can be changed through secular or religious therapies: the data is almost entirely anecdotal, based on what people say and believe has happened in their lives. For example, a prominent American psychiatrist, Robert Spitzer, recently told a convention of his colleagues that he believed a small number of people who had gone through "ex-gay" programs had changed sexual orientation. However, his contention was based on "ex-gay" testimonials given by telephone, with no independent corroboration or objective measures of sexual orientation either before or after the self-reported change.

Shidlo and Schroeder [2002] surveyed 202 people who had undergone reorientation therapy. A majority reported no change to sexual orientation. Of the 14% who reported that they had been helped, a third claimed a degree of reorientation and two-thirds said the therapy had helped them remain celibate or to struggle more effectively to control their desires. Other benefits reported included a greater sense of belonging, improved insights, self-esteem, and communication skills, relief at being able to talk about sexual feelings, confirmation of one's gay or lesbian identity with less guilt, and improvement in religious and spiritual life. Of those who experienced no change, many reported having suffered harm from the "therapy," citing increased depression, suicidal ideation and attempts, internalized homophobia, lower self-esteem, distorted perception of homosexual orientation, intrusive unpleasant imagery, sexual dysfunction, greater fear, shame, alienation, loneliness, loss of social supports, interference with intimate relationships, and spiritual harm.

From social science research a pattern may be discerned: for a small number of people, usually those more bisexual than homosexual, some changes of uncertain duration, more in behaviour than in feelings, may follow some treatments. However, there remains no scientific substantiation that "reorientation" therapies of any sort change homosexual orientation to heterosexual.

That treatment attempts are not always positive or even neutral in their effects, but may be harmful, raises important ethical concerns. Where churches sponsor counselling programs for those with problems related to sexual orientation or behaviour, only the highest ethical standards should be expected. Are counsellors well trained and subject to a stringent code of ethical conduct? Do participants give informed consent to treatment, having received all the relevant information about strategies, outcomes, and risks in an accurate and unbiased manner? Is the whole truth told or is it selective toward a particular point of view? Are counsellors equipped to deal with harmful outcomes?

How should Christians regard people's deeply-felt life stories? Can we conclude from their accounts of their sexual journeys that things happened exactly as they perceived? Psychology would suggest we all construct our personal histories prompted by many motivations, some not fully conscious to us. Also, science cannot objectively verify people's feelings and dreams. In the spirit of our baptismal covenant to respect the dignity of all persons, I suggest that we should receive their stories by listening respectfully, and then wishing for them the very best: to be authentic, to love and be loved.

"Homophobia" is an awkward term coined by psychologist George Weinberg [1973]. Embedded in the word is what he thought caused people to discriminate against homosexuals — fear. He elaborated that homophobia included dread, revulsion, loathing, and the "desire to inflict punishment as retribution" [113]. Other psychologists have suggested different words to describe anti-gay attitudes, such as heterosexism (the belief that heterosexuality is superior to homosexuality) or sexual prejudice (negative attitudes based on sexual orientation) [Herek 2003].

There are those who complain that they are not homophobic, but nonetheless disapprove of homosexuality for philosophical or religious reasons. However, merely claiming one is not homophobic does not necessarily make it so. Psychologists have documented the human inclination to see and portray ourselves with a "self-serving bias." Jesus provides us with a principle by which to discern the truth: "By their fruits you shall know them" [Matthew 7:13]. Homophobia should be judged from the evidence: the fruit of people's attitudes in their speech and action.

You may recall Matthew Shepherd, a young gay man and Anglican server, who was beaten and left hanging, broken and bleeding, on a fence in Wyoming. He died, and a fundamentalist Christian group picketed his funeral carrying signs that said, "God Hates Fags." Myers quotes church historian Martin Marty in a Los Angeles *Times* article of 1998. Reflecting on the murder, Marty likened today's homosexuals to the lepers of Jesus' day, who were shunned by the religious but not Our Lord. "I believe that much anti-gay and anti-other activity is inspired by Christian rhetoric, but by now we must know that the attempt to love sinners while stirring hate about the sin which, after all, has to be done by those called sinners, contributes to the atmosphere in which crime occurs."

Recently two boys in British Columbia have helped further to put a human face to the effects of homophobia. One killed himself after prolonged anti-gay harassment at school, and the other sued his school board, unsuccessfully, for not protecting him from years of such harassment. Parenthetically, in neither case did the boy self-identify as gay.

Hearing Diverse Voices also spoke of healing of communities — families, social networks, and churches — overcoming fear and hatred, renouncing persecution, and accepting gay and lesbian people, with qualification or without. Anglican Church leaders have repeatedly stated that gay and lesbian people "as children of God, have a full and equal claim with all other persons upon the love, acceptance, concern and pastoral care of the church" [*House of Bishops Guidelines,* 1979].

Can homophobia be cured? asks Bruce Hilton [1992]. He begins by considering what might cause it: it is taught by word and example to the young; people may automatically be biased against those who are different; the media often present negative images of gay and lesbian people. He thinks sexism is part of the problem, as for instance when a person asks, "How could a man lower himself to be 'like a woman' in an intimate relationship?" He suggests that people tend to think about homosexuality chiefly as genital sexual activity. Also, in the context of widespread anxiety about all issues of sexuality, some seek the reassurance of over-simplified rules. Anyway, since only a small minority of people is directly affected, homosexuality can be attacked at little cost, and can be dealt with abstractly without having to engage its human face. Weinberg [1973] suggests homophobia may arise from religious motivations, from the secret fear of being homosexual, from repressed envy of the freedom from cultural conventions that lesbians and gays are perceived to enjoy, and from the threat that gays and lesbians are felt to offer to cultural conventions. Finally, he says some are disturbed by the gay person's "existence without (the) vicarious immortality" conferred by having children.

Weinberg [1973] describes his attempts three decades ago to open the minds of some of his psychoanalyst colleagues to the possibility of "healthy homosexuals." He invited them to his home for dinner together with some gay friends. His colleagues were excessively polite, but once the gay guests had left, they complained about them and made it clear they wanted no further contact. He felt compelled to conclude: "Once an attitude is formed, in some cases at least, it may not be dislodged by evidence alone. You can lead an expert to the source of his fear and disgust, but you cannot always make him drink of his observations" [39]. In psychology, the term for this phenomenon is belief perseverance, defined by Myers [2003] as "our tendency to cling to our beliefs in the face of contrary evidence" [396].

Nonetheless, our efforts to overcome homophobia continue to focus on presenting the whole truth in place of selective information or outright distortions and errors, and on offering opportunities to meet real, live lesbian and gay people. The effect of prejudice, and one of the ways in which it is perpetuated, is to render the out-group "less than fully human." Presenting a human face is so powerful that it is both encouraged by those who seek openness to attitude change, and actively resisted by those who do not.

Identity and Maturing

Psychologists regard an integrated, well-formed identity as a characteristic of psychological health. Psychologist Erik Erikson regards the establishment of a coherent identity as a key developmental task of the adolescent, focusing around questions such as "Who am I?' and "Who am I becoming?" This involves individuation from family of origin, the process of coming to know oneself as distinct and separate, though in relationship. Family therapists describe healthy families as ones that allow for this individuation. We learn early that we are gendered — male or female. The vast majority of lesbian and gay people studied, like heterosexual people, have a gender identity consistent with their biological sex.

Another feature of our sexual identity is our social sex-role behaviour, the degree to which we act "like a man" or "like a woman." This collection of traits is highly culture-dependent. Again, the research shows gay and lesbian people inhabiting the same range of socially-constructed feminine or masculine characteristics as heterosexual people. The extent to which gender typical or atypical social sex-role behaviour characterizes gay or lesbian populations cannot yet be determined.

The third element of sexual identity is sexual orientation: our characteristic affectional-sexual attraction to, and our potential to fall in love with, people of the same, the other, or either gender.

The Process of Coming Out

Gay or lesbian identity is neither conferred nor evident from earliest childhood, but discovered, then owned and integrated in a process called "coming out." Psychologists have developed models of coming out. Most begin with a stage of feeling different from one's peers, usually in budding adolescence with its unbidden erotic dreams and body reactions. Then follows a stage of wondering and worrying: "Could I be gay?" After varying lengths of time and degrees of turmoil, most gay and lesbian people reach a stage of accepting the truth of their sexual orientation. Then they begin exploring how to integrate their sexuality with the rest of their lives. The journey of experience, learning, and self-discovery, of living more and more authentically, may lead to seeing the positive potential of being gay or lesbian, to affirming and even celebrating it: Gay is good. Gay is gift.

For good mental health we need not only a coherent and integrated sense of ourselves, but also to value ourselves. Psychological research shows a clear positive relationship between self-esteem and good psychological function. A positive gay or lesbian identity has also been found to be associated with higher self-esteem, greater ego strength, less depression, and fewer symptoms of neurotic or social anxiety [Garnets and Kimmel 2003].

We have been told that in the new creation, our Christian identity transcends all others: Jew or Greek, slave or free, male and female. "And gay or straight!" adds B. Barbara Hall [1996]. For gay and lesbian Christians, "coming out" is a path to both psychological and spiritual maturity and wholeness. The gay Christian almost inevitably asks: "As I come to know myself as gay or lesbian and integrate this aspect of myself into the totality of who I am, do I still hear God calling this newly-discovered 'me' by name? Does God still recognize me as God's own child and love the real, whole, sexual me?"

I once had a greeting card that read: "The irony is this: if you don't go in, you can't find out." I add: "and you can't come out!" The "going in" part of the "coming out" process is a spiritual act. We go in to find out what is true, authentic, and real about ourselves, and also what is true about God and what God intends the world to be. In this act of discernment we ask, "Who is speaking to me? Who gives me my name: my culture and its conventional wisdom, or God? Who knows my truth and can help me find it?" As Christians, we know that God breaks through to us with the truth when our guard is down, when the world has no explanations that work or make sense, when we are at our wits' end and most powerless, defenceless, and empty — when we gay and lesbian people have, in John Fortunato's [1982] words, finally "embraced our exile" from the world.

John McNeill [1988] says that God's self-revelation is first as parent; then as brother and fellow human being, more accessible to us, yet still outside; finally as Holy Spirit of love, dwelling within us. "God writes the law deep within us, on our hearts ... and every human being, from the least to the greatest, is able to find the will of God within himself, within her experience" [23]. So we lesbian and gay people receive living water from our own well, and with it we receive the knowledge that God is for us even more than we are for ourselves, loves us even more than we love ourselves. Our hearts are converted, we are honoured and cherished, and with gratitude we can begin moving outward.

McNeill quotes Father Jacques Perotti, a leader in the gay Christian movement in France, who says that now is a *declic*, a special time in history, in which there is "a revelation of the slow emergence of positive gay/lesbian identity from the heart of the world. McNeill adds that this is "part of the great dialectic of human liberation that God is working out" [McNeill 1995, 160].

In the words of the responsorial prayer found in the introduction of the Diocese of New Westminster's rite of blessing for gay and lesbian couples:

> *Holy and Eternal One, in the quiet night you have called us each by our own name.*
> *In our very heart, you have named us beloved.*
> *You surprise us by your grace; we are the fruit of your boundless love.*
> *On our exodus way, you nourish and free us.*

Being Couples

You give us companions for our journey.

Psychologists recognize the ubiquitous human motivation to establish intimate pair relationships. In Erikson's psycho-social model of human development, the central challenge of young adulthood after we have developed a coherent identity is the successful resolution of Intimacy versus Isolation. We discover and develop our capacity to love and be loved intimately.

Peplau and Spaulding [2003] have summarized the research on same-sex couples. In the samples studied, a majority of gay men and lesbians are found to be in couple relationships with perhaps a higher percentage for lesbians. We can't estimate the typical duration of committed relationships, but they can extend decades. Like their heterosexual counterparts, gays and lesbians look for people who are affectionate and reliable, who share interests and religious beliefs. The research finds that both gay and heterosexual men are more interested than lesbians and heterosexual women in the physical attractiveness of potential partners. Women seem more concerned about personality characteristics. Gay men tend to prefer other men with traditionally masculine traits, while lesbians don't show as clear a preference for masculine or feminine traits in potential mates.

Research shows marked similarity in self-reported love and satisfaction in couples, regardless of their being lesbian, gay, or straight. Both same-sex and heterosexual couples report equally often that similarity between partners is a factor in the success of their relationship. Same-sex couples tend to look for equality of involvement, commitment, power, and decision making. The division of household labour is more equitable among same-gender than among other-gender couples. Same-gender couples who strongly value interpersonal attachment in their relationship also report greater satisfaction, closeness, and love, than those who value attachment less. Bell and Weinberg [1978] also found their "close-coupled" sample had very few social or personal problems, were more self-accepting, the happiest, and best adjusted of all the groups they studied.

Evidence is inconsistent about the stressful effects on relationships of one or both partners being still "in the closet." It is as yet unclear whether there is any significant difference in frequency of sexual activity between same- and other-gendered couples. Gay male couples are much more likely to have non-monogamous relationships than heterosexual and lesbian couples in the samples studied.

As far as managing conflict in relationships is concerned, same- and other-gendered couples are similar in frequency and intensity of arguing, and there seems to be similarity even over what these conflicts concern. There is some evidence that gender-role expectations play out in unique ways in lesbian and gay couple conflict, with the former more focused on intimacy issues and the latter on competition. Same and other-gendered couples showed no difference in the likelihood of using positive problem-solving strategies. In recent years, some attention has been paid to domestic violence in same-gender relationships and it appears thus far that the rate is similar to that found in samples of heterosexual couples. Blumstein and Schwartz [1983; cited in Peplau and Spaulding 2003] examined stability in relationships of lesbian, gay, and heterosexual couples. They found that differences in the break-up rate of couples who had lived together only a short time lay not between same- and other-gendered couples, but between legally married and unmarried couples, heterosexual or homosexual. That finding has been replicated, which suggests that there is something about being married that encourages relationship stability. Interestingly, reports from the Netherlands show that, since same-sex marriages were first recognized, the divorce rate among same-sex couples has actually been lower than the divorce rate among other-sex married couples. Peplau and Spaulding conclude, "Many lesbians and gay men are involved in satisfying, close relationships. Contemporary same-sex couples in the United States often prize equality in their relationships and reject the model of traditional male-female marriage in favour of a model of best friendship. Comparisons of heterosexual and same-sex couples find many similarities in relationship quality and in the factors associated with satisfaction, commitment and stability over time. Efforts to apply basic relationship theories have been largely successful. There is much commonality among the issues facing all close relationships, regardless of the sexual orientation of the partners" [468].

A new documentary film, *Trembling before G-d,* concerns the struggle of lesbian and gay Orthodox Jews to integrate their faith and sexuality. After a recent screening a rabbi offered a *midrash* on the first creation story in Genesis. He reminded us that G-d created the human from the earth and placed this earth creature in the Garden. At some point, G-d recognized that the human was lonely. ("It is not right that the human should be alone.") Then the rabbi said, "G-d brings by various animals, to see if they'd be the right companion for the human to ease his loneliness. I can just see G-d, like a typical Jewish parent, waiting up for Adam to come home from his date and asking eagerly: 'So, how was it? Did you like (the giraffe or whatever)?' "

In this creation story, G-d's first concern was that the human needed companionship and community — the instruction to go forth and multiply came later! I was once challenged to produce the "biblical warrant" by which I could justify same-sex spousal relationships. My answer: "The Bible tells us that God saw that we humans get lonely for someone to love and share life with. Like any loving parent, God wants that for gay and lesbian people, too."

The delegate asked, "What is sex for?' Or maybe he asked, "What is sex good for?" This question brought an uncomfortable silence to the floor of General Synod in 1995 during a discussion of sexuality. Procreation would be the most obvious answer, but human sexuality experts suggest that sexual activity within "pair-bonded" couples is also "relationship glue." An evolutionary psychologist would look for the evolutionary advantage of any human behaviour — its survival value for the species. Again, procreation is clearly a good answer. However, is pair-bonding in humans primarily or only good because it establishes a stable context for procreation? Could it have another value, a good that contributes to our species' survival in some other way?

Canadian Roman Catholic theologian André Guindon [1986] says that our sexuality "speaks of who we are" and that our human sexual communication aims at establishing relationship based on the totality of who we are. He holds up "fruitfulness" as the mark of healthy and holy sexuality, describing as fruitful that which promotes humanly tender/sensuous life, self-identity, personal worth, and community. James B. Nelson [1979] describes sexual love as life-serving, "always meaning the transmission of the power of newness of life from one lover to the other; sometimes it also means the procreation of children" [118]. St. Augustine saw the divine in human sexual loving: "Show me a human in love, and I'll show you a human on the way to God" [cited in McNeill 1985]. McNeill adds: "The ultimate drive in the human psyche toward the intimacy of love is a built-in drive toward oneness with the infinite reality of God" [157].

A writer from a theology school here in Vancouver has contended that gay men should marry women. He opined that it wasn't necessary for the woman to know who her husband was fantasizing about during their sexual relations. A parallel might be heterosexual men in all-male environments fantasizing women while having sexual relations with other men. There is nothing in this of sharing one's deepest self in a tender and sensuous expression. It isn't sexual intimacy at all. It also shows that you can't infer people's sexual orientation from their sexual behaviour.

Being a Couple with Kids

Some studies suggest that about half of lesbians and between a quarter and a half of gay men who marry partners of the opposite gender have children. To this we can add the unknown number, more lesbians than gay men, who are biological and functional parents but have never been in heterosexual marriages. We have no systematic study of the prevalence of gay and lesbian adoptive and foster parents. But children all over Canada assert that they have two mommies or two daddies. Here in British Columbia, awareness of this is high as the result of recent court cases over the availability in schools of literature depicting families headed by two men or two women parents.

Gay-unfriendly organizations frequently claim that social science research supports their contention that a household headed by a mother and a father together is best for children. The research that they cite often reveals, however, that what is being compared are broken versus intact homes, or homes that are headed by a single parent versus those headed by two. To study the relative adequacy as parents of same-gendered versus other-gendered couples requires that samples of these two populations be compared. A Vatican document recently asserted that the absence of "sexual complementarity" in same-sex parents would interfere with the normal development of children, and that "violence" would be done to children by placing them in such an environment.

The president of the Canadian Psychological Association, Dr. Patrick O'Neil, replied publicly: "Psycho-social research into lesbian and gay parenting indicates that there is no basis in the scientific literature for this perception. The research leads the CPA to conclude [as follows]: (1) Available evidence indicates that the children of gay and lesbian parents do not differ significantly from the children of heterosexual parents with regard to psycho-social and gender development and identity. (2) Statements that children of gay and lesbian parents have more and significant problems in the area of psycho-social or gender development and identity than do the children of heterosexual parents have no support from the scientific literature. (3) If gay and lesbian parents encounter unique stress as parents, it is more likely the result of the public's beliefs and perceptions about their fitness as parents and obstacles created by social systems such as the courts, than it is the result of any deficiencies in their actual fitness to parent" [CPA 2003]. The American Association of Pediatrics has stated, "A considerable body of professional literature provides evidence that children with parents who are homosexual can have the same advantages and the same expectations for health, adjustment and development as can children whose parents are heterosexual" [see www.aap.org/policy/020008.html]. The American Psychological Association provides an annotated bibliography of research into lesbian and gay parenting at htpp://www.apa.org.

Good Fruits: Gay/Lesbian Gifts to Church and Society

We have raised the question, "What is sex good for?" so it seems right to go another step and ask: "What is homosexuality good for?" Evolutionary psychologist J. D. Weinrich [1990] described ways in which homosexuality may contribute to species survival. First, homosexual members act altruistically by helping their kin raise children rather than having their own. Second, in societies where everyone marries, homosexual people help by being more willing to marry whomever is chosen for them and by generating fewer extra-marital pregnancies. Third, the highest reproductive success is hypothesized for bisexuals, who have genes for both heterosexual and homosexual orientation.

John McNeill [1985] considered the positive contribution of homosexual people from the perspective of the human sciences. To the extent that gay and lesbian people are able to integrate masculine and feminine social sex-role characteristics, he thought they helpfully challenge the "partial and dehumanizing aspects" of the masculine/feminine stereotypes of the day. He quotes Jung [1959] as applauding gay men's great capacity for same-sex friendship and tenderness, suggesting also that they "may even rescue friendship between the sexes from its limbo of the impossible."

From both a psychological and a religious perspective, one of the most important gifts gay and lesbian people bring to the church and the world is the psycho-social and spiritual path to maturity called "coming out": our coming to self-affirmation and wholeness, trusting in God's word of love and truth as against the dehumanizing message of the world. Guindon [1986] asks, "Can gay/lesbian sexual language be fruitful for the whole human community?" He suggests that the "gratuitous celebration of love" that characterizes much gay and lesbian intimate loving is another gift we have to offer. It is "gratuitous" because lesbian and gay people do not enter into committed relationships to fulfill social expectations or to gain economic or career advantage or to carry on a family name. Given the few supports and many obstacles to sharing a life together over the long haul, he suggests that our fidelity is a witness to "love's power to endure." Guindon says also that gay and lesbian people can help the wider community to "liberate sensuousness from shame, to reclaim our sensual bodies, and to learn from them who we are and how to act humanly" [165]. He thinks perhaps gay men can be helpful to other men by showing how sensuality can be humanized through tenderness.

Another gift is the friendship model which gay and lesbian relationships predominantly follow, emphasizing companionship, sharing, and equality. These relationships are relatively free from social-sexual stereotypes and may be developed creatively according to each person's nature and talents. It is interesting that the same-sex union ceremonies of premodern Europe uncovered and discussed by Boswell [1994] reflect a model of mutual commitment of equals, with no sense of either being the possession of the other.

Among many lesbian and gay people, our friendship network is our "family of choice," our community. There is often a special cherishing and honouring of friendship that has partly emerged out of being obliged to live in a hostile socio-cultural environment. McNeill [1988] observes that "from the first calling of the disciples to the inauguration of the church at Pentecost, God's call to conversion was always simultaneously a call to community" [187]. The care and love of friends and communities of friendship demonstrate and anticipate the reign of Christ. McNeill also suggests that gay and lesbian people have been generously endowed with hospitality. Perhaps our having been lonely and having feared rejection makes us sensitive to the weariness of the stranger. Perhaps because we don't easily belong, we recognize others who don't and respond with empathy. Perhaps because many of us have no children we are left with much love and care to give.

Another gift we offer is different-ness. It makes us a disquieting minority, but it can be fruitful in bringing something new to life. If engaged, the stranger may draw us out of ourselves, challenge our worldview, and open us to *metanoia*, a transformation of perspective. For Christians in particular there is significance in being at the margin of things, about being outsiders or identifying with them. Father Richard Rohr, OFM, said in a lecture some years ago, that being in the place of powerlessness, disestablishment, and insecurity holds us close to longing and thirsting for the truth, for the coming reign of God. Being a small minority, gay and lesbian people can never compel or overpower by force of numbers. The wider world is called to acts of gratuitous justice-making in affirming us.

I close with the final phrases of the responsorial prayer in the rite of blessing, which were inspired by Episcopal priest and theologian, M. R. Ritley:

> *You set us apart, shaped by our love, yet call us into the midst*
> *of your people*
> *Where we will be your word of blessing.*

Works Cited

Anglican Church of Canada. 1994. *Hearing Diverse Voices, Seeking Common Ground*. Toronto: Anglican Book Centre.

Anglican Church of Canada. 1997. House of Bishops statement.

Bell, A. P., and M. S. Weinberg. 1978. *Homosexualities: A Study of Diversity Among Men and Women*. New York: Simon and Schuster.

Bell, A. P., M. S. Weinberg, and S. K. Hammersmith. 1981. *Sexual Preference: Its Development in Men and Women*. Bloomington: Indiana University Press.

Blumstein, P., and P. Schwartz. 1983. *American Couples: Money, Work, Sex*. New York: Morrow.

Boswell, J. 1994. *Same-Sex Unions in Premodern Europe*. New York: Vintage Books.

Canadian Psychological Association. 2003. Press Release: "Gays and Lesbians Make Bad Parents: There is no basis in the scientific literature for this perception."

Diocese of New Westminster. 2003. *Rite for the Celebration of Gay and Lesbian Covenants*.

Fortunato, J. E. 1982. *Embracing the Exile: Healing Journeys of Gay Christians*. San Francisco: Harper and Row.

Garnets, L. D., and D. C. Kimmel, eds. 2003. *Psychological Perspectives on Lesbian, Gay and Bisexual Experiences*. 2nd ed. New York: Columbia University Press.

Guindon, André. 1986. *The Sexual Creators. An Ethical Proposal for Concerned Christians*. Lanham, MD: University Press of America.

Hall, B. B. 1996. "Homosexuality and a New Creation." In C. Helfing, ed., *Our Selves, Our Souls and Bodies*. Boston: Cowley Publications.

Herek, G. M. 2003. "The Psychology of Sexual Prejudice." In L. D. Garnets and D. C. Kimmel, eds., *Psychological Perspectives on Lesbian, Gay and Bisexual Experiences*. 2nd ed. New York: Columbia University Press. 157–164.

Hilton, B. 1992. *Can Homophobia be Cured? Wrestling with Questions that Challenge the Church*. Nashville: Abingdon Press.

Janus, S., and C. Janus. 1993. *The Janus Report on Sexual Behavior*. New York: John Wiley and Sons.

Marty, M. 1998. Los Angeles *Times*. 18 October.

McNeill, J. J. 1985. *The Church and the Homosexual*. New York: Next Year Publications.

———. 1988. *Taking a Chance on God: Liberating Theology for Gays, Lesbians and Their Lovers, Families and Friends*. Boston: Beacon Press.

———. 1995. *Freedom, Glorious Freedom: The Spiritual Journey to the Fullness of Life for Gays, Lesbians, and Everybody Else*. Boston: Beacon Press.

Meyers, I. H. 2003. "Minority stress and mental health in gay men." In L. D. Garnets and D. C. Kimmel, eds. *Psychological Perspectives on Lesbian, Gay and Bisexual Experiences*. 2nd ed. New York: Columbia University Press. 699–731.

Myers, D. G. 1999. "Accepting What Cannot be Changed." *Perspectives* June/July.

———. 2003. *Psychology*. 7th ed. New York: Worth.

Nelson, J. B. 1979. *Embodiment: An Approach to Sexuality and Christian Theology*. Minneapolis: Augsburg.

Peplau, L. A. 1993. "Lesbian and gay relationships." In L. D. Garnets and D. C. Kimmel, *Psychological Perspectives on Lesbian and Gay Male Experiences*. New York: Columbia University Press. 2nd ed. 395–415.

Peplau, L. A., and L. R. Spalding. 2003. "The Close Relationships of Lesbians, Gay men and Bisexuals." In L. D. Garnets and D. C. Kimmel, eds., *Psychological Perspectives on Lesbian, Gay and Bisexual Experiences*. 2nd ed. New York: Columbia University Press. 449–474.

Remafedi, G., J. A. Farrow, and R. W. Deisher. 1993. "Risk Factors in Attempted Suicide in Gay and Bisexual Youth." In L. D. Garnets and D. C. Kimmel, eds., *Psychological Perspectives on Lesbian, Gay and Bisexual Experiences*. 2nd ed. New York: Columbia University Press.

Ritley, M. R. 1991. "Set Apart, Called into the Midst." In M. Boyd and N. L. Wilson, eds., *Amazing Grace: Stories of Lesbian and Gay Faith*. Freedom, CA: The Crossing Press. 116–130.

Shidlo, A., and M. Schroeder. 2002. "Changing Sexual Orientation: A Consumer's Report." *Professional Psychology: Research and Practice* 33 (3): 249–259.

Siegelman, M. 1974. "Parental Background of Male Homosexuals and Heterosexuals." *Archives of Sexual Behavior* 7:1–11.

Spitzer, R. 2002. "200 subjects who claim to have changed their sexual orientation from homosexual to heterosexual." Presentation at meeting of American Psychiatric Association.

Weinberg, G. 1973. *Society and the Healthy Homosexual.* Garden City, NY: Anchor Press/Doubleday.

Weinrich, J. D. 1990. "The Kinsey Scale in Biology, with a Note on Kinsey as a Biologist." In D. P. McWhirter, S. A. Sanders, and J. M. Reinisch, eds., *Homosexuality/Heterosexuality: Concepts of Sexual Orientation.* New York: Oxford University Press. 115–137.

Church, Society, and State

Reconciling with Gays and Lesbians

STEPHEN J. TOOPE *is President and CEO of the Pierre Elliott Trudeau Foundation. (The views expressed should not be attributed to the Foundation.) On leave from the faculty of law at McGill University, where he has worked since 1987 and of which he is a former dean, his scholarly interests include family law and public international law. He was law clerk to the Right Honourable Brian Dickson, Chief Justice of Canada, has served as chair of the Primate's World Relief and Development Fund, and was a member of the Jurisdiction Task Force of the General Synod of the Anglican Church of Canada.*

———✦———

In June 2003 the Ontario Court of Appeal issued a unanimous judgement in *Halpern et al.* vs. *Attorney General of Canada* [Halpern 2003] that changed the political dynamics surrounding the legal status of homosexuals in Canada. In one sense, the court was merely following a well-trodden path. Courts in three provinces — the supreme courts of British Columbia and Quebec and a lower court in Ontario — had already declared that the common law definition limiting access to marriage to heterosexual couples was unconstitutional, in that it breached the guarantee of equality contained in section 15 of the *Canadian Charter of Rights and Freedoms* [Charter 1982]. The Law Commission of Canada had previously recommended that the legal prohibition on the marriage of same-sex partners be eliminated [Law Commission 2001, 131]. The

Ontario Court of Appeal simply joined the growing throng marching along that path of analysis. In a significant addition, however, the Ontario judges declared that, because the definition of marriage was a rule made by common law judges and not by a legislature, judges should change it as soon as the decision had been taken that the rule was in breach of constitutional rights. It was not necessary to provide for a delay in the implementation of the judgement to allow Parliament to act, because no direct Parliamentary action was required; judges could change judge-made law, and they could do it immediately. The old rule was erased forthwith, and gay and lesbian people in Ontario were entitled to marry.

How does this decision, and others like it, affect the church? The superficial answer is that the decision to authorize legal marriages between homosexuals has nothing to do with religion, or with religious ceremonies or sacraments. The Ontario Court of Appeal was careful to state:

> In our view, this case does not engage religious rights and freedoms. Marriage is a legal institution, as well as a religious and social institution. This case is solely about the legal institution of marriage. It is not about the religious validity or invalidity of various forms of marriage. We do not view this case as, in any way, dealing or interfering with the religious institution of marriage [Halpern 2003, para. 53].

Similarly, in another case declaring the right of same-sex couples to have access to the legal institution of marriage, the British Columbia Court of Appeal emphasized that:

> There is no merit to the argument that the rights and interests of heterosexuals would be affected by granting same-sex couples the freedom to marry.... I cannot conclude that freedom of religion would be threatened or jeopardized by legally sanctioning same-sex marriage. No religious body would be compelled to solemnize a same-sex marriage against its wishes and all religious people — of any faith — would continue to enjoy the freedom to hold and espouse their beliefs. Thus, there

is no need for any infringement of the equality rights of lesbians and gays that arises because of the restrictions against same-sex marriage [Barbeau 2003, para.130].

These statements are strong signals that Canadian courts are unlikely to interfere with the decisions of religious denominations on the question whether or not to perform marriages involving homosexual couples, much less on the question whether or not same-sex unions should or should not be blessed.

In Quebec the position is even clearer. Article 367 of the *Civil Code* states expressly that no minister of religion may be forced to celebrate a marriage that his or her religion does not recognize. In the Quebec case that also required the legal recognition of gay and lesbian marriage, the court concluded that the equality rights of same-sex couples cannot displace the rights of religious groups to refuse to solemnize same-sex marriages. At the same time, however, the rights of religious groups to freely practise their religion cannot trump the rights of same-sex couples seeking equality. Religious definitions of marriage cannot dictate the appropriate definition in secular law.

No one would dispute that religions have played a major role in marriage since their beliefs and rites have governed the development of the institution's framework. The secularization of marriage has forced our legislatures to take into account the fact that the institution is civil and cannot be defined solely in religious terms. We are no longer living in the homogenous community of the last century. Multiculturalism, various religious beliefs, and the secularization of several institutions testify to the openness of Canadian society. The state must ensure compliance by each individual, but no single group can impose its values or define a civil institution [Hendricks 2002, paras. 164–66, in translation].

In this decision, the Quebec court followed the landmark decision of the Supreme Court of Canada that "what may appear good and true to a majoritarian religious group, or to the state acting at its behest, may not, for religious reasons, be imposed upon citizens who take a contrary view. The *Charter* safeguards religious minorities from the threat of 'tyranny of the majority' " [Big M

Drug Mart 1985, 337]. The Law Commission of Canada is entirely correct, therefore, in suggesting that the "history of marriage regulation in Canada [is] characterized by a progressive uncoupling of religious and legal requirements, reflecting the growing emphasis upon the separation of church and state in a secular and pluralistic political community" [Law Commission 2001, 23].

In its recent reference to the Supreme Court of Canada on proposed legislation authorizing same-sex marriage, prompted by the Halpern decision, the federal government specifically asked the Court to consider the following question: "Does the freedom of religion guaranteed by paragraph 2(*a*) of the *Canadian Charter of Rights and Freedoms* protect religious officials from being compelled to perform a marriage between two persons of the same sex that is contrary to their religious beliefs?" [Department of Justice 2003]. Given the powerful statements of the Ontario and British Columbia Courts of Appeal, and the existing protections of Quebec law, it is hard to imagine the Supreme Court answering this question in anything but the affirmative. The draft legislation that the Supreme Court has been asked to consider is itself explicit on this question. It emphasizes that only "civil" marriage is at issue, and it states that "nothing in this Act affects the freedom of officials of religious groups to refuse to perform marriages that are not in accordance with their religious beliefs" [Department of Justice 2003]. Whatever the final version of the legislation that Parliament passes concerning same-sex marriage, it will not undermine the freedom of religious officials to refuse to perform a religious marriage between homosexuals.

The Supreme Court has already offered an expansive vision of religious liberty. In interpreting s. 2(a) of the Charter, which guarantees the freedom of conscience and religion, former Chief Justice Dickson described the "essence" of freedom of religion as follows:

> ... the right to entertain such religious beliefs as a person chooses, the right to declare religious beliefs openly and without fear of hindrance or reprisal, and the right to manifest religious belief by worship and practice or by teaching and dissemination [Big M Drug Mart 1985, 336].

The emphasis upon the protection not only of beliefs, but of "worship and practice," would provide a compelling defence against any argument that a minister of religion would be required by the state to act against his or her conscience in either blessing a same-sex union or performing a marriage between homosexuals. This issue is entirely separate from the question how a particular denomination might handle issues of discipline among clergy who refuse to abide by a decision taken by duly authorized constitutional structures of the church.

One can therefore conclude with some confidence that recent cases affirming a right of equal access to the legal institution of marriage for homosexual couples do not directly affect Canadian churches. This conclusion does not imply, however, that the changing social and legal context is irrelevant to debates within the church. Indeed, one of the odd features of the current travails in the Diocese of New Westminster is that, while a nasty fight continues to rage over the propriety of simply blessing same-sex unions, gay and lesbian couples can already get legally (though not religiously) married. Almost immediately after the release of the Halpern decision, the BC Court of Appeal decided to bring the law of British Columbia into line with the new law of Ontario [Barbeau 2003a]. The BC Court of Appeal had previously suspended its own judgement that the exclusion of homosexuals from the legal institution of marriage was unconstitutional. The goal had been to allow Parliament time to act on the question. The Ontario decision, which was not suspended, prompted the BC Court to lift its own suspension. Add to this oddity the fact that British Columbia is now the only province in which the number of couples choosing civil marriage is greater than the number who choose religious ceremonies each year [Law Commission 2001, 128], and one must question how the church relates to the society in which it is embedded.

Social attitudes toward homosexuality are changing across Canada, especially in major urban centres. These changes are part of a broader trend wherein Canadians are increasingly committed to principles of equality and autonomy in choices about close personal relationships [Law Commission 2001, xxiii and 13]. Such attitudinal changes have begun to affect the constitutional and legal traditions of the country. In turn, decisions within the law, particularly in relation to expanding notions of human rights for gays and lesbians, feed back into social normative change. Nor is Canada alone in these processes of change that are also playing themselves out in northern Europe [Lund-Anderson 1998; Waaldijk 2000].

Human rights for homosexuals are now commonly viewed in Canadian law as fitting within the framework of "human dignity" [Law 1999; Gosselin 2002]. The Supreme Court decided in 1995 that sexual orientation is an "analogous ground of discrimination within the equality rights guarantee of the Charter"[Egan 1995]. In reaching this conclusion, the Supreme Court emphasized "the historic disadvantage suffered by homosexual persons." Justice Cory went on to detail how the human dignity of gays and lesbians has been attacked in our society:

Public harassment and verbal abuse of homosexual individuals is not uncommon. Homosexual women and men have been victims of crimes of violence directed at them specifically because of their sexual orientation.... They have been discriminated against in their employment and their access to services. They have been excluded from some aspects of public life solely because of their sexual orientation.... The stigmatization of homosexual persons and the hatred which some members of the public have expressed toward them has forced many homosexuals to conceal their orientation [Egan 1995, 600].

Since then, Canadian courts have formally concluded as a fact that homosexual orientation is not a free choice, but is "a deeply personal characteristic that is either unchangeable or changeable only at unacceptable personal cost" [M. *vs.* H. 1999, para. 52]. Many decisions of courts and legislatures across the country have awarded gay and lesbian couples access to social benefits, including bereavement leave, health care benefits, pensions, and spousal support previously available only to heterosexual couples [Vriend 1998; M. *vs.* H. 1999]. In many communities across Canada, stable homosexual couples now adopt children. The Law Commission of Canada has pushed the parameters of the debate even further, by suggesting that the law should stop focussing on conjugal relations of any kind as the basis for obligations of support or for access to social and economic benefits. The commission argues that a wide variety of close personal relationships between adults, such as sisters who live together, inter-generational families, and families of homosexuals living in non-conjugal relationships, give rise to mutual benefits and dependencies that should generate legal protection [Law Commission 2001].

After the extension of economic and social benefits to gay and lesbian couples was largely, though not entirely, complete, Canadian courts addressed the question of marriage head-on. In doing so, due recognition was accorded to the "momentous" nature of the extension of the institution of marriage to same-sex couples:

> Whatever one's point of view, the fact that previous legislative changes and changes to the common law have expanded the rights of same-sex couples does not make the further expansion of those rights any less significant to those who, by reason of religious beliefs, or otherwise, view these changes as momentous. Applying the rigour of a full Charter analysis to a challenge to the law in these circumstances recognizes the importance of the rights at stake and the significance of those rights not only to the appellants, but to other members of society who have an interest in this issue [Barbeau 2003, para. 79].

In concluding that the limitation of legal marriage to heterosexual couples was a violation of the constitution, four different courts in three provinces expressly rejected arguments that the extension of marriage to gays and lesbians would undermine the institution of marriage for heterosexuals. In fact, each of the courts concluded that there was simply no necessary rational connection between marriage and heterosexuality. In particular, the oft-expressed justification that "natural" procreation is the central reason to exclude homosexuals from the legal institution of marriage has been resoundingly rejected [Halpern 2003, para. 122]. In the words of the British Columbia Court of Appeal:

> Advances in alternative means of conception have decreased reliance upon marriage as an opposite-sex relationship required for the purpose of procreation. Children are conceived by, born to, and raised by opposite-sex, unmarried couples. They are also adopted and raised by same-sex couples....
>
> Given this background and dramatically shifting attitudes toward marriage and the family, I have a great deal of difficulty accepting that heterosexual procreation is such a compelling and central aspect of marriage in twenty-first-century post-Charter Canadian society that it — and it alone — gives marriage its defining characteristic and justifies the exclusion of same-sex couples from that institution. It is, of course, the only characteristic with which such couples are unable to conform (and even that inability is changing) [Barbeau 2003, paras. 82 and 87].

It is instructive to note that, although the overall childbearing rate has declined in Canada over the last several decades, the non-marital childbearing rate has increased sharply [Law Commission 2001, 127]. The link between marriage and having children is now tenuous at best.

Similarly, the idea that marriage is historically exclusively heterosexual, and for that reason should continue in its traditional form, has also been rejected by Canadian courts. The Ontario Court of Appeal held that "stating that marriage is heterosexual because it has always been heterosexual is merely an explanation for the opposite-sex requirement of marriage; it is not an objective that is capable of justifying the infringement of a Charter [equality] guarantee" [Halpern 2003, para. 117]. Finally, Canadian courts have determined that simply because marriage has traditionally furthered mutual reliance and companionship between heterosexuals is not a good reason to deny that possibility to homosexuals. To do so merely "perpetuates the view that persons in same-sex relationships are not equally capable of providing companionship and forming lasting and loving relationships" [Halpern 2003, para. 124]. In its report on how Canadian governments should address close personal adult relationships of all kinds, the Law Commission of Canada emphasized that for "many Canadians, the relationships that they hold dear ... as varied as they are, constitute an important source of comfort [that help] them continue to be productive members of society" [Law Commission 2001, xxvi]. This observation is as true for gays and lesbians as it is for heterosexuals.

The central message of all the recent changes in Canadian law relating to homosexuals is that gays and lesbians are "acceptable" in our society and that their reasonable life choices fall firmly within the protection of the law. Systematic efforts have been made to reconcile a previously hostile society to the reality of homosexuality in our midst. Courts and legislatures have constantly rooted these changes in recognition of cultural change within Canada. Quite simply, Canadian culture, or more precisely Canadian urban culture, seems to be more accommodating to homosexuality than ever before. Polls indicate that this trend is growing, and expanding in geographic scope. There are periodic incidents that call into question the cultural evolution toward greater acceptance of homosexuals, some of them violent, but these incidents are exceptions to a broader trend. The legal pressure toward the recognition of same-sex marriage is part of that trend. The British Columbia Court of Appeal made the point clearly:

> Viewed in the context of legislative change and social and cultural evolution, and notwithstanding the material distinction between opposite-sex and same-sex couples with respect to reproductive capacity, the omission to provide some form of legal status for same-sex couples enhances, rather than diminishes, the stereotypical view that same-sex relationships are less important or valuable than opposite-sex relationships. There is now sufficient practical similarity between the economic and social consequences of opposite-sex and same-sex relationships

that affording one but not the other the opportunity to acquire a legal and formal status discriminates in the substantive sense of the word [Barbeau 2003, para. 82].

The claim is that the legal changes that protected homosexuals within human rights law, and that extended benefits comparable to those available to unmarried heterosexual couples living "common law," have not gone far enough. Homosexuals must be allowed the full social inclusion represented by marital status.

The legal argument of full social inclusion is probably the greatest practical challenge to the church in decisions concerning homosexuals. After all, it is the church that has argued, in Jesus' name, for inclusion of the prostitute, the prisoner, and the sinner. We confront a certain irony when the law, an expression of the state and its relationship with society, takes on the prophetic role so often claimed by the church. How will the faithful respond?

One can certainly imagine a response grounded in the idea that the church must remain a bastion of truth against the false claims of secular society and the state. This argument is relatively easy to put forth when one casts the problem as resistance to sexual immorality or societal degradation. But how to address the legal claim that equality and justice are being pursued through recognition of same-sex marriage? Given the broad consensus that seems to have emerged in the courts of Canada, and even in the legislatures, that homosexuals have historically been the victims of discrimination, it would not be easy simply to refuse to acknowledge that conclusion, or to attempt to overturn it.

Does the church then simply say, "So what? These are not people that we care enough about to prompt us to dislodge our traditional commitments." Is it possible to imagine a different response? Perhaps a recognition that the church is a part of a changing culture, and that some reconciliation with gays and lesbians is now possible? If the law, an institution encrusted with its own doctrines and traditions, can change, why not the church? Change need not mean a wholesale rejection of the past. Even if civil marriage between homosexuals is possible, marriage in the church need not follow — though it might. In the context of the cultural evolution that is taking place in Canada on issues of homosexuality, the idea that same-sex relationships might be blessed emerges as a modest recognition by the church of the need to reconcile with gays and lesbians over past discrimination. It also upholds a commitment to stable close personal relationships of mutual support, an unquestioned social good. At the same time, blessing is not marriage. Marriage will remain an institution, and a sacrament, that the church can define for itself, but mindful of the society in which the church lives and to which it addresses its message of hope.

Works Cited

Beaudoin, G.A., and E. Mendes, eds. 1996. *The Canadian Charter of Rights and Freedoms*. Toronto: Carswell Publishing.

Charter. 1982. *Canadian Charter of Rights and Freedoms*, being Schedule B of the *Constitution Act, 1867*, enacted as Schedule B to the *Canada Act 1982*. UK. c.11.

Davies, Christine. 1999. "The Extension of Marital Rights and Obligations to the Unmarried: Registered Domestic Partnerships and Other Methods." *Canadian Family Law Quarterly* 247:17.

Department of Justice: Reference to the Supreme Court of Canada. *Online:* http:// www.canada.justice.gc.ca/en/news/nr/2003/ doc_30946.html

Lahey, Kathleen. 1999. *Are We "Persons" Yet? Law and Sexuality in Canada*. Toronto: University of Toronto Press.

Law Commission of Canada. 2001. *Beyond Conjugality: Recognizing and Supporting Close Personal Adult Relationships*. Ottawa: Minister of Public Works and Government Services.

Lund-Anderson, Ingrid. 1998. "Cohabitation and Registered Partnership in Scandinavia: The Legal Position of Homosexuals." In John M. Eekelaar and Thandabantu Nhlapo, eds., *The Changing Family: Family Forms and Family Law*. Oxford: Hart Publishing. 397.

Waaldijk, K. 2000. "Civil Developments: Patterns of Reform in the Legal Position of Same-Sex Partners in Europe." *Canadian Journal of Family Law* (62):17.

Cases

Barbeau et al. vs. *British Columbia (Attorney General) et al.* 2003. BCCA 251.

Barbeau et al. vs. *British Columbia (Attorney General) et al.* 2003. BCCA 406 [Barbeau 2003a].

Big M Drug Mart. 1985. 1 S.C.R. 295.

Egan vs. *Canada.* 1995. 2 S.C.R. 513.

Gosselin vs. *Quebec (Attorney General)*. 2002. S.C.C. 84.

Halpern et al. vs. *A-G Canada et al.* Dockets C39172 and C39174.

Online: htpp://www.ontariocourts.on.ca/decisions/2003/june/ halpernC39172.htm

Hendricks vs. *Quebec (Attorney General)*. 2002. J.Q. 3816 (S.C.).

Law vs. *Canada (Minister of Employment and Immigration)*. 1999. 1 S.C.R. 497.

M. vs. *H.* 1999. 2 S.C.R. 3.

Vriend vs. *Alberta.* 1998. 1 S.C.R. 493.

Leadership
and Dialogue
in a Time of Crisis

Prophecy, Leadership, and Communities in Crisis

WALTER DELLER *(BMus, MDiv, ThD) is Principal and Professor of Old Testament and Congregational Life at the College of Emmanuel and St. Chad in Saskatoon, Saskatchewan. Raised in western Manitoba, his experience includes living and working as a community musician in Nova Scotia, with Cree people at the Henry Budd College for Ministry in northern Manitoba, and in Toronto, where for ten years he was Coordinator of the LOGOS Institute, then Director of Program Resources for the Diocese of Toronto. Beyond regular reading and study of the Bible, his primary theological and intellectual sources include Jacques Ellul, Dorothy Day and the Catholic Worker tradition, George Grant, Emmanuel Lévinas, Jewish midrash, and the writings of the Church Fathers.*

———◆———

Beyond providing Leviticus grenades to lob, does the Old Testament have anything else to offer to the Anglican Communion as it tries to carry on a corporate conversation about the place of gay and lesbian people in God's plan for creation and the church?* I find myself reflecting more and more on one set of biblical narratives in which a pair of utterly contradictory personalities appear as characters in a drama that unfolds over a period of about fifty years. The style of these narratives indicates that they originate in folk-tales or popular hagiography (stories about heroic holy people). This suggests that part of their value lies in passing on communal wisdom about valued human qualities. It is wisdom to which we might well attend.

The stories have come into the scriptures already collected and ordered, and they have been inserted into a still larger collection of historical material in a way that makes them the centrepiece of the entire structure. We might conclude that the collectors and editors of the scriptures intended us to reflect on these legends in a broader historical and theological framework, and to ponder the differences between the personalities as revealing something significant. Our struggle over the full inclusion of gay and lesbian people in the life of the church is not simply a struggle over a category of people — it is a struggle about how our community understands God's will for the world, about styles and models of leadership, about how we interact with the world and its many cultures, and ultimately about what it means for Anglicans to live faithfully with the God of Abraham and Moses who is also the God of Jesus.

The book in which these stories were included came to be part of that section of the Jewish Bible known as the Former Prophets. So I interpret these texts not simply as legends or history but as prophecy, holding before us both God's equally demanding judgement and promise, with all the questions that implies. The narratives in question are the Elijah-Elisha cycle found in 1 Kings 17 to 2 Kings 9.[1] What leads me to consider these stories?

---

* Some of the material included here is drawn from *A Double Portion: Reflections on the Elijah/Elisha Cycle,* a set of unpublished retreat reflections originally prepared in 1998 for the Montreal Diocesan Theological College Orientation Retreat. I want to express my gratitude to Dr. John Simons and the college for having offered me the original opportunity to reflect on a set of issues in the life of the contemporary church (calling and leadership), which alerted me and focused for me the richness of this material from 1 and 2 Kings.

Two Kinds of Crisis: Within the Community and Between Communities

First, *they portray a period of crisis and upheaval* in the life of the northern Kingdom, Israel. There are two types of crisis involved. One is a huge controversy about what Israel's true faith is and who the true God is. The question at issue is: What is the community's identity within itself? We might characterize this as a crisis about *orthodoxy and **intra**-communal identity*. The other crisis is about how Israel is to remain faithful and secure under pressure from more powerful surrounding nations and cultures, and about how it should interact with those other nations and cultures. We might characterize this as a crisis about *relationship and **inter**-communal identity*. These, it seems to me, are identical with the issues we find ourselves faced with in our life together as Anglicans.

The second reason I am led to these stories is that, in the manner characteristic of hagiographic legends and folklore, *they portray strong personalities* with exaggerated traits. So they offer us room to reflect on different types of people and styles of leadership, how such people seek to live out faithfulness, and also how leadership styles succeed and fail. These texts may have something to offer us as we discern whom among our leaders to trust and why; and if we are leaders, they may warn us of the dangers contained in our own choices and personal predilections.

Finally, I am drawn to these stories because *they are about the life of the breakaway and apostate kingdom* of northern Israel, a kingdom that, according to the entire biblical tradition, has fallen under the judgement of God. Yet the same biblical tradition, by focusing almost the entire book(s) of Kings on this apostate kingdom and by insisting on the continued presence of God's activity in its history, reminds us that God is at least as complex, unpredictable, and obstinate as we are. God's will and design are never as transparent as many of us would like to think — which is one good reason why so many Christians prefer not to read most of the Bible.[2] In the rush to judge each other as faithless and damned and to set up Golden Bishops as idols to mark the boundaries between true and false Anglicans, I find it salutary to remember that ancient Israel did the same and discovered that God continued, in the words of the collect, "to carry out in tranquillity the plan of salvation" for all the descendants of Israel.

Meet the Prophets

So who are these two great prophets who fill this narrative landscape? Their names tell us all. The name of the first, *'eliyyahu* (or sometimes *'eliyyah*), Elijah, means "YHWH is (my) God." His entire life is the embodiment of stubborn witness to the insistence that there is one and only one God, and one and only one truth. The event by which most of us remember Elijah is his confrontation with the prophets and priests of Ba'al on Mount Carmel. The name of his successor also gives us a glimpse of the prophetic personality: *elisha*, Elisha, means "My God is salvation" or "My God is deliverance." The event by which most of us remember Elisha is the story of his healing of the foreign general Naaman, suffering from leprosy.

Is there a more prickly or eminently unlikable figure in scripture than Elijah the Tishbite? The legends portray him consistently as self-centred, whining, rigid, isolated, demanding, violent, blood-soaked, deaf and unheeding even to the direct command of God. Conversely, how can we not respond to the sociability of Elisha — fond of a decent party with the neighbours, impetuous, eager, self-conscious about his baldness, constantly getting folks out of scrapes, shrewd, able to see beyond the surface, and above all, deeply aware of how humans suffer at each other's hands.

The Crisis of Elijah's Day: The Evil in Ba'alism

While the contrast between the two personalities is evident throughout the text, I would argue that the portrayal of Elijah is ambivalent. Later tradition regards him as the prophet *par excellence*, the one who was swept up to dwell with God in heaven and who will return before the coming of the Messiah. But the stories in Kings depict him with a complex mixture of awe and humour, homage and critique. He provides an essential intervention in a profound crisis, but whether the Kings narratives view his intervention as effective is, on close reading, a matter of doubt.

In 1 Kings 16:29–33, immediately preceding the first appearance of Elijah on the scene, Ahab, king of the northern kingdom of Israel, marries a Phoenician princess, Jezebel. In doing so he accepts the role of patron of her god Ba'al. Superficially it is easy to see the crisis here as conflict over who is the true god — Yhwh, God of Israel, or Ba'al, god of the Phoenicians. Alternatively the issue is often presented as one of syncretism — the attempt to reconcile and synthesize diverse religious practices and beliefs. I think the complete collection of texts makes clear that in the crisis lies a much more profound confusion.

The very word "Ba'al" could not be uttered without automatically conveying several meanings. Ba'al was an alternate name for the thunder and storm god Hadad, associated in the northwest-semitic mythological pantheon with the coming of the rains and the renewal of the agricultural cycle. Ba'al was also a dying and rising god, representing the cyclic inevitability of nature. Thus Ba'al religion was bound up in a theology that sacralized the natural and that viewed the natural pattern and order of things as inviolable truth, controlling and determining a corresponding set of right and proper relations and patterns for humans and human society.

Ba'al also had two other ordinary and interconnected everyday meanings. It was one of the common terms for "husband." It was also a common term for an "owner" or a "proprietor." Thus Ba'al as a term for husband also conveys a social ideology of marriage and partnership that implies male control, ownership, and domination.

The great achievement of the Omride dynasty that ruled Israel was its having built the immensely successful city Samaria and having brought in a period of economic prosperity. This involved a major change in Israelite society from a subsistence-farming mode of life to an urban import-export focus combined with the development of a large military establishment. This change had been achieved through alliance with the seacoast cities of Phoenicia, which took both a religio-cultural and an economic form. The king's marriage to Jezebel is the symbol of, and actual effecting of, this alliance; she represents the triumph of the new over the old values, not only in religion but in social and economic matters as well. In the episode of Naboth's vineyard [1 Kings 21], Jezebel masterminds the manipulation of the citizens of Samaria to scapegoat Naboth, in order to alienate and seize his legitimate tribal inheritance. The stolen vineyard is symbolic of the overturning of traditional economic order, and also of the effective subversion of the power of the traditional structures of law and justice. The shift of property and wealth away from traditional familial and clan ownership to an urban elite led to resentment and political upheaval as witnessed by repeated dynastic coups and increased rural poverty [1 Kings 17:10–12, 1 Kings 21].

Elijah criticizes the new socio-economic structures from the perspective of the older, more egalitarian Israelite religion and tradition. He intervenes in the episode of Naboth's vineyard, which classically represents the transfer of socio-economic power. What inflames Elijah more is the conjunction of the socio-economic upward mobility and the dominance of the Omride party with the ideologies and practices of Ba'al religion. The new religious system undergirds an unjust economic system with an ideology of power and ownership rooted in the inviolability of the natural order.

Furthermore, its cultic practices divert attention away from what is actually taking place. The ideology of Ba'alism involved, among other things, a powerful emphasis on male-female sexuality and on male potency. (Ba'al's symbolic visual form was a bull.) Whether sexual intercourse (with other humans or with objects) formed part of the cultic ritual is increasingly a matter of debate.[3] I would argue that, whatever view we take of the matter, the faith crisis in northern Israel resulted from the official adoption of a religious ideology founded on male-female sexual congress as essential for upholding the stability of the natural order, together with a social ideology of male domination and possession in sexuality and society. In marriage (and, if it existed, in the practices of cultic prostitution), the man was conceived as "owner," the "ba'al," of the woman, just as he might own land. The theology diverted attention from the suffering that resulted from the economic displacements and justified powerful men possessing whatever they could get. The cultic practices and symbols reaffirmed the theology.

This powerful focus on sexuality (presented as essential to maintaining the natural and social order) combined with the worship of power, domination, and success (used to cover up or justify oppression) is the evil in Ba'alism. The folk-tradition and the later literary traditions revere Elijah because he confronted this ideology of power, sexual control, and big money. In honouring him as the prophet *par excellence*, scripture reminds us that all God's people who seek to live faithfully must challenge such Ba'alisms in whatever place and generation they appear.

Challenging a Complex System of Religion, Economics, and Power

The biblical text tells us almost nothing of Elijah's origins, suitability for the task, or call. In fact, it is not clear whether Elijah actually had any authentic call whatsoever. He appears on the scene unheralded and announcing that there will be no dew or rain except at his bidding, thereby binding God by his oath. So begins his education into the realities of being a prophetic religious leader.[4] It is all very well for Elijah to commit God to causing a drought, but he hasn't grasped that already impoverished people will go hungry [1 Kings 17]. Nor has he grasped that his direct entry into competition with King Ahab endangers the lives of other faithful people — such as Ahab's servant Obadiah [1 Kings 18]. He hasn't even grasped that he himself is courting disaster, if we judge by his own complaints when he encounters God on Mount Horeb and tells God, "I have been very jealous for the Lord ... and they seek my life to take it away" [1 Kings 19].

Almost never in the text do we hear of the word of the Lord coming to Elijah and Elijah relaying it. Rather, we hear Elijah making pronouncements that he formulates as divine communication.

Even in the single instance in which Elijah receives a direct prophetic commission from God, he fulfills only one of the three
commands given him. Wearing his distinctive leather belt, Elijah
strides through the parched, sun-beaten landscape of Israel, sum-
moning fire from heaven onto water-soaked sacrificial offerings,
onto threatening troops of soldiers, and ultimately onto the chariot
that sweeps him away into the heavens. Elijah is driven by a fire
within, and the fire within creates destruction around him.

Apart from his encounter with God on Mount Horeb, when
the Lord speaks, not in the wind and fire that Elijah understood,
but in a still, small voice, the two most extensive elements of the
Elijah tradition tell of his confrontations with the prophets of Ba'al
on Mount Carmel and with Ahab in the stolen vineyard of Naboth.
All three confrontations play out the socio-economic, political, and
religious tensions of the northern kingdom during the Omride
dynasty.

In a time of confrontations, Elijah offers a leadership of confrontation. The texts nowhere suggest that his choice of mode of
action was wrong, although I think they do illuminate the problems caused by confrontation as a way of doing things. There may
be times when an interlocked set of social and spiritual evils allow
no other alternative. Elijah's rigid and uncompromising opposition to injustice and heresy gave rise to a popular hero-story
tradition that became a symbol of resistance for the future as well.
In the short and medium term the biblical text would indicate that
the great gesture of Carmel, the showdown with and murder of
the prophets of Ba'al, yielded no significant result. In the long term
Elijah's witness provided a backbone to a movement of social criticism and allegiance to the old ethical and economic order linked
to the YHWHistic tradition. The judgement of history was on his
side.

The texts also point to three problems associated with confrontation as a mode of acting. First, questions are always framed
in extremes, as black or white, as yes or no decisions. Reality is
rarely made up of such extremes, as God reminds the depressed
and frightened Elijah on Mount Horeb. In response to his com-
plaint, "I alone am left, and they are out to take my life," God replies,

"I will leave in Israel seven thousand." Second, until the arrival of Elisha on the scene, Elijah is manifestly isolated, a lone operator. Third, confrontation tends to restrict the ability to shift frame. How does Elijah deal with Jezebel's violence? By murdering more prophets in his turn!

A classic demonstration of the impasse caused by confrontation occurs in 2 Kings 1, when King Ahaziah of Israel sends two detachments of troops to order Elijah to "come down" at the king's command. Neither their captains nor Elijah can reframe the confrontation, and Elijah zaps the detachments with fire from heaven. When the captain of the third detachment sent is able to reframe the confrontation as mediation by pleading for the life of innocent people, the impasse is broken. The biblical text implicitly reveals Elijah's erroneous assumptions, for nowhere does it state that in sending the soldiers Ahaziah was seeking to harm Elijah.

On the one hand, the text seems to invite us to admire Elijah for his single-mindedness, his willingness to confront power, his commitment to the one God. On the other hand, the text embodies a recurring current of critique. Despite the grand demonstration and bloodshed on Mount Carmel, the Ba'alists are still there in 2 Kings 9, thirteen chapters later, for Jehu to eliminate. If anything, the showdown only increases the polarization [1 Kings 19:1–2]. If nothing else the biblical texts reminds us that it is possible for faithful people to be simultaneously right and wrong. We may be confronting the wrong thing, or the wrong person, or at the wrong moment, and we may become so locked in our logic of the necessity of confrontation that we leave mayhem and death in our wake wherever we go.

So What is God Telling Elijah?

Elijah thrives on these gestures of power — an irony since the Ba'alism he opposes is grounded in a theology of power. Here is a question for us to ponder: Does the confrontational mode deceive and trap us into imagining the world in the same false terms as the thing we are opposing? Not only is the language of power

Elijah's first choice, but also he is a violent man. Whenever the biblical texts present violence, we are invited to consider the ethics of means and ends — the Bible is intimately aware of the dark nexus linking violence, purity, and orthodoxy. From Cain and Abel onwards, we cannot avoid contemplating how our own desire to make an offering acceptable to God leads us inevitably to the murder of our brother or sister [Matthew 5:21]. Because of his adoption of violence, can we even consider Elijah a genuine prophet? For Elijah, other humans always seem to be objects to be removed in his single-minded commitment to the purification of Israel for God.

The text in several instances portrays Elijah as unable to hear or understand God. For example, when God summons Elijah to go to Ahab after the judicial murder of Naboth and the seizure of his property, the word Elijah receives to convey to Ahab is this: "Thus says the Lord: 'Would you murder and take possession?' Thus says the Lord, 'In the very place where the dogs lapped up Naboth's blood, the dogs will lap up your blood too.' " But when Elijah meets Ahab, he says this: "Because you have committed yourself to doing what is evil in the sight of the Lord, I will bring disaster upon you. I will make a clean sweep of you, I will cut off from Israel every male belonging to Ahab, bond and free. And I will make your house like the house of Jeroboam son of Nabat and like the House of Baasha son of Ahjiah [the previous two dynasties], because of the provocation you have caused by leading Israel to sin. And the Lord has also spoken concerning Jezebel: 'The dogs shall devour Jezebel in the field of Jezreel. All of Ahab's line who die in the town shall be devoured by dogs, and all who die in the open country shall be devoured by the birds of the sky' " [1 Kings 21:19–24]. To present this revised message, as commentators often do, simply as a matter of "prophetic practice" in expanding messages, avoids the fundamental dissonance set up between the two utterances, separated from one another in the text by only one intervening verse. Evidently Elijah has not heard what God said (a judgement on Ahab alone, matching his crime) and instead presents as God's intention an elaborate and violent project involving many deaths and dynastic overthrow. As our own righteousness becomes self-evident, how prone do we become to mis-hearing the God of the scriptures, the Jesus of the gospels, and the carefully crafted messages of the tradition, and to elaborating anathemas suited primarily to our own preoccupations?

So it is difficult not to read the great encounter on Mount Horeb, in which Elijah figures as a new Moses, as perhaps a biblical joke. We read of wind, earthquake, fire (Elijah's own favourite divine manifestation) — the divine world of great gestures, and yet the Lord is not present in them! What must it mean for someone as zealous for the Lord as Elijah to discover that meeting God requires listening to a still, small voice — an almost inaudible muttering — listening for the voice and secret of another instead of being endlessly preoccupied with his own self-righteousness? Elijah is certain that he is the only righteous one left in a synod of sinners, but then God tells him that, unknown to him, there are seven thousand other faithful people present (in other words, many or most of the rest!) What God does *not* tell him is to lead out that faithful remnant to found a new, more holy community. And how faithful is Elijah really? Of the three tasks given him, Elijah never completes the first two (anointing Hazael and Jehu). He accomplishes only the third and simplest, anointing Elisha as his successor. Is God suggesting something about Elijah's style by ordering him to anoint a replacement prophet?

Elijah lives out his name, his unswerving commitment to the truth of Israel's one God. But with typical biblical irony, none of our texts ever indicates that God wants or commands Elijah to defend such a singular truth.

The Mantle of Elijah Falls upon Elisha

Elisha, anointed to succeed Elijah, is a much more conventional but also much more complex prophetic figure. He fits with much of what we know about patterns of ancient Near-Eastern and Israelite prophesying. He is "called" by divine word mediated through Elijah, through symbolic action, and out of his own inner compulsion and willingness. He serves an apprenticeship as the servant of Elijah, and he lives in a community of prophets [2 Kings 2, 4, 6].

Like other prophets he lives on the margins, yet at the same time he has access to people of power and influence. The traditions about him bear rich evidence of a Spirit-filled presence, ranging from trivial problem solving and near-magic, through subtle discernment of proclivities of the human spirit and its desires.

What is the Crisis in Elisha's Period?

The crucial issue during Elisha's time as prophet is how Israel is to remain faithful and secure under pressure from more powerful surrounding nations and cultures, and how it should interact with them. Thus many of the Elisha stories have a political or diplomatic dimension. The economic backdrop of drought, famine, and increasing poverty remains [2 Kings 2, 3, 4, 6, etc.], but the primary focus shifts to interactions between Israel and its powerful neighbour to the northeast, Aram. They are often at war, and both are also involved in diplomatic relations or war with other surrounding states [2 Kings 3, 8]. One of the stories portrays Elisha as anointing Hazael to be king over the enemy Aramaeans — one of the most unusual prophetic moments in the Bible, comparable only to Second Isaiah's proclamation of the Persian king as God's anointed one. Earlier I characterized this as a crisis about *relationship and inter-communal identity*: Whom do we trust? With whom might we have common cause? What are the risks of not being in relationship?

Elisha symbolizes this problematic web of interactions by his own huge range of interactions, crossing many boundaries. He associates with the poor and with the wealthy; he appears to be welcome in the royal circles of both Israel and Aram; he also appears to spend considerable time with a marginal community of prophets. The stories portray him both as stable and propertied, and as peripatetic and on the move — alone, with his servant, and with armies. Elisha has received twice the portion of the Spirit that Elijah possessed [2 Kings 2]. In representing the startling range of ways in which the activity of the Spirit is present in and through Elisha across boundaries of nationality, wealth, and social status, these biblical texts powerfully testify that God's Spirit is active across bounds, cultures, and taboos, against all our cherished expectations and assumptions.[5]

Even Elisha's name points up the symbolism; it means, "My God is salvation" or "My God is deliverance." All the Elisha narratives (with perhaps one exception) draw our attention to the activity of God in the world, delivering people or communities from conditions that trap them, from the prison of their own assumptions, from dangers that face them. Wherever Elisha goes, he embodies moments and actions that show forth God's intention for deliverance.

The problem is that Elisha's God seems to have very little interest in "orthodoxy" — in being proved "true." Elisha's God seems to want even to deliver Israel's enemies and to heal people who have harmed the faithful. Elisha himself seems rather uninterested in the great struggle over orthodoxy. It is as if Elisha understands that the God he serves wants to deliver all humanity, that God's mission for salvation is not confined to one nation or community, or even limited to those who are good, just, and faithful.

The story of the healing of Naaman [2 Kings 5] illustrates this divine desire to deliver and Elisha's own acceptance of how blurred orthodoxy and orthopraxy can become when one is totally obedient to such a God. Beginning with the desire of the Israelite slave girl for another's betterment, passing through a series of episodes in which kings, generals, and even Naaman discover their assumptions exposed and upturned, the story comes to rest, after Naaman's healing and recognition of the God of Israel as the only true God, in a dilemma about how to worship this true God to whom he now owes allegiance. Would a token, two mule-loads of Israelite earth have passed muster with Elijah? Could Elijah even have imagined a God who could pardon Naaman for bowing low in the idolatrous temple in the company of his foreign king? But what does Elisha say in response? "Go in peace!"

Elisha as an Alternative Model of Prophetic Leadership

The varied narratives in the Elisha sequence present three key modes of action: problem solving, collaboration and mediation, and illusion.

In several cases, Elisha appears to solve problems by knowing how people and the natural world work. Speaking to the woman who is in a panic about the death of her husband, the arrival of the creditor, and the potential loss of her two children to slavery, he tells her to borrow all the pots she can from her neighbours and to pour oil from the one pot she owns into the others. The pot never runs out of oil! The story is miraculous, but as clever as the miracle is, Elisha's approach to the woman's concerns shows clear good sense. Being in a flap does not help her to solve the problems; getting busy and doing something does. In a moment of deep discernment Elisha says, "What can I do for you?" — and then puts her to work doing something for herself. Knowing how things work — people, systems, and the natural order — and knowing how to cut through anxiety and put other people to work on constructing solutions for themselves are critical leadership skills that a community needs when the moment of crisis involves relationships and inter-communal identities.

For the most part, Elisha's prophetic leadership, in striking contrast with Elijah's, makes use of collaboration and mediation. I have already noted how he moves across economic, class, national, and cultural boundaries, arranging collaboration and mediation. Two episodes among the Elisha traditions show how he tailors his mode of action to the context, and highlight his gifts as a leader able to see what lies beneath the surface and able to reframe situations where groups are in conflict.

In one episode [2 Kings 6:8-23], the king of Aram learns that his whereabouts are constantly being revealed to the king of Israel, and that Elisha is the source of the damaging information. He sends soldiers to seize Elisha, they surround the town, and his attendant discovers them early the next morning. This is a problem that Elijah, in a parallel episode in 2 Kings 1, handled with fire from heaven. Elisha treats it as an opportunity to teach his servant about perceiving beyond the obvious. Elisha prays that God will realize the insight within the servant who comes to see the mysterious protecting presence of God. But there is more. Elisha treats the enemy soldiers as suffering equally from misperception. They think they have to seize Elisha. He astutely reframes their understanding so that they see themselves as soldiers involved in a squabble between two kings. His prayer that they be blinded by light is a realization of their actual state of confusion. They are looking for the wrong person, because they are part of a wrongly framed problem. So he leads them into Samaria, and when they open their eyes they realize they are inside the enemy stronghold. At this point the king of Israel comes on stage. "Shall I kill them?" he asks Elisha. Once again Elisha shifts the frame by questioning the king's assumptions. To kill may be an appropriate response to enemies after a battle, but not to people who have just walked into your capital city blind and had their eyes opened to its splendours. This is party time! So a feast unfolds, after which they return to their Syrian master. The text closes the tale by observing that the Aramaean bands stopped invading the land of Israel.

Elisha's God is a God of deliverance, of multiple possibilities, of imagination, of a world in which all assumptions about the natural rightness of things can be questioned and turned upside down. Prophetic leadership, as modeled in Elisha, requires discernment about people and their assumptions and gifts, the ability to help them shift their frame of references, and a seemingly endless ability to move the focus and perspective on the problem so that it is transformed into opportunity.

Another Elisha tale illustrates illusion, a mysterious skill that also characterizes his leadership. In 2 Kings 3 we hear about the expedition of the three kings of Israel, Judah, and Edom to quell the rebellious vassal king of Moab. After a week's march in the salt sea wilderness on the recommendation of Israel's king Jehoram, they find themselves in a pickle — no water for themselves or their pack animals. The kings have a kind of corporate anxiety attack and look for oracular help. Elisha begins in confrontation mode: let Jehoram consult his own Ba'alite prophets! When Jehoram ups the anxiety ante by asserting that the Lord has brought the kings together so that they may all be slain by the Moabites, Elisha, clearly somewhat piqued, shifts into action. He puts the kings to work finding him a musician.

We might adequately read this against the background of Near-Eastern prophetic practice and suppose that the purpose of the musician is to enable Elisha to fall into a trance in preparation for oracular utterance. However, I think an alternative reading is possible. Here we have three kings armed for battle, in a volatile mood, disputatious with one another, highly anxious, one suffering from the shame of having suggested a strategy of folly. The three kings are now in genuine danger, not only from their external foe but from their internal divisions. Whom exactly does Elisha hope the music will calm? Who needs to be in a trance state? The enemy Moabites ultimately make their false step because they are tricked by the illusion that the water in a flash-flooded streamed in the early morning sun is the blood of the squabbling kings. The other half of the illusion is Elisha's ability to induce a trance not in himself, but in the anxious royal players through the adept use of diversion. Perhaps the Anglican Communion would be strengthened by singing the *Magnificat* a little more often and writing pastoral letters a little less.

God will be Faithful to God's Word — Speak Cautiously on God's Behalf

The final narrative to which I wish to turn our attention is the rounding out of the cycle in 2 Kings 9. Here, at long last, we see the carrying forward of the divine command originally given to Elijah on Mount Horeb [1 Kings 18], to anoint Jehu son of Nimshi to be king over Israel.[6] The first thing to which the text points is that sometimes it will be necessary to intervene directly in the unfolding political interactions of the community. So dangerous is this task that Elijah simply did not do as directed. Likewise, although Elisha has already carried out the charge to anoint Hazael as next king of Syria, he is shrewd enough to understand that the anointing of Jehu should be delegated. Knowing the risk for the young apprentice prophet to whom he delegates the task, he gives cautious and explicit directions. The young man is to get Jehu away from his companions, anoint him swiftly with the words, "Thus said the Lord: I anoint you king over Israel," then flee for his life. Elisha, after a long career, knows the danger of both paranoia and ambition.

The sequel illustrates the tremendous power of suggestion in political events, the dangers and damage that can be wrought by the eager and zealous. When the keen young prophet-in-training arrives and anoints Jehu, what does he say? "Thus said the Lord, the God of Israel: I anoint you king over the people of the Lord, over Israel. You shall strike down that House of Ahab your master; thus will I avenge on Jezebel the blood of My servants the prophets.... The whole House of Ahab shall perish.... The dogs shall devour Jezebel in the field of Jezreel, with none to bury her...." After all, why let all those months of practice in forms of oracular utterance go to waste on a trite little "I anoint you king over Israel..."? Phrase by phrase, clause by bloody clause, Jehu systematically carries out the improvised prophecy in a bloodbath of murder and mayhem. There are no surprises here. Elijah, Elisha, and also God must have known that Jehu, the one chosen for the final confrontation with Ba'alism, would be a literalist orthodox rigorist.

Those who intervene to direct the course of events need a clear understanding of the force of human ambition and the forward thrust of the uncoiling political spring. The text highlights not merely the virtue of discretion but the necessity of caution. It reminds us, simple as it may seem, of the value of attention to precisely what we are directed to do when charged with a weighty task of intervention. The text in its final canonical structure reminds us that Jehu's coup unfolds in explicit fulfillment of the message delivered by the young prophet, which triggers Jehu's most violent and destructive instincts.

What is striking in the texts is the degree to which the prophetic interventions in politics are oblique and indirect. These episodes offer sound advice to religious leaders who must intervene or take part in complex situations: Attend to the complexities and confusions in our own and others' intentions and interpretations. Be aware both of the randomness and logic that unfold simultaneously as events take their course. Confidently offer a concrete word of faith, trust, and hope in situations of crisis. Judge situations acutely, understanding the potential for releasing chaos and violence.

But most of all, the Elijah and Elisha cycle of tales reminds us that at certain moments in history, the faithful witness and the religious leader may be called by God to *act*. For centuries, folk passed on these legends and tales to remind themselves and one another that their time of crisis, testing, and ambiguity was not unique. Elijah and Elisha had been there before them, and God was with them still.

Prophetic Leadership and the Crisis in the Contemporary Church

The entire Elijah-Elisha cycle offers a rich mine for reflection on appropriate modes of prophetic leadership. I have singled out a few examples that illustrate the manner in which context and leadership are linked. They also reflect the issues and problems of four important modes of leadership that might be of value in crises of orthodoxy and intra-communal identity, and of relationships and inter-communal identity:

1. *confrontation on fundamental issues of value*, with all the risks and polarization, it entails;

2. *practical problem solving*, through application of knowledge of how things work and discernment of when and how to put people to work to help themselves;

3. *collaboration and mediation*, with their concomitant skills of discernment of human motivation and ability to reframe; and

4. *the art of illusion*, requiring the ability to displace anxiety and to capitalize on the unforeseen eventuality to enhance the community's capacity for effective corporate action.

We might view this entire cycle of texts from Kings then, as presenting two contrasting figures. Elijah is ill formed, irascible, graceless, a lover of the grand gesture, and his career of religious leadership can be read as a near-disaster. Elisha is well schooled and mentored, alert, connected, aware, sympathetic, and politically adept, sure in all his ways. His career is a chain of effective interventions. People call Elijah "a man of God," "my lord, " "troubler of Israel," and "my enemy." People call Elisha "man of God," "my lord," and "my master."

We might choose to accept the text's seeming critique of Elijah's confrontational mode and prefer Elisha's conciliating mode. But the text does not allow us to reject the one and accept the other. It holds us firmly to honouring both. It binds the two together in a large and cohesive narrative sequence, and it binds the two prophets in terms of family, formation, and — difficult as it may be to imagine — perhaps even affection. At the moment when Elisha receives the mantle of prophecy, he sees, not Elijah's disappearance in one last grand stage gesture, but the angelic chariots and horsemen of Israel, and he cries out, "My father, my father." *Both Elijah and Elisha are God's gift to the Israelite community at this moment in its history.*

The community needs its Elijahs, though they may well be ignorant, uneducable, single-minded, undisciplined, narcissistic, narrow, impatient of others, and prone to leave bloody destruction in their wake. Frequently they have a passion for reform. But whether we like them or not, the fire that burns in them to speak for God's singleness and truth, and to demand of the community that it be pure and holy, is a genuine Spirit-kindled fire and Spirit-given call. The text, ambivalent as it is about Elijah's call and effectiveness as a prophet, indicates that God stands with him and unfailingly fulfills his word and his prayer.

The community also needs its Elishas, in whom mentoring, formation, and communal life have created and nurtured leaders who are capable of effective action and intervention, who exercise deep and subtle discernment, and who see beyond the superficial to the mystery within, who are alert to suffering, deprivation, and the need for compassion. Frequently they cross boundaries and disturb long-standing taboos; sometimes they confuse friends with enemies; sometimes they seem to be engaged in the trivial or even the superficial. But the desire that burns within them to heal the world, to introduce everyone to the God who is deliverance, to imagine new ways of being community, and to see the world through the eyes of a God who is totally salvation — that too is a desire fuelled by the Spirit.

First and Second Kings suggest that the Elijahs and the Elishas may need each other to survive in the church and the age in which they are called to live, witness, and provide leadership.

Finally, we might note that despite everything, it is Elisha the gifted and successful one who knows that to live out his call faithfully will require the extra gift of "a double portion" of Elijah's spirit, and he is wise enough to ask for it. Yet the subsequent tradition, despite everything, remembers the solitary Elijah as the one who will return as the herald of the messianic age, and who, oddly enough, "will turn the hearts of parents to their children and the hearts of children to their parents, so that I will not come and strike the land with a curse" [Malachi 4:5-6]. Only the one true God who is the God of salvation and deliverance in all times and all ages, the God of Elijah, of Elisha, and of Jesus Christ the crucified and risen one, can transform confrontation and rejection into reconciliation and hope.

Notes

1. It makes some sense to see the cycle beginning at 1 Kings 16:29, which tells of the ascent of Ahab as successor in the Omride dynasty (880–841 BCE), his marriage to Jezebel, a Phoenician princess, and the particular religious changes they introduced. Others might also wish to extend the cycle through 2 Kings 13 in which, after a lengthy interlude in which the prophet plays little part, Elisha and Hazael of Aram both die.

2. In choosing to read these texts in this way, my great model is the little known *Politics of God and Politics of Man*, by the French historian, sociologist, and Reformed lay theologian Jacques Ellul. Written in the 1960s, Ellul's book explores how these texts can illuminate for Christians questions of intervention in social and political life. I choose to adopt his supposition that careful attention to different aspects and dynamics of the biblical text may offer us probing questions and guidance for our participation in the life of the community of faith and in the world.

3. See most Bible dictionaries for a traditional view that sexual congress with multiple partners was an element of the Ba'al cult; some biblical texts are understood to suggest that there were passive male sacred prostitutes as well. One supposition is that this was a form of "sympathetic" activity — humans having sex encouraged the earth to renew its fertility. More recent scholarship argues that cultic prostitution was nonexistent in the ancient Near East. See Jacob Milgrom's article on Leviticus 19:29 for a concise review of the recent literature and the questions involved, *Anchor Bible 3A,* Leviticus 17–22.

4. I draw here on a reading of these narratives by the gifted contemporary orthodox rabbi and teacher David Silber. My verbal account of his lectures came from the late Dr. Katharine Temple, a Canadian Anglican scholar and social activist who studied with Silber in New York for several years.

5. Here I am indebted to Michael Welker's superb *God the Spirit*, both in its exposition of the biblical presentation of the Spirit and in Welker's rich and nuanced understanding of the inspiration of scripture, of the function of scripture as testimonies, and (as developed also in his *What Happens in the Lord's Supper?)* of the hermeneutics of contradiction among the biblical testimonies.

6. Again, I echo some of Ellul's salient observations in *The Politics of God and the Politics of Man*, post-modern before its time in its careful reading of the two prophetic utterances against each other, and reflecting on what this episode has to offer a religious leader in a politically tense and fraught period.

Abandoning Silence in Favour of Dialogue

Faith, Vocation, and Intimacy

My Journey from Secrecy to Openness

PETER ELLIOTT *is a graduate of Trent University in Peterborough, Ontario, and the Episcopal Divinity School in Cambridge, Massachusetts, USA. Ordained in 1980, he has served in the dioceses of Niagara and Toronto. Presently Dean of New Westminster and Rector of Christ Church Cathedral in Vancouver, he is also Deputy Prolocutor of the General Synod. He and his partner live in Vancouver.*

———

When I was asked to write this essay, it was assumed that the writer would be anonymous. On reflection, I realized that this assumption was at the heart of the challenge to our church. Why would a priest have to hide his name when writing an essay that told his story? As a priest, I have always valued the Anglican pastoral tradition of being a "parson" — an old English word that means "person." It is our identity as persons that shapes the way we minister as priests, and my identity as a gay man has been both a help and a burden in my priestly ministry. I offer my story as a way to reach out especially to lesbian and gay young Christians who feel called to ordained ministry, but are anxious about living in a church that may not accept their gifts. My hope is that one day we will be able to live in a church that celebrates openly the gifts that lesbian and gay laity and clergy bring to it.

———

When I was in my twenties, the rector of our parish shared some wisdom that has guided me for thirty years. He said that young adults had to face three critical questions: What would be your life's faith? What would be your life's work? Who would be your life's partner? Faith, work, and intimacy: three areas of life that call for serious thought. Through my life's experience, I have learned that all three are closely linked.

My life's faith was set early on. I was baptized as an infant and nurtured in a Christian home. The church was part of our family's life — a place for worship and community where the deepest concerns of life were addressed. My parents and siblings were actively involved in the life of our parish church, and as a family we engaged in discussions about theology and spirituality. I also was actively involved, singing in the choir, serving at the altar, participating in the youth group, and teaching Sunday school. But much of parish life seemed more social than spiritual. It was the presence of God I sought, not a comfortable pew. So I got involved with evangelical and charismatic young Christians in my hometown. Jesus Christ was a living reality for these people, and I became aware of Christ's presence in my life, especially when together in the group, we lifted up our lives in prayer.

It seemed natural to consider ordained ministry as my life's work, but there was a problem: I could not find a way to resolve my deep faith with my homosexual feelings. I prayed about this. I guess I was bargaining with God. In my journals I wrote about praying that God would take away my homosexual feelings. I gave thanks whenever a day passed without experiencing attraction to men. But the feelings were as strong and persistent as the call to ordained ministry, and it seemed that my sexuality made it impossible to embrace my life's faith and work. I did not seek counsel or help because I was ashamed of my feelings and worried about speaking of them out loud. It was a lonely and confusing time.

Just before graduating from high school, my best friend was killed in a plane crash. Everything I had believed seemed trivial compared with the shock and grief that resulted. Although I carried on with church activities, my faith was shattered, and the easy answers that had seemed so compelling no longer made any sense.

I wanted to get away from God. So I chose to go to a university that had no particular religious affiliation to study literature and philosophy.

Surprisingly, I found a renewed faith through intellectual pursuits. Philosophy and English literature opened up a world of ideas and raised deep questions. The university community offered a mix of pleasures and pain: the parties were great, but finding a balance between social life and study was a challenge. I dated women, but my homosexual feelings persisted. Then I began a relationship with another male student. When he dropped out of university, I felt abandoned, and the pain and depression lasted for the balance of my university days. Yet a tiny flicker of faith remained. As I read and wrote and thought and walked and prayed, my life's faith emerged again more strongly: Jesus Christ continued to be a living presence in my life, and a call to serve Christ through the ordained ministry would not let go of me. I decided to study theology.

Seminary days were exciting — a time of profound spiritual, personal, and emotional growth. I loved the combination of academic life with daily prayer, and was challenged to grow in my understanding of the Bible, theology, and ethics. In the parish, where for two years I worked as a student intern, I found that my gifts and skills could flourish. My life's faith seemed to be meeting my life's work, and the depression of university years was lifting at last.

But there was a new reality with which to deal. At the seminary there was a strong gay and lesbian community of faculty and students. For the first time I met people who were Anglican and Christian and also self-affirming gay men and lesbians. At first I wanted nothing to do with them. Deeply hurt by my only gay relationship and feeling more and more called to ordained ministry, I assumed that it was impossible to be both gay and a priest. By my second year at seminary, I was fortunate to have a steady girlfriend, but all my prayers and even the love of a beautiful young woman were not enough to stop my attraction to men. I broke off the relationship and sought psychotherapy.

At the university health clinic I described to a doctor, for the first time out loud, the struggle I was having. So began a long process of therapy. When the psychiatrist told me that many homosexual people lived productive and happy lives and were able to sustain healthy, life-long partnerships, an avenue opened that I had never considered. Through therapy, first with a psychiatrist, and later with a Jungian analyst, and through spiritual direction, I began to discern that God loved me, and that being gay may have been God's gift to me. In the final year of seminary, I met with an eminent priest, a scholar both in psychology and spirituality. When he heard my struggles with sexuality, he responded that Christ would use my whole self so that God's name would be glorified. He told me to put my fear away and let God work through me. It was a life-changing conversation.

So I presented myself to the bishop for ordination. I was anxious going into the candidacy process, even though I knew I met the guidelines of the church that allowed homosexuals to be ordained as long as we were celibate. I was ordained and appointed to a parish, where I soon learned that the practice of ministry was indeed my life's work. There I met many lesbian and gay parishioners, and in time came out to them. I didn't date, and although I attended parties at the homes of some gay parishioners, I couldn't imagine having a significant relationship with another man while remaining a parish priest. I moved into educational and administrative positions, hoping that this ministry, removed from the public nature of parish life, would provide an opportunity for me to develop a significant relationship.

As with many of my heterosexual friends, my first experience of an intimate partnership did not last for long, nor did the second. The ending of both relationships was very painful. The decision to keep my relationships secret from most colleagues, especially from ecclesiastical authorities, contributed to the stress that ended these relationships. Yet the church also gave me wonderful opportunities to meet gay and lesbian people with great faith — faith that sustained me through some very difficult times in my life, particularly during painful periods following the end of my first two long-term relationships. Many people within our church — clergy and lay, straight and gay — are supportive and caring to gay clergy, and I appreciated the care I received.

The position I held just before returning to parish life offered the privilege of travelling across Canada representing and working for the General Synod. In almost every visit to dioceses and parishes across the country, I met — although it was not my plan to do so — lesbian and gay people, clergy and laity, who were longing for a day when our church could be more honest about who we are. We dreamed of a day when we would be able to abandon enforced celibacy and silence, and speak the truth about our lives without fear of rejection or persecution. Knowing the stories of lesbian and gay deacons, priests, and bishops, and hearing of the pain they carry, I have felt like a keeper of family secrets. This culture of secrecy has caused deep pain in the church.

The cost of secrecy came to the fore when a former colleague, Father Warren Eling, was brutally murdered in Montreal in the early 1990s. At his funeral, the homilist reminded the congregation that Warren had wanted nothing more than to live with a committed same-sex partner, but unwilling to depart from our church's official policy, he had lived a single and lonely life. Sadly the church's silence and secrecy contributed to his death, and we lost his great gifts in ministry. His death coincided with the end of my second attempt at a long-term relationship, and I despaired for our church and for my ministry within it.

Yet, as I have found so often in my life, God transforms pain and despair into new life and possibility. I was encouraged to apply for the position where I currently serve, and have found life as a parish priest to be fulfilling. Long before my arrival, the cathedral parish had faced issues of inclusion and decided to welcome all. It is a community where all — old and young; single, married, and partnered; straight and gay; rich and poor — together seek to follow Jesus Christ. To be accepted as a priest who is a partnered gay man and be included as a couple in social events is a great joy.

As with many gay men my age, it takes time to make the transition from not speaking about one's sexual orientation to feeling included and therefore comfortable enough to be open. There are others in our church who have been more publicly open than I about their sexual orientation, and I have always admired them. My journey toward openness has been a long one. But recent events in church and society have created a climate where I believe that it is important to speak the truth about my life.

Some years ago while presiding at a eucharist for Integrity, the gay Anglican organization, I spoke publicly for the first time of *our* community, *our* struggle, and *our* hopes. Describing to a counsellor some time later this first experience of being public about my sexual orientation, I found myself speaking about God's Holy Spirit encompassing me and knowing that I was loved by God as a gay man. I believe that all the baptized are one in Christ, who was named at his own baptism as God's beloved son. In the community of the baptized, we are all beloved by God, and I believe that Christ's love transcends all our differences. In Christ, as St. Paul says, we are one body.

I had come out to my parents and family sometime before moving to Vancouver. Within my family, acceptance did not come easily at first, but we have grown to appreciate being able to speak the truth in love to each other. It was a great joy when my family came to Vancouver when I was installed as dean, and our visits back and forth were, and continue to be, very important. On one of those visits to Vancouver my father suddenly took ill and died. As sad as it was, I had a sense that his work was done when he saw that all his children were settled in their lives, and that he knew who we were. I am grateful that he was able to know who I am and that he honoured and respected my sexuality. One of my sadnesses is that he did not know my present partner.

At the personal level, then, at last I can celebrate a faith that I find sustaining, work that I find challenging and fulfilling, and a partner with whom I can share the good and bad things that life inevitably brings.

I believe that when God calls a lesbian or gay man to ministry, great gifts are made available to the church — not only for the gay community, but also for all. Our journey toward self-acceptance has taken us to difficult places, and we can therefore identify with those who live on the edge of society and bring compassion and caring to those that Jesus particularly loved: the poor, sick, weak, and lonely. The spirituality and sensitivity of lesbian and gay clergy are gifts greatly needed by the church in our time.

In my ministry, I have been accepted by people who know I'm gay and by people who don't. As relationships in ministry deepen, it is often tough to know whether or not to be open about my sexual orientation, but when I have, a deeper level of acceptance often follows, together with a greater honesty in talking about our lives. On occasions when this openness has been too difficult for people to accept, it has been painful when they have distanced themselves from me. In fact, it is seldom easy to know how best to express oneself in the church. I remember a meeting of bishops and senior diocesan executives at the national office, which began with each person sharing something about their home and family life. I was living with a partner at the time. What was I to say? How could I be honest about my domestic life without disclosing my sexual orientation?

Being a priest in the Diocese of New Westminster through our much-publicized debates and decisions on the issue of blessing same-sex unions, has often been distressing. One of the early dialogue days on sexuality was organized to encourage everyone to participate. Lesbian and gay clergy were in a difficult position because we knew that we were supposed to "share" in the groups, and to share honestly would mean that we would "out" ourselves. Most of the gay clergy chose not to attend. In the debates at our synod meeting, there was anxiety that some that were opposed to the blessing of same-sex unions would "out" one of the gay clergy. To their credit, those opposed kept the debate focused on principles.

Our diocesan decision to bless same-sex unions was an acknowledgement that homosexuality is a normative variation of human nature, morally neutral in and of itself. Therefore, to bless same-sex unions would serve as a way to support and encourage all committed long-term faithful relationships. New Westminster's decision and the subsequent election of Gene Robinson as Bishop of New Hampshire have created one of the most exciting periods in recent church history. But painful divisions have emerged. It is hard to find grounds for reconciliation between those who support inclusiveness and those who believe that gay people are going to hell because of who we are. Some of those who claim a "traditional conscience" on matters of sexual orientation hold that their integrity is at stake. For some of them, homosexuality has been elevated to being a "salvation issue." They take the view that remaining in a church that supports gay and lesbian people and our committed relationships makes them complicit in a sin and places their mortal souls in danger. Reconciliation is difficult for people who take such an extreme position.

However, I have met and spoken with people who are theologically conservative, yet choose to stay connected with their lesbian and gay sisters and brothers in Christ rather than to separate. The relationships with them are among the most precious ones that I have in the church these days. Being able to be open about my life's faith, work, and intimate partnership with someone who may have some questions but would rather keep in relationship is a great privilege and gift. I believe that it is possible, within Anglicanism, to have an asymmetrical pattern of relationships, where some parishes and communities welcome and affirm lesbian and gay people and bless our partnered relationships, while others do not. This ability to be in communion with those with whom we differ has always been characteristic of Anglicanism. Long before issues of homosexuality dominated debates within our church, we have lived in a state of impaired communion. While some dioceses and provinces of the church ordain women to the episcopate, others do not. Yet we have, as Anglicans, found a way to stay together in a state of impaired communion.

Anglican history has always found a middle way, a broad path that holds people who choose to stay together, even if we have deep disagreements with each other and even if the path is uncomfortable to walk on. We can, if we will, choose to find our unity in Christ, rather than in shared theological propositions, and continue the way forward, even in this difficult time. We can choose to look beyond our differences to the one who was among us as a servant, calling us to serve and love one another.

The secrecy that has plagued our lives endangers not only our individual health, but also our health as a community. The divisions that have emerged are painful, but the truth that is now being set free is more powerful still. That truth is a vision of the church that includes all people. In this church we would witness to our baptismal covenant by telling the truth about our lives, by seeking and serving Christ in all persons, and by respecting the dignity of every human being. In a world of suspicion, separation, and enmity, this church would bring people together. In this church, the gifts of gay and lesbian clergy, always valued by the church with the proviso that secrecy be maintained, would flourish and be gladly received by a truth-loving community. Anglicans are especially well situated to build on a history of avoiding extremes of religious intolerance. In a church that embraces diversity, a great diversity of people can find a home.

I long for that vision of the church to come true. I still long for a time when it will no longer be necessary to listen to the painful stories of young lesbians and gay men who have been told that they are sinners who need to change their sexual orientation or go to hell. I still long to be a priest who is gay, not just a gay priest. I still long to take my place with other clergy, gay and straight, women and men, living our lives openly with our partners.

One day, I hope to be able to pass on the advice given to me so many years ago, and counsel younger people about the importance of life's faith, life's work, and life's partner, straight or gay.

Finding Acceptance as a Gay Person and Priest

JOHN SAYNOR, *after a career as a funeral director, was ordained a priest and served in parishes in Toronto, Peterborough, and Harwood, Ontario. He has had a special ministry to those living and dying with AIDS. Now in partial retirement, he lives with his partner in Warkworth and continues work as a grief counsellor.*

———◆———

Before I formed you in the womb I knew you,
and before you were born I consecrated you
[Jeremiah 1:5].

Harwood, Ontario, is a lazy resort village on the southern shore of Rice Lake. During the winter months those who haven't gone to Florida number about two hundred. The summer population explodes as people come from all over North America to enjoy the scenery and the abundance of fish that still lurk among the reeds of the lake. I was asked to assume responsibility for the local Anglican church, St. John's, which had been closed for a number of years. The bishop gave me a free hand to revitalize it.

After nine years of ministry I retired. At the retirement dinner in the community centre my partner and I sat at the head table with the wardens and other parish leaders at their request. Paul, my partner of twenty-two years, although not an active church-goer himself, supported wholeheartedly my ministry at St. John's. He often attended and participated in the services. The people had grown to love him, and at the dinner they thanked him for his contribution to St. John's over the years.

It seems like an eternity since the gay issue came to the fore-front of the Anglican Church's consciousness. At this point there is welcome and acceptance of gays and lesbians in some churches, while in others it is best not to reveal one's sexual orientation. We ordain gay and lesbian priests but deny them the privilege of openly having a partner with whom they can share their life. How then did I, a priest in the Anglican Church of Canada, arrive at that table with my partner at my retirement? I welcome the opportunity to share my story and my reflections.

I was born in 1942 in Hamilton, Ontario. And I was born gay. I had nothing to do with it, nor was I given a choice. It was years before I began to wonder about my sexual orientation, more years before I understood what it was, and even longer before I was able to come to grips with it.

All my life I have believed, more or less, that in some unique way God cared for me. I wasn't always convinced, but when the chips were down, I held on to that belief. My parents were Christians, members of the Plymouth Brethren, a group that broke away from the Church of England about four hundred years ago in re-action to its liturgy and formality. They wanted to get back to the simplicity of the Bible, Holy Communion, and personal faith in Christ.

The Plymouth Brethren held to very strict rules around personal behaviour: no drinking, no smoking, no card playing, no theatre going, and a strict observance of Sunday. They were hard workers, and many of them were wealthy. Theologically they were Calvinistic, with a strong sense of the sovereignty of God and of predestination. The services on Sunday included the Lord's Supper (which only members of the congregation could attend), Sunday school, and an evening gospel meeting. They were very exclusive, separate from all other denominations, sometimes even other Brethren groups that they deemed more liberal than themselves. Their preachers often railed against the clergy of other denominations who were "draped in the rags of Rome!"

Right from the beginning, I knew that as a sinner, I was bound for hell. The only chance of escaping that destiny was an act of sincere repentance. So when I was nine years old, I made a personal confession of sin and accepted Jesus as my Saviour. With that act I was "saved." At thirteen I was baptized by immersion and admitted to communion.

My high school days were some of the loneliest of my life. My father died when I was fourteen. This in itself made me different from other kids. I took my new responsibilities at home seriously. Also, I had known all through my childhood that I was somehow different without understanding why. With the onset of adolescence, I began to understand. In those days the word "homosexual" wasn't in common use. I remember when someone accused the popular pianist Liberace of being a homosexual. I went to my dictionary to find out what that was and was horrified to know that Liberace and I had something in common! Up until then I thought I was the only person who had these feelings. I began to wish I could have a serious boyfriend, not a girlfriend, and I had crushes on some of my male teachers.

Once I began to realize how society in general and the church more specifically looked on gays, I did everything I could to keep from looking effeminate or from saying anything that would give me away. My whole life was motivated by guilt over being gay, and my increased involvement in the church and our high school Christian club was an attempt to please God and somehow earn forgiveness. I dated girls like everyone else, and it suited me just fine that in those days premarital sex was taboo. I was afraid I would be forced by family and society to marry.

O Lord, thou hast searched me and known me.... Thou art about my path and about my bed, and art acquainted with all my ways.... Thou didst knit me together in my mother's womb ... and in thy book were all of them written, even the days that were planned for me..." [Psalm 139]. Please, God, why am I like this? Did you make me or not? Whose mistake was I? Who is

responsible, You or me? It wasn't my idea to be born. I didn't ask to be gay;
it would have been so much easier to be heterosexual.

The funeral directors who looked after my father's funeral made
such an impression on me that I decided to become a funeral director following high school. While being trained for the job in
Toronto, I realized there was a whole gay world waiting to be discovered. True to form, however, I avoided it and continued to
suppress my sexual desires and live in the closet.

Working in funeral service, I felt fulfilled and comfortable, but
inside the struggle continued. I became a leader of the youth group
in my home church, and it grew to over one hundred young people. This I took as an indication that God hadn't given up on me.
I gained a lot of respect and acceptance through my work with
young people, but I was terrified that anyone might think I was
gay. If people asked me when I was going to get married, I told
them I was too busy doing the Lord's work. Finally, the struggle became too much for me. I made a deal with God:

I know I am not what You want, but I can't seem to do anything about it.
So I will give my life to serving You. I will go to Bible college and prepare for
ministry. All I ask in return is that I will be healed of my homosexuality.

So I resigned my job and went to Bible college in Toronto to prepare for ministry. At graduation four years later I was lauded as
the student in my class most likely to succeed in evangelism. I
wanted to evangelize the world! One of the highlights of those
years was meeting Evangelist Billy Graham, who was my hero. After graduation from Bible college I was appointed director of a
large Christian boys' and girls' camp in the Muskoka Lakes dis-
trict of Ontario.

The camp grew enormously in those years. We developed teens,
college, and careers camps, and a ministry to youth in downtown
Toronto. We developed discipleship programs for young people
and did anything we could to get the ear of young people and win
them for Christ. We tested God in any way we could. We developed programs and then watched as the funding miraculously

appeared from nowhere. I bought a large home in downtown Toronto and used it as my headquarters for ministry in the city in the winter, then moved to the camp for the summer months. These were heady years. I prided myself in working day and night seven days a week for the Lord, and was highly regarded by those I worked with.

But at the end of six years things began to fall apart. During the camping season of my sixth year I became depressed, anxious, and confused about what I was doing. I was thirty-five years old and had never loved anyone intimately. I was only five years away from the age my father was when he died. Would I die at forty like him? I didn't have much time left!

God, I don't understand what is happening. After all I have done for You, why haven't I been healed yet? All these miracles I see around me, and You haven't healed me yet. I've kept my part of the promise. Why didn't You keep yours?

That fall, I took a sabbatical. Those were the darkest days of my life. I didn't know what was happening or where I was going. I spent many days alone. I began to doubt that God existed, but I promised myself that I wouldn't discard what was left of my faith until I had worked this through.

I remembered reading about an Anglican monastic community not far from where our camp was located, one of the houses of the Society of St. John the Evangelist (SSJE). Knowing people could go there for rest and renewal, I made a phone call and was encouraged to pay them a visit. One dark and rainy evening in September I arrived and was greeted by Father Brian Bostwick, who took me to the guest house, a beautiful, old building of Muskoka field stone and pine beams. A fire burned in the stone fireplace in the living room. Handel's *Messiah* was playing in the background. Father Brian made me a cup of tea and we chatted for a few minutes before he invited me to Compline in the chapel. A strange sense of peace descended.

The chapel was magnificent in its simplicity. The only windows were high up, and through them you could see the branches of the trees swaying in the autumn wind. The brothers filed into the chapel in silence and the service began:

Into thy hands, O Lord, I commend my spirit....
Preserve us, O Lord, waking, and guard us sleeping, that awake we
may watch with Christ, and asleep we may rest in peace....
We will lay us down in peace and take our rest....
For it is thou, Lord, only, that makest us dwell in safety.

God, is it possible you know where I am after all? Have You brought me here? I have always trusted You; can I continue to trust You? I am feeling a peace come over me that I haven't felt for weeks. I haven't slept for weeks, is it possible I may sleep tonight?

Little did I know how significant that visit would be. I visited SSJE many times during the next year and was introduced to Anglican liturgy and theology and to the writings of Thomas Merton, Henri Nouwen, and St. John of the Cross.

On one visit I was quite depressed, and Father Ted Weare, one of the priests whom I had gotten to know quite well, asked me what was wrong. I bit the bullet. I told him I was gay. I told him about the praying, the fasting, the promises I had made to God, and my frustration that nothing had happened. He put his arms around me and said, "John, you are okay and you are going to be okay!" With that he laid his hands on my head and prayed that I would be relieved of depression. The depression left me that night and has never returned. That was twenty-five years ago.

So, God, if I could be healed of my depression with such ease, why not heal me of my homosexuality? Maybe You don't want to. Maybe You don't need to. Maybe I need to have a new understanding of who I am — and who You are!

I was now headed in a new direction. During a visit to my sister in Germany I made a pilgrimage to the Taizé Community in France, an ecumenical community of priests, nuns, and brothers of Roman Catholic, Lutheran, and Reformed traditions. The journey there was complicated and I was travelling alone with no idea of what lay ahead. Just north of the town of Cluny, once a great monastic centre, the bus stopped in the middle of nowhere, and the driver indicated that it was time for me to get off. "Where is Taizé?" I asked. "Up there, over the hill" was his response. I stood alone on the side of the road with a lump in my throat, and then with a sigh, began to walk. Over the crest of the hill, a magnificent, French country village unfolded before my eyes. I had arrived at Taizé!

My home for the next week was a small stone cottage, its garden alive with spring flowers. In my tiny room on the second floor there was a bed, a table, a chair, and a sink. Meals were taken in silence in the dining room — on the ceramic floor! It was spread with a tablecloth and colourful napkins, and in the middle were bouquets of freshly cut flowers. Quiet music played in the background. Two or three brothers would come and eat with us. We spent the days in silence except for the services.

Two significant events occurred that week. The first came while I was praying before one of the services. I looked up to see a man standing off to the side. He was dressed in white and was smiling at me. We looked at each other for some time, then he motioned at me to come toward him. As soon as He made the motion, He disappeared. For a moment I thought I had been seeing things. But then I realized who He was! What was He trying to tell me?

Lord, You must be trying to tell me one of two things. If You are telling me to keep following You, it must mean You are pleased with me and with who I am. Perhaps there is still work for me to do! If You are saying my life is almost over and I am coming to be with You, that is fine, too. Whatever it is, I'm willing.

There have been many times of testing in the last twenty-five years when I have remembered that moment.

The second event took place on the back porch of the little cottage overlooking the Burgundy countryside when I was getting ready to leave and return to Canada. It was a year since I had resigned from the camp, and in that year only one person from my past attempted to make any contact with me to find out what was going on. I now know that rumours about me were rampant, but of all the people I had ministered with and to, only one came to minister to me. Before I had left for Europe, I had begun to find a community with the SSJE. I knew I needed to find a Christian community in Toronto when I returned. As I sat there in the stillness, this verse from Hebrews came to my mind. "By faith, Abraham ... went out, not knowing where he was going" [Hebrews 11:8]. That was it! I was going I didn't know where, but I was being called again to go on in faith.

I returned to Canada and to the only work I knew how to do — funeral service. At the same time, I began to explore life as a gay man. During this time I met many wonderful gay people, who formed another tightly knit community. I began to worship in an Anglican church in Toronto. It was during this time that I met Paul, who would become my life partner. I had no idea where our meeting would lead, but I knew I loved him and he loved me. This was, after all, what I had been waiting for all these years.

Soon I began to sense the call to do ministry again. Before I knew it, I was enrolled at Wycliffe College in Toronto and became a postulant in the Toronto diocese. It was now the early 1980s, when AIDS entered the world's consciousness. The gay community was being hard hit, and soon Paul and I found ourselves immersed in caring for people living with AIDS, people dying with AIDS, and their partners, families, and friends. My two professions brought me in touch with them: funeral homes and the church. Both institutions were unprepared and often unwilling to care for this group. I found myself, along with others, advocating for people with AIDS even though a number of priests advised me not to. Their reasoning was that if the bishops found out I was involved with the gay community, they wouldn't ordain me since they would assume I was gay.

It seems to me that You ministered to prostitutes, lepers, and all sorts of outcasts while You were here? Shouldn't we be doing the same thing? It is impossible for me to ignore this great need in my community. I will do what I have to do. You risked Your reputation, I'll risk mine.

During my years at Wycliffe, I was appointed student assistant at the Church of the Redeemer in downtown Toronto. Canon Tim Foley was rector at that time. Right near the beginning of the AIDS crisis he called a meeting of those interested in creating a Christian response to AIDS. It was a radical step since no one had yet come forward to respond to this crisis, and it allowed me to bring together my faith and who I was in response to human need.

When it became apparent that the Church of the Redeemer was responding to the need, gays and lesbians began to attend. They were gifted, talented, and committed, and they were welcomed and accepted by people who had been in that church for fifty years or more. It was a relief for many to find a place to worship where they were accepted.

For the next few years, my ministry was focused around AIDS-related issues. I listened to the stories of young men who had been excluded from the church but who still believed in God. "Will God still accept me when I die?" they would ask. Parents, brothers, and sisters wept with me as they expressed their concern that their son or brother would go to hell because he was gay. Many young men were baptized and confirmed before their inevitable deaths. Personally I felt surrounded by God and by the love of the Christian community in a way I had never felt it before.

For a number of years Paul and I seemed to spend most of our time in Casey House Hospice (the AIDS hospice in Toronto), funeral homes, and hospitals. Everything was set aside for this: personal time, holidays, money. We were only two of hundreds of people who gave of themselves unselfishly. By now millions of dollars had been raised by the gay community for AIDS research, financial support for those who were most deeply affected and for the building of Casey House and other residences for people living with AIDS. I was amazed at how people accepted and helped each other.

Isn't this what the church is supposed to be about? How did we get bogged down in debating what service book we should use or whether women should be ordained? Why have we given silent assent to all kinds of racism and prejudice? Jesus, it seems as if You are stepping out of the stained-glass windows and teaching us to live like You again.

Five years after entering Wycliffe College I was ordained. I was never asked if I was gay. I decided to live my life as a gay man and not make a big deal about it. Although I didn't announce that Paul and I were a couple, people recognized that we were, and both at the Redeemer and in other parishes outside Toronto, they simply accepted us.

When James Ferry, a priest of the diocese, was suspended from active ministry because he was living with a gay partner, I was so angry that I considered resigning from the diocese to fight for Jim and the issues that were at stake. Canon Edgar Bull, my mentor for many years, advised me against that move. "John, keep on living the way you are. You will do more to change people's attitudes by living the way you do than if you resign."

My curacy was served at All Saints, Peterborough. When I told the rector about the AIDS work I had been doing in Toronto, his response was, "Well, there isn't any AIDS in Peterborough." Within a week of arriving there, a nurse phoned. She had heard about me from the AIDS Committee of Toronto and wanted to know if I would be interested in helping a young man who had AIDS. A great deal of networking among Peterborough doctors and other professionals was soon taking place, and Paul and I, along with others, set about developing the Peterborough AIDS Resource Network — a flourishing organization that, unfortunately, still exists today.

There were drawbacks to being a gay male priest. Perhaps they were really my own issues. At a time when reports of sexual abuse by priests of young boys were beginning to surface, I felt limited in my work with young people. And being an unmarried male didn't make dealing with some of the women particularly easy either. However, I have never been aware of any serious opposition when my sexual orientation became known, and I have been able to exercise a special ministry to gay and lesbian people, just as other clergy have had special ministries to children, Chinese, Hispanics, and others.

In his book *Embracing the Exile* [NY: Seabury Press, 1982], John

Fortunato compares the spiritual journey of the gay Christian to the Israelites' Babylonian exile. Of course the experience of exile isn't exclusive to the gay community. There are many outside the accepted social norms who share it. Yet it is in the exile that many people find God or find God again. I did. Not only did I rediscover God, but also I rediscovered myself, and that brought me healing and helped to make me who I am today.

In a world full of hypocrisy, people long for integrity from community leaders — politicians, clergy, teachers, doctors, or whoever. People long to be able to live with integrity themselves. I believe that God requires us to live with integrity and loves us for who we are. For me there can be no genuinely Christian alternative to living with integrity as a gay person. Living with a partner who supports and encourages me has strengthened my ministry. And our relationship has been an example of how two people of the same sex can live together in a committed relationship and be a sign to the world of the love and acceptance of God.

Continuing
the Dialogue

Community and Diversity

The Role of Perspective in Debates about Human Sexuality

ERIC BERESFORD *serves as Consultant for Ethics and Interfaith Relationships for the Anglican Church of Canada, and as Consultant for Ethics for the Anglican Consultative Council. In his work for the Anglican Church of Canada he deals with a broad portfolio of ethical issues including those related to biotechnology, the environment, and medical ethics, as well as ethical issues related to human sexuality. Before taking up his current appointment, Canon Beresford was Assistant Professor of Ethics in the Faculty of Religious Studies at McGill University. He has recently finished a term of office as President of the Canadian Theological Society.*

O ne of the most frequently repeated concerns in the debate concerning the place of gay and lesbian people in the life of the church is the experience of bias in positions presented, not only by lobbyists on either side of the debate, but also by those from whom, it is felt, we should expect neutral, balanced information. Bias, it seems, is endemic. This concern about lack of balance appears again in the studies undertaken by the consultants preparing for the 2004 General Synod. Repeatedly they heard concerns about processes that were considered manipulative because they were inherently biased to particular conclusions and about information that was biased because it did not reflect the full range of views. Bias, we are told, is present in our leaders, in our institutional structures, in the resources that have been produced to support conversation in this area, and in the mechanisms through which that conversation proceeds. This perception of widespread bias undermines trust and means that any decision, however carefully it proceeds, will have doubts cast upon its validity. Those who do not see their views reflected in the outcome will inevitably believe that the outcome is a product of bias. It is therefore crucially important to answer the charge of bias.

How might the charge be answered? It is surely the case that there is no view from nowhere. Each of us occupies a particular place in the world that is the product of our culture, background, education, religious faith, experience, and the nexus of relationships within which we live. Our place in the world determines our perspective. What we see is shaped not only by what is there to be seen, but also by the perspective from which we view it. The philosopher Hans Georg Gadamer gave expression to this in the paradoxical claim that "all understanding inevitably involves some prejudice" [Gadamer 1985, 239ff.]. More than this, while Gadamer accepts the possibility of destructive prejudice, he argues also for the positive role of prejudice in shaping our openness to reality [245ff.]. Gadamer's point is that our experience of reality is made possible by certain assumptions — prejudgements — that orient us to the world around us. They are the starting points for our understanding of the world. In Gadamer's view, this understanding is not static; it grows as our experience either confirms or challenges and reshapes our assumptions. Gadamer is far from being the only thinker to recognize that there is no view from nowhere. But if our ways of understanding the world are shaped by assumptions derived from our own particular experience of the world, how can we communicate across those different assumptions? This is especially problematic if we are dealing with differences between groups of people with sharply different perspectives, especially cultural or religious perspectives.

Such is the reality across the Anglican Communion at present, and to a lesser degree even within the Anglican Church of Canada.

In a recent chapter on the history of Anglican discussions of human sexuality, I argued for a greater attention to the communal context of the conversations on the subject. My central thesis was that we can only understand those conversations by paying careful attention to the history, character, and organization of the community in which they are taking place. I drew a distinction between debate and dialogue that I hoped might encourage a greater recognition of the common ground between those on different sides of our current disagreements.

> By their very nature, debates are cast in oppositional terms. The purpose of debate is to clarify the truth and separate it from positions that are erroneous or incomplete. It may indeed turn out that neither side is in possession of the whole truth, but debate focuses its attention on the arguments being deployed and proceeds by eliminating options that prove to be untrue or inadequate. By contrast, dialogue begins in a recognition of the community of dialogue partners. We belong together as members of a single community. As such, we share interests and concerns that often go unnoticed, but which from time to time bring us into conflict. Dialogue is not in the first place about winners and losers; it is about relationship and mutual responsibility. To understand a debate it is enough to explain the basic premises at stake for each side, and the arguments used. To understand a dialogue it is important to tell the story of how the community arrived at the place it finds itself in [Sider Hamilton 2003, 178–179].

Embedded in this distinction between debate and dialogue are both a moral commitment and an interpretive assumption. The moral commitment arises from the observation that our disagreements are about the nature of particular relationships and about communal responses to those relationships. Given this, moral responsibility will require us to pay attention to the effects of our moral discourse on the communities of which we are a part. It makes no sense to seek to articulate the values embedded in the relationships we are speaking about in ways that are disruptive of the relational structure of the community. Indeed, I would suggest that all helpful argument about moral issues needs to take responsibility for the way that moral arguments sustain or undermine the possibility of moral community. In practice, debates pay little attention to moral community. Because they are cast in terms of winners and losers, they tend to fragment communities based on friendship, trust, and intimacy by elevating assertion, suspicion, and competition. Further, because debates are about excluding incorrect, untrue, and therefore untenable positions, they do not encourage outcomes that support diversity of perspective and insight. There is even, perhaps, an authoritarian element in them. If we are able to show through debate that a particular conclusion is "right," then it seems legitimate to enforce such "true" conclusions upon others in the community, whatever their private misgivings might be.

The interpretive assumption is that no individual or group can claim possession of the truth in all its aspects. This is practically true in an institution such as the church, where there are no effective means of enforcing conformity. Even churches that might be more energetic than Anglicanism in seeking uniformity cannot achieve it, and dissent is a reality in all church communities. However, the point I am making goes further. I am arguing that a recognition of the limits on knowing imposed by the human condition implies the refusal of all absolutist claims to truth. We cannot know everything, or know absolutely, because we cannot see without seeing from particular perspectives. The only one who could see everything, or know absolutely is, by definition, God. As Paul puts it, "we walk by faith, not by sight" [2 Corinthians 5:7].

This position is obviously attractive to many of us who have been shaped by liberal democratic institutions and who are suspicious of demands for conformity to narrowly defined truth claims. Moreover, a widespread recognition of the need for humility in our truth claims has arisen, at least in part, from our historical awareness of intolerance and its social consequences, especially for minorities and marginalized groups. This humility, while clearly shaped by the secular culture of which we are a part, is not unique to it. Rather, I shall argue, a certain tolerance of plurality of approaches is embedded within the very foundations of Anglicanism as it came to be defined at the Elizabethan settlement.

The obvious danger of this position is relativism — a reluctance to make any truth claims whatsoever, and a reduction of all claims to *mere* opinion. Such a position would in my view be at odds with historic Christianity. In what follows I will attempt

- to argue for the necessity of recognizing the role of perspective in all theological reflection;
- to show that the recognition of the role of perspective does not lead to a moral relativism; and
- to see the significance of perspective for understanding the way we disagree with each other about complex moral issues and also the way in which we might resolve those disagreements over time.

Perspective in Theological Reflection

At first it might seem odd to claim that perspective is an important element of all theological reflection. We are more used to thinking of the theological task as the working out of God's self-revelation. If we say that God has revealed God's self, then surely this means that we know something about God. I think few would dispute this claim; nonetheless, the sixteenth and seventeenth century reformers spoke of the need to "proclaim the gospel afresh in every generation." They did not doubt that the gospel was true, and true for all times and places, but the need to constantly proclaim afresh surely contains within itself the recognition that different aspects of this truth will be particularly significant to different social and historical contexts. Just as those contexts frame our perspective, so they frame the possibilities within which we will be able to hear and understand the gospel message. In an earlier definition of theology, St. Anselm (1033–1109; scholar and Archbishop of Canterbury) describes theology as "faith in search of understanding"[1] [Anselm, 83]. In indicating a relationship between the lived experience of faith and the theological task, Anselm was not doubting the possibility of true knowledge of God. Rather he recognized that the life of faith gives rise to questions, and that theology needs to pay attention to these questions if it is to help our faith to grow and mature. Once again, perspective is important because the *particular* experience of faith in the life of individuals and communities shapes the questions that direct and shape the theological task. Neither of these descriptions of the theological task claims that God is revealed through experience, but both assume that experience shapes the way in which revelation is received, understood, and responded to.

More controversially, we need to consider the role of perspective in our reading of scripture. Many of the debates about the blessing of same-sex relationships focus on alternative readings of scripture. Accusations of bias in the reading of scripture assume that there is one true interpretation of scripture that would resolve our difficulties if only we would get our biases out of the way. We are told that we need to pay attention to "the plain sense of scripture" that alone constitutes the meaning of scripture for the lives of Christians. This suggestion misses several important points.[2]

In its most extreme form the claim that we are simply to pay attention to the plain sense of scripture renders interpretation redundant. It assumes that the meaning of a text is simply a property of that text and the task is simply to make clear what the words mean. This meaning should, it is inferred, be plain to all people of good sense. Disagreement becomes a symptom of willful blindness. One problem with this is that it makes the relationship of the Hebrew Bible to Christian thought extremely problematic. When Isaiah says, "Therefore the Lord himself will give you a sign. Look, the young woman is with child and shall bear a son, and shall name him Immanuel" [Isaiah 7:14], Isaiah is referring to a sign that he fully expects King Ahaz to see, despite the unwillingness of Ahaz to put God to the test. This sign is to be proof to Ahaz of the truth of Isaiah's prophecy. The plain sense of this text refers to an event in the lifetime of Isaiah, not to the incarnation of Christ. Yet the New Testament itself links this prophecy to the coming of the Messiah. Is the New Testament wrong to interpret this passage in this way? No. The point is surely that the meaning of the text is complex, and that texts are interpreted not in the abstract but in the context of the concerns and interests of readers. "What emerged is an unbroken dialogue or discourse between a book and a people, between Scripture and tradition, between letter and the spirit, and between the word and the experience of those hearing it" [Kugel and Green 1986, 157].

Perspectives shape how we read scripture, and this is true for all of us. One of the problems in the current debates is the gap between claims that are made for the importance of the plain meaning of scripture and the actual practices of reading that we engage in. Scripture teaches clearly and repeatedly that the lending of money at interest is wrong and sinful. This was the universal teaching of the church for almost 1500 years, until John Calvin advanced the claim that it was not interest that was sinful, but excessive interest. Calvin's context in Geneva is surely important for understanding this shift in interpretation. Geneva was not an agrarian society such as the one within which the scriptural passages were written. Agrarian societies hold their wealth primarily in land. But the social and economic impact of lending money is quite different in a mercantile economy of the sort that surrounded Calvin and shaped the moral and theological questions that Calvin asked in his reading of scripture. There are few modern Christians, however committed they may be to reading scripture in its "plain sense," who have no involvement in the practice of lending money at interest. This does not necessarily mean that we do not take scripture seriously. On the contrary, it can mean that we take scripture so seriously that we pay careful attention to the meaning of particular scriptural injunctions in their own social and moral context before simply importing them into our very different context.

What this means is that we can never draw a simple straight line between scriptural texts on the one hand and the convictions that Christians hold or the way in which they shape their lives. Rather, as Fowl notes there is a complex interplay. "Christians will find that interpretations of scripture have already shaped convictions, practices, and dispositions which have, in turn, shaped the ways in which scripture is interpreted. Not only is it impossible to undo this process, it is not clear how one would ever know that one had done so" [Fowl 1995, 7]. Put simply, if scriptural interpretation is shaped by our perspectives, there is going to be no perspective-free way of separating our perspectives from the way in which we have come to understand scripture.

None of this should be taken as a denial of the authority of scripture, or as an attempt to undercut the centrality of scripture in shaping the moral life of Christians. Fowl's point, and mine, is that this centrality is expressed precisely in the commitment to continually bringing our beliefs and practices into relationship with our reading of scripture as the primary benchmark for Christian life and witness. Again, "for Christians at least, biblical interpretation will be the occasion of a complex interaction between the biblical text and the varieties of theological, moral, material, and ecclesial concerns that are part of the day-to-day lives of Christians struggling to live faithfully before God in the contexts in which they find themselves" [Fowl 1995, 60].

Of course concerns arise from the insistence on the inevitability of interpretation. For, as Elizabeth Schüssler-Fiorenza notes in her important essay on the ethics of biblical interpretation, all interpretation involves interests, values, and visions, and those interests and values can distort as well as support our interpretive practice [Schüssler-Fiorenza 1999, 28]. Scriptural texts have been used not only to legitimate good and worthy insights and actions, but also to support war and colonialism, and to justify anti-Semitism, misogyny, and the exploitation of slavery. Given this history, Christians need to be responsible not simply in their interpretation of biblical texts, but also for the social and ethical consequences of their interpretation of these texts. In order to do this, we need to pay careful attention to our assumptions and biases, something we are unable to do if we fail to acknowledge their role in our readings of scripture.

Fowl also draws attention to the problem of abusing scripture to justify our sinful attitudes and practices, and he acknowledges that this is one of the motives for seeking to limit the range of acceptable scriptural interpretation. The fear is that the failure to limit the range of interpretation will result in doctrinal and moral anarchy [Fowl 1995, 34]. Yet we need to remember that diversity is not the same thing as arbitrariness. Neither Fowl nor I would imply that scripture could bear *any* meaning. The meaning of scripture is understood in the life of the community of faith, and the contexts within which that community lives limit its interpretations. Of course, scripture can be distorted to serve particular sinful interests, but the real question is what strategies will effectively prevent this. What will help will be the recognition that interpretation is a task that takes place within real historical communities with all the limitations that implies. What matters is that these communities recognize and accept their accountability both for the practices of interpretation they engage in, and also for the ethical consequences of those practices both within the church and for the wider community. In Fowl's view this is made possible by the centrality of the practices of forgiveness, repentance, and reconciliation within the life of the community of faith. He concludes:

> Therefore, if Christians are to combat their well-documented tendencies to read scripture to underwrite their sin, then they must attend to themselves. That is, they must primarily be concerned with their own common life, and with the voices of those both inside and outside the community which offer words of prophetic critique of the community and its interpretive practices [Fowl 1995, 85].

We cannot interpret scripture responsibly if we do not pay careful and critical attention to ourselves, to the perspectives we assume, and to the interests embedded in those perspectives. What is it we seek to legitimate? And what does that say about our understanding of God and about the interpretive practices that legitimate that understanding? Once again,

> context is as important as text. What we see depends on where we stand. One's social location or rhetorical context is decisive for how one sees the world, constructs reality, or interprets biblical texts [Schüssler-Fiorenza 1999, 19].

We cannot escape bias in our interpretation of scripture, but we can become responsible for being attentive to its impact on ourselves, on the life of our community, and on those around us.

Perspective and Moral Commitment

Yet the question still remains: Is the account I have given of the relationship of perspective to the theological task, particularly the task of scriptural interpretation, adequate to resist the challenges of moral relativism? This is a complex question to which I can give only the briefest of responses here.

In asking this question it is important to be clear about the nature of the threat posed by moral relativism. Strictly, relativism proposes not simply that there are multiple moral perspectives, but that it is in principle impossible to adjudicate between them. Moral positions become mere expressions of personal preference, to which may be added expressions of the hope that others should share one's position. Where this link is present, moral claims become what Alistair MacIntyre has described as "emotivist" [MacIntyre 1984, 11ff.], and the difficulty with emotivist claims is that they cannot be sustained by rational public argument. It is this failure that invites the suspicion that claims about what is good or bad, right or wrong, virtuous or vicious, are essentially empty. If moral beliefs are emotivist in MacIntyre's sense, then they have no publicly available meaning, and moral judgements are mere expressions of personal points of view, none of which is more valid or true than any other. It is no longer possible to say that the holocaust was evil on an unprecedented scale, or that slavery is wrong. Or at least, such statements simply express a point of view no more valid than their opposites.

Richard Bernstein, in his book *Beyond Objectivism and Relativism* [Bernstein 1983, 19, cf. 37ff.], argues that we need not limit ourselves either to the belief that moral values are relative and therefore arbitrary, or to the belief that they refer to some objective moral order beyond the particularities or history, culture, and social context within which our moral views are expressed and lived out. He agrees that relativism is problematic, but argues that it is possible to understand ethical judgement as shaped by the social and cultural contexts within which they are made without their becoming merely arbitrary. Moral claims cannot be proven, but they can be rationally defended. Particular moral claims can be called into question, analyzed, and weighed. Further, it is possible to talk about moral progress. The changes in the role and status of women in North American society, and the abolition of slavery, would both be examples of this. They represent moral positions that, once achieved, call into question all previous positions, and throw light on why those positions might once have appeared attractive, as well as on why they failed. What is being suggested here is that moral claims are justified not by appeal to some established and unquestionable moral foundations, but through the complex interplay of commitments and insights grounded in the historical development of the social and cultural perspectives out of which they come. It is precisely the insights drawn from our cultural context that allow us to question the assumptions that our culture takes for granted. This questioning can then give rise to changes in particular moral positions, allowing us to see new possibilities and ask new questions that in turn may lead to new understandings of, or even shifts within, our moral world view.

Once we challenge the idea that objectivism and relativism are the only alternatives, then we can see that it is possible to acknowledge that all moral insights are shaped by our historical realities, and by our social and cultural context, without concluding that these moral insights are simply arbitrary and therefore irrational. On the contrary, we can recognize and acknowledge the actual historic and communal processes by which moral arguments proceed. We can pay attention to the role of culture and socio-economic factors on moral arguments, without claiming that these factors reduce moral arguments to the assertion of the interests of particular groups. Moral arguments may reflect the biases of particular cultures, but this does not mean that there is no way to adjudicate the strengths and weaknesses of particular moral claims in ways that may be generally accessible. It does mean that moral agreement will not always be available on all matters in the short term. Yet this is surely simply a description of the realities that we experience in all moral discourse.

I am also drawing a distinction here between relativism and what might be called pluralism. In the final analysis, relativism undermines moral commitment, but pluralism need not. Indeed it may be grounded on moral insights and commitments. For example, pluralism may reflect the greater value given to community and relationship, rather than to assertion and argument. It may reflect the high value given to a humility based on a recognition of human fallibility, and on the historical experience of limit and failure in the insights of individuals and communities. Not only have individual Christians got it wrong in the past, but church communities have supported positions they later found to be morally reprehensible, as in the case of the support given to Apartheid by the Reformed Church in South Africa, or the support given by Canadian Christians to the attempt to assimilate indigenous peoples. Pluralism may be embraced not because we think *any* moral position is acceptable, but because we see the value and importance of leaving real space for moral disagreement and dialogue. Pluralism makes it possible to exercise an interpretive charity towards positions we ultimately disagree with. It is not necessary to see such positions as the result of moral or intellectual failure, but rather as a different balancing of the complex issues associated with particular moral judgements.

It might be objected that the values embedded in this sort of pluralism reflect the individualist liberalism of the modern West. However, one might also argue that the tolerance of diversity and acceptance of a plurality of perspectives is one that is found in the very roots of Anglican polity. The Anglican Church under Henry VIII, while it split from Rome, remained essentially catholic. A translation of the scriptures was authorized, and prayers were to be in the vernacular, but what Henry authorized was simply a translation of the Latin mass. There is no evidence that he intended to authorize substantial alterations of the rite in line with protestant ideas. The service that appeared in 1549 after Henry's death went somewhat further and is an obviously, if moderately, protestant document. The Church of England moved even further in a protestant direction in the prayer book of 1552. These changes were short lived, and after Edward's brief reign, Mary attempted to bring the Church of England firmly back into the Catholic fold.

By the time Elizabeth ascended to the throne there was a huge diversity of religious opinion in England. Elizabeth believed that a single church was necessary to the life of the nation, but realized that this could not be achieved by enforcing a closely defined conformity. She sought to shape a church that did not "make windows into men's souls." As a result the Elizabethan settlement was an attempt to produce a church that could be home to all but the most uncompromising puritans and most committed Roman Catholics. The church of the Elizabethan settlement recognized that some disputes could not be settled and ought to be treated as "matters indifferent" — matters upon which conscience could not and should not be compelled. These disputes were not seen as indifferent in the modern sense of the word. Often people were passionate in their support of one position or another, but the disagreements were deemed about issues insufficient to justify the breaking of communion. The church that grew out of the Elizabethan settlement acknowledged that individual members might have different perspectives, and it allowed for diversity within its shared life. It acknowledged some of the values and virtues that I have associated with pluralism.

While relativism reflects the somewhat cynical attitude that one moral position is as good as any other, pluralism begins in the embrace of quite specific moral commitments. Ironically, pluralism may also provide a more effective alternative to moral relativism than most objectivist positions can, precisely because it is better able to describe the actual context, possibilities, and limits of moral reason. Objectivism and moral absolutism may in the end lead to relativism because they are unable to provide the sort of moral certainty they promise. What is more, there is little evidence that they can bring about the closure of complex and troubling moral debates. It is precisely the interminable character of much moral debate that lends weight to the claims of relativists. If we cannot resolve our differences, perhaps they are not claims about any state of affairs in the real world, but expressions of personal and essentially arbitrary and ungrounded preferences, of no more significance than a preference for blue over green.

Perspective and Moral Conversation

Positive gains are offered by the pluralist perspective, with its acceptance of the role of diversity and its positive evaluation of the dialogues that arise in a diverse community. I have been arguing for a way of thinking about those dialogues that does not see difference as a bias to be eradicated, but as a positive expression of the theological and moral commitments of the community to be embraced. To acknowledge the particularity of individual perspectives is to affirm the value and contribution of perspectives other than our own to the shaping and enriching of the life of the church. There are practical ways of shaping moral conversations in a church characterized by such different points of view.

First, the acknowledgment of perspective allows for the possibility of real moral disagreement within communities. Acknowledging perspective permits us to see that scripture and tradition may look different from different perspectives and yet be read faithfully by all. Even where we agree on the theological concerns at stake in coming to conclusions around issues of human sexuality, we might decide to support different practices in different historical and social contexts. For example, it is clear that marriage is a quite different institution at the beginning of the twenty-first century than it was in Jesus' day; whatever our reading of scripture, we can agree that none of us lives a first-century pattern of marriage. Disagreement remains about how to interpret what our first-century scriptures say about marriage in our twenty-first century context.

Second, the acknowledgement of the role of perspective allows us to see that we are communities not because we agree, but because our disagreements are based on shared values, dispositions, and practices. Often it turns out that our disagreements are themselves premised on much more important and deeper agreements.

One of the agreements that unites many who would disagree about the appropriateness of same-sex unions is the belief that sexual intimacy is not simply a private matter, but carries profound implications for our public life and for the wider network of relationships of which we are a part. The service for the solemnization of marriage recognizes that the love and intimacy shared between a couple has implications for the new life they enter in the community, not simply as separate individuals but as a couple. The disagreement about the appropriateness of same-sex intimacy is here worked out in the context of a much deeper recognition that appropriate intimate relationships have a public face.

Often we speak of living with our differences as a matter of compromise, "for the sake of unity." This can be very misleading. On the one hand, unity is not a product of compromise. Rather compromise is a response to the recognition that unity is not a goal to be achieved but a gift. It is the grace of God already present in our common life which we are called to recognize, accept, and live out. On the other hand, when we acknowledge the role of perspective, we begin to see living with diversity not as a compromise, but as a reflection of the true character and texture of our common life and of the contexts within which it is lived out.

Third, acknowledging the role of perspective allows us to see that solutions to our disagreements cannot be found in abstract moral argument. Rather we must pay attention to the shared commitments to common life in community. As part of this, we need to practice charity in interpreting the aims and intentions of those with whom we disagree. Acknowledging perspective as an essential element of the moral issues that confront us sets limits on the role of argumentative models based on suspicion and critique. Such arguments are poor strategies because sustaining community life requires that we pay attention to the character of our common life, rather than to simply exposing and articulating our differences. We need to be clear about what is at issue between us, but we will never be fully clear unless we understand something of the context of the disagreement. Only then can we understand both the content and the emotional weight of our differences. Only then can we see why our difficulties are often so hurtful, yet also why this hurt, by bringing us back to the acknowledgment of the character and importance of our common life, can be a sign of hope.

Is it possible to make contributions to the conversations on human sexuality that are free from bias? I would have to say no, but I would also have to say that the presence of bias need not be viewed as destructive to the possibility of principled, reasoned, moral thought. Nor need moral disagreement be destructive of community. Indeed, I would suggest that it is impossible to be a truly moral community without admitting, more than this, without welcoming, principled moral disagreement. Our disagreements cannot be resolved by fiat. The attempt to resolve our disagreements through the external application of institutional authority, or the attempt to exclude perspectives other than our own by appeal to particular applications of scripture or tradition, is doomed to failure.

The debates concerning the blessing of same-sex relationships have brought us to a point in the life of the church that is painful and difficult, and it is tempting to seek a quick and easy solution. However, if my analysis of the role of perspective is accurate, then such solutions are simply not available. Any attempt to impose such solutions can only have the effect of marginalizing, or worse, excluding those who take minority positions in the life of the church. If we are to find a way forward in our current debates, it must come from the acknowledgement that there are real and sharp differences of perspective between Bible-believing Anglicans whose desire is to live lives of holiness, and faithfulness to God in the community of the church. While we need to be as fair and balanced as possible in our assessment of the issues, we need to acknowledge that none of us is, or can be, free from the biases we bring from the many factors that have made us who we are. While we need to challenge perspectives that are distorting or incomplete, we need to recognize also that much of what we too readily call bias is not a failing to be rejected, but an inescapable fact of our human reality. More, it is a gift. It is the means through which the work and grace of God, lived in the diversity of the community of God's people, enriches our common understanding of the problems we face and the lives that we are called to lead.

Note

1. I am grateful to Stephen Fowl for shaping my thinking for much of what follows on the reading of scripture. See Stephen E. Fowl, *Engaging Scripture* (Malden, MA: 1998).

Works Cited

Anselm of Canterbury, Saint. 1998. *The Major Works*. Brian Davies, and Gillian Evans, eds. Oxford: Oxford University Press.

Bernstein, Richard. 1983. *Beyond Objectivism and Relativism: Science Hermeneutics and Praxis*. Philadelphia, PA: University of Pennsylvania Press.

Fowl, Stephen E. 1998. *Engaging Scripture*. Malden, MA: Blackwell Publishers.

Gadamer, Hans Georg. 1985. *Truth and Method*. New York: Crossroad Publishing.

Hamilton, Catherine Sider. 2003. *The Homosexuality Debate: Faith Seeking Understanding*. Toronto: ABC Publishing.

Kugel, James, and Rowan Greer. 1986. *Early Biblical Interpretation*. Philadelphia: Westminster Press.

MacIntyre, A. 1984. *After Virtue*. South Bend, IN: Notre Dame University Press.

Schüssler-Fiorenza, Elizabeth. 1999. *Rhetoric and Ethic: The Politics of Biblical Studies*. Minneapolis: Augsburg Fortress Press.

Discerning the Spirit in Our Experience

Living Together with Difficult Issues

CARROLL GUEN HART *is a founding member of the Dialogue Group in the Diocese of Toronto, and is struggling to come to terms with the perception that dialogue never ends. In her spare time, Carroll reads, knits, and works for the Province of Ontario. She is a parishioner at St. Thomas's, Huron Street.*

⚊➤⚊

I have been privileged to take part in an extended conversation arranged by the Archbishop of Toronto about the place of gay and lesbian believers in the church. In the Anglican Church of Canada, versions of this dialogue have been in progress for some years. As might be expected, the dialogue has often been highly divisive and ideologically split, between those who believe deeply that homosexuality violates God's created order, and those (including myself) who have come to believe that a homosexual orientation may well be a variant within God's created order, and that gay and lesbian sexual expression within long-term committed relationships may be blessed by the Body of Christ.

Dispersed Authority

In struggling to continue this conversation, we have often referred to the fourfold authority of scripture, tradition, reason, and experience. That we find authority dispersed into four sources suggests that God's Word to us is not a monolithic, monotonous drone, but has internal diversity. As the author of the epistle to the Hebrews has it, God has spoken to us "in many times and in many ways." That is, God's Word comes from a number of sources, and the different sources may carry a somewhat different nuancing of the Word. I think this is a wonderful insight that needs to be preserved.

However, it is clear that we differ, often quite strongly, as to the range of sources and voices, and the weighting that we might assign to each. In principle, this difference of weighting is normal and is a fruitful topic for conversation. However, in practice those legitimate differences can often deteriorate into unfruitful antagonisms. For those of us who have come gradually to a more positive view of gay and lesbian sexual orientation and expression, our journey has often included a significant experience of a gay or lesbian person whom we could not reject — a son or daughter, a respected leader, a close friend, and so on. Sometimes we have claimed that, in accepting the sexual orientation of this person, we are being true to reason and experience, and sometimes we have implied that scripture and tradition belong to the other side of the debate. Likewise, for those who believe that scripture and tradition forbid the legitimate and blessed expression of homosexual activity, it is easy to claim that scripture and tradition are orthodox, whereas reason and experience represent secular departures from orthodox Christian faith. This turns the notion of dispersed authority into the notion of secular authorities at war with God's Word, and warps the dialogue in the direction of condemnation and distrust.

This divisive use of the model of fourfold authority has caused me deep distress and has forced me to articulate more clearly my own approach: to hold reason and experience together with scripture and tradition, and to articulate them more clearly, as Rowan Williams says, "in terms of the common language of the faith" [Williams 1999]. In a very short space, I will try to suggest a way of conceiving the "appeal to experience" that might preserve the internal diversity of God's Word to us while not splitting us into warring camps. I will try to suggest a way of conceiving the appeal to reason and experience that roots them in scripture and tradition and also allows for the internal diversity of God's Word to us. Specifically, I want to consider the doctrine of the Trinity as a basis for accepting the notion of dispersed authority, and I want to explore the theology of Spirit as a basis for accepting the newness of contemporary experience as one way in which God speaks to us. I hope that doing so may offer us a way beyond the impasse in which we are apt to be caught so that we can continue our dialogue more fruitfully.

The Trinity as the Basis for Dispersed Authority

When we name the triune God, we are saying a lot of things all at once. On the one hand, we want to say that, on a very basic level, the three Persons of the Trinity all point in the same direction. Jesus does not say something other than what Yahweh says; the Spirit does not take us in a direction other than that of Yahweh and Jesus. Jesus does not tell us that shalom or the decalogue no longer matter, just as Spirit does not tell us that the peace of Christ is now passé. In a profound sense they are all saying the same thing to us. On the other hand, we also want to say that each has a different angle or perspective on our calling as People of God. And each angle is rooted in a different historical and cultural context, and hence in a different stage of the economy of salvation.

Yahweh in the older testament provides us with that large, all-encompassing vision of shalom that involves all life, not just what we do at worship. In scripture we see the history of Yahweh's shalom: that all-inclusive vision of peace, justice, and right relationship expressed through Torah, histories, wisdom, and prophets. We see that the people of God, having been slaves, are to be particularly welcoming to strangers, widows, orphans, and the poor, in every area of life. For example, God's people are to leave sheaves in the fields and to forgive debts every few years. At the heart of the law lies the command to love God and our neighbours. The prophets detail the results of abandoning or pursuing shalom, and help to reconfigure a faith based on the promised land for a people in exile.

Jesus focuses all that shalom on the Body of Christ, which is to be a microcosm of life in the new heaven and the new earth. The Body of Christ is called to exemplify the "peace of Christ," both in its willingness to bridge all prior differences in the one body, and in being an agent of sacrificial reconciliation, a bearer of peace, justice, and right relationship in the world at large. Jesus and the church are new and yet not totally different from what has gone before. They are a radical focusing of the heart of the law in a way that frees us from bondage to laws.

When Jesus leaves this earthly life, he sends the Spirit to lead us into all truth. Spirit, too, is not a total departure from what has gone before, but rather the Spirit of God and of Jesus. And yet Spirit has its own mode of being. As foretold in Jeremiah and Joel, the Spirit will fall on all humankind, young and old, male and female, slave and free, will produce dreams and visions, and will cause us to sing new songs. Jesus himself says in St. John's Gospel, the Spirit blows where it wills and cannot be stopped or controlled. Spirit, who breathed on the face of the deep at creation, continually brings to birth the new creation. Through Peter's dream-vision of the unclean animals, the Spirit presses the Jerusalem Council to let go of the dichotomies of circumcision/uncircumcision, clean/unclean and to accept the Gentiles as equal members in the body. The Spirit continues now to give birth to the new creation, as it did in Genesis. I hear the Spirit in Martin Luther King's "I have a dream," and in John McNeill's *Taking a Chance on God* [1993].

As Christians, we read the Torah deeply from the perspective of Christian freedom from the letter of the law and Christian focus on the heart of the law, which is love of God and neighbour. We also understand that the Spirit is the Spirit of Jesus, forming the new creation, the Body of Christ, as the focus of God's reconciling actions in the world. What that body does, in its gathered as well as in its dispersed life, is still a sign to the world. Most importantly, anything that we recommend to the body as appropriate to Christian life and witness needs to proclaim good news in a way that sounds like the authentic voice of Jesus.

This internal diversity in God's Word to us means that there are healthy internal tensions in our faith: the pull between the gathered body and the whole of society; the pull between honouring the goodness of the whole large creation and acknowledging its need for redemption; the pull between God's Word as it comes to us in the ambiguities of contemporary life and other comings of the Word written up with the certainty of hindsight. Even within each stream, there is a diversity of positions: the tension in the church, for example, between being a community of holiness and a community of inclusion, the tension between grace and works, tensions within the law, and tensions among different strategies for renewal. These are normal and healthy, and are part of the dynamic of our faith.

Experience as Movement of Spirit

To speak of the "appeal to experience" and the "appeal to reason" is a shorthand way of talking about the profound experience of being moved and challenged by our contact with something mysterious which, on reflection, we have discerned to be God's Spirit. I say "mysterious," because I think that spirit is as mysterious as breath and potentially as frightening as wind.

The contact with spirit is often mediated through contacts with persons. When a group comes together for a common purpose, spirit may quicken us, drawing us together in a common effort. When I meet someone who is profoundly moving and congenial to me, I may feel that we are one in spirit, that there is a meeting of spirits. When a new political party comes to power, a spirit may sweep across the electorate, drawing people together and carrying them along. This is the realm of spirit: dreaming and envisioning, coming together and moving to different places. It is mysterious and risky, because we do not always know where we are being blown, and we're aware that there are many spirits in creation, some of them evil. Yet we are called to a willingness to open ourselves to this mysterious realm, so that we may be blown about by God's Spirit and opened to new dreams, new visions, new forms of connection and movement.

But let me be more specific. Many of us who are not gay (especially those of us over a certain age) have probably never spent much time thinking about gay people, but when we have, we were more or less against homosexuality. There was no issue until we actually got to know some gay and lesbian people. We heard their wrenching stories of growing up "different," often considering suicide as an option, painfully coming out to parents and friends. We heard what it felt like to be made to realize that something as profoundly constitutive of self as basic sexual orientation could be wrong. We learned of the damage done by this realization to psyche and self-worth. Over and over again we heard, "I never chose this; I fought against it." I remember a gay man asking, "If I could choose my sexual orientation, why would I choose one that would cause people to beat me up and ostracize me?" We heard how unloved gay and lesbian people felt when even their desire for loving, faithful, and monogamous sexual expression was forbidden as wrong in its very being, not merely in its mode of expression. We heard about the pain of hearing over and over that gay people are pedophiles and perverts, one step away from bestiality. And from those who were trying to maintain faithful and loving sexual relationships, we heard of the strain of having to censor all public expression that might give away the relationship. And, above all, we heard the despairing conviction that "God created me, but did not create me good."

As we have continued the conversation about homosexuality, we have returned to scripture, especially to those passages in the Bible that are used to condemn homosexuality. But when we spoke those words of condemnation or mentally applied them to our gay and lesbian friends, we grew to believe that they were not a good enough answer to the human anguish that we had heard expressed. In short, they were not God's highest and best answer. We then took the risky step of looking elsewhere in scripture. Rather than looking at isolated passages, we began to look at the larger story of the new creation, where old barriers fall down and the formerly alienated are welcomed into the body of Christ. And in so doing we came to see Gentiles, black people, women, Aboriginal people, and now gay and lesbian people being welcomed into the church, not in spite of who they are, but rejoicing in who they are.

Many of us have felt uneasy about this new realization: we can't be absolutely sure whether we are crossing one more cultural barrier in the ongoing new creation of the body, or whether we are crossing the one great divide that will take us definitively away from faith. However, I must say that, so far, it doesn't seem like the latter.

Still, some of the results of our acceptance of gay and lesbian believers can be disconcerting. My sense of the importance of sexual intimacy has been heightened so that I see it now, not as usurping the central role of procreation, yet as equally important in its own right. I now see sexual intimacy as a joining of two different persons, whose "otherness" from one another is not wholly or necessarily the result of difference in gender. One consequence is recognizing that marriage is different from parenting. Another is recognizing that God's shalom includes sexual intimacy, which has the power to offer a glimpse of the new heaven and new earth. I continue to be amazed at gay couples who have maintained their loving commitment when everything in society, even the church, worked against it. For people like me, brought up in the fifties (or earlier), all this is somewhat disconcerting and still feels uncomfortable at times.

Nothing could be further from the truth than that this process of realization was merely a matter of effortlessly going with the flow of secular culture. We did not ask for this revealing experience; we did not seek it. I know that I ran from it for years. But I was chased by something more compelling, something embarrassingly like Francis Thompson's "hound of heaven." I felt driven deeper and deeper into the heart of our faith, far beyond my comfort level, until I had to confront myself too, realizing that the questions are as much about *us* as they are about *them*. Yes, this discomfort has produced in many of us a feeling of community with all those who have struggled with hard decisions in the history of God's people. It has also quickened our faith. It has given rise to a sense of deeply engaging with something of tremendous importance, of seeing God at work in the everyday situations of our lives. Paradoxically, taking our experience and our feelings seriously has led us deeper into scripture and deeper into our tradition.

The experience of being changed by looking into the eyes of

our gay and lesbian fellow believers, of hearing their stories and observing the quality of their lives, recalls similar moments in the history of the church. Word has it that the abolitionist movement in the United States was started by a slave owner who heard the cry of a slave being beaten and suddenly thought, "That sounds human." Out of that experience came an increasing need to struggle against a church and a society that insistently regarded slavery as part of God's divine order. The horrors of the Nazi persecution led finally to a similar awakening and to a shift in the church's regard for Jews. In like instances, going back through Peter's dream to Jesus' welcoming of Gentiles and sinners, a pattern emerges.

I would put it this way: Spirit makes another person so present to us that we are required to return to our faith and find new resources for dealing with the experience. Sometimes we feel bound to revisit our understanding of what is created good and what is not, what is legitimate variation and what is culpable deviation. For example, when pedophilia or murder are at issue, we have concluded that our sympathy for the person does not allow us to accept their actions. Through all of this, we have concluded that our experience of God working in and through our feelings, our dreams, and our connections with other people is one enduring way in which God works in the world and makes God's Word known to us.

"Revisionism" and the Gift of Experience

Those of us who assert the authority of reason and experience as necessary components of theology are sometimes called "revisionists." There's something accurate about the label. We do acknowledge that contemporary experience presses us to look at scripture and tradition in different ways and to find different resources in them. However, "revisionism" is not accurate when it implies that scripture and tradition have been always the same from the beginning, and are only now being suddenly challenged from within the church by a spirit of secularism that does not accept their authority. Of course we accept the authority of scripture and tradition. Indeed, we are formed by scripture and tradition. Scripture provides the fundamental stories and images that shape us as People of God and as Body of Christ, inhabiting our imaginations and enabling us to see the world through eyes of faith.

But scripture and tradition are not somehow opposed to contemporary experience. They are themselves records of other generations' vividly contemporary experience, experience which was every bit as risky and uncertain then as ours is now. When God told Abram to leave Haran and go toward an unknown promised land for the sake of an uncertain progeny, he didn't have written scriptures to rely on. He took a risk, believing that it was God who was encouraging him to go. When the disciples followed Jesus, there was nothing written down to tell them that this was the right thing to do. They took a risk, believing that this person was of God, even though the newness that he represented could seem unacceptably presumptuous. And the apostles, deliberating on Peter's dream, set aside vast tracts of written scripture because of a powerful new experience of God's working among the Gentiles. Beyond the closure of the canon, Christian communities have continued to move out in faith, to allow contemporary experience to draw out the newness of gospel again and again. In fact, the reason the scriptures are written down for us is not to limit us to a perusal of other people's experience, but precisely to train us to look for those moments in our own lives where God might be pushing us to move beyond our comfort zone into a new connection or a new manifestation of life.

Charles Wood says that scripture is an untidy collection of homely stories, examples, and analogies, drawing out different strands of scriptural tradition and ordinary experience, designed to point out God's ways with the world in many different times and contexts. This very untidiness and ambiguity are signs of "the Word made flesh," because to be flesh is to enter into the diversity of times and places. The internal diversity of scripture, says Wood, provides different possible "construals" of exactly what God is saying to us [Wood 1993]. This means that scripture itself is full of different responses in different situations, and a new experience may be the catalyst that reconfigures these into a new resource for a new time.

The diversity of situations and faith responses throughout scripture and tradition is meant to stimulate our imaginations so that we can see other possibilities in our own situations. By the same token, it is the pressure of contemporary experience that forces us to look for possibilities that we had not seen before, as resources for dealing with new situations. So if it is our task to study the scriptures and learn about our tradition, it is also our task to open our senses and feelings to the situations and people around us right now. It is precisely the gift of experience to be rooted in the here and now, to be blown about, to be moved and changed and pushed. This is why New Testament scholar James Dunn notes that we must always beware of "discounting *the creative force of religious experience.*"

> Perhaps the biggest challenge to twentieth-century Christianity is ... to start not from what now is by way of tradition and institution, but instead to be open to that experience of God which first launched Christianity and to let that experience, properly safeguarded as Paul insisted, create new expressions of faith, worship and mission at both individual and corporate level. One thing we may be sure of: the life of the Christian church can go forward only when each generation is able creatively to reinterpret its gospel and its common life out of its own experience of the Spirit and word which first called Christianity into existence [Dunn 1975, 360].

Dunn concludes that the presence of the Spirit will always mean "paradox and conflict" as we allow contemporary experience to interact creatively with scripture and with traditional Christian formulations. Moreover, this paradox and conflict are "the marks of healthy religious experience," and as such are to be nurtured [339]. For this reason, I believe that our contemporary experience of the Spirit is not an option, to be left to charismatics who happen to like that sort of thing, but a necessity for all Christians in all times and places.

It is right, then, to hear the Word in the words spoken by those who have been marginal to the church, black people, women,

Aboriginal people — and gay and lesbian people. The Word that comes through them pushes the prevailing view of the content of faith as it leads us to consider them fully human and full members of the Body of Christ. Our own faith is enriched in turn. No doubt an energetic, explorative reconstrual of the content of faith produces mistakes and errors as well as reflecting genuine movements of God's Spirit. However, I believe that we are called to take that risk. I believe that the polyphonic harmony sung throughout the ages can accommodate some discordant notes, and allow them to expand and deepen the harmonic counterpoint. I believe that opening ourselves to the potential working of the Spirit in our own contemporary experience is *essential* to our identity as Christians; it is not an option.

Discernment as Ongoing Dialogue

The process by which tradition develops in scripture is the dialogue of current reason and experience with past reason and experience. I like the term "discernment" to describe this process. It is a communal process of recognizing what is an authentic expression of God's redemptive work in our world and what is to be recommended to the church as a standard of faith and witness. It is open to the movements of Spirit, and it invites us to follow the directions opened to us by Spirit. Discernment calls us to move past the barriers of custom and habit, to live into the new and unfamiliar, and to test the spirits by seeing what fruits they bear.

After years of dialogue with gay and lesbian people, and now with others in the Dialogue Group, it seems to me that discernment happens in a very concrete way, through the varied responses and comments of other people in the process of dialogue. As many of us struggled with our attitude toward gay and lesbian believers, we heard them say, "That doesn't sound like the voice of Jesus; it is not a life-giving, redeeming word." Troubled by those comments, we had to look for God's own better answer to these people, and in the process changed our own minds and moved to places we had never before anticipated.

From my conservative colleagues in the Dialogue Group, I have heard that the ideal of "love" that I was propounding didn't sound enough like Christ's ideal of love. As I tried to say what I meant, I had to go back to scripture. In that process, I struggled very much to understand Jesus' sacrificial love for us, as well as Yahweh's stern love which calls us to shalom — that all-encompassing ideal of peace, justice, and right relationship. I also had to rediscover the ordinary creaturely importance of love and intimacy in healthy human life. So I arrived back where I began, but with a much more nuanced view of love that is more rooted in the great themes of scripture.

My own ongoing attempt to articulate what we mean by an appeal to experience has been greatly stimulated by the criticism that "experience" is not recognizably Christian language. So it has been very helpful to be driven to find what in scripture and Christian tradition we might be trying to hold onto with the term "experience." The same criticism has been made of language about "human rights," for that too is not of itself biblical language. I have been driven back to scripture and Christian tradition, to find what is perhaps a more complicated way of speaking of human rights, but one which is more firmly rooted in our tradition's concern for the outsider and the Gentile who may well bring a new word from God. I myself believe that human rights language was originally rooted in a Christian conviction that every human person, as a creature of God, had a legitimate claim on — a right to — some degree of fair treatment and quality of life. I understand that we may have expanded the notion of rights to include anything that people want, and that some putative rights may be difficult to enforce legally. But I do believe that if we let go of the language of rights and return to the fundamental Christian concerns out of which rights language developed, we may be better able to talk about what is due to persons in a way that sounds authentically Christian to all of our people.

Nurturing Discerning Dialogue

True dialogue is hard work, made harder by the dawning realization that dialogue, like discernment, will never end. Too often we think that a finite period of dialogue will be followed by a decision that, if it is the right decision, will end the conversation. It is far more likely that dialogue continues as we act, reflect on our actions, make midstream corrections, and keep talking. So it is important to ask ourselves how best to nurture the sort of ongoing dialogue that can produce true Christian discernment.

Respect Another's Experience of Spirit
One of the gifts of experience is a respect for another person's report of having been moved by the Spirit. Yes, we can and should ask critical questions, but we should never slam the door on something that God might be doing in that person's life and, potentially, in ours. Too often our culture teaches us to go for the jugular and to exploit all signs of vulnerability. However, signs of vulnerability or of conceptual confusion are often places of questioning and growth, and they need to be treated with respect. That delicate combination of respectful tenderness and tough critical questioning is one of those life skills that we need to develop if we are to engage in fruitful Christian dialogue.

Continue to be Open to Spirit
I have noticed that most words used in connection with Spirit describe us as being drawn or moved or pushed or blown. This shows that we do not control Spirit; it blows where it will. It means we need to be open at all times to the movement of Spirit, which is likely to come upon us at the most inconvenient times. And it never really ends. When I first joined the Dialogue Group, I had already opened myself to the stories of gay and lesbian people, and my opponents in the Dialogue Group appeared to be just that — opponents. However, as I hear hints of stories that might begin to explain why some Christians feel that the prohibition against homosexuality is essential to their faith, I understand that it is possible

for me to be moved in some way by those stories also. Although I am not convinced at this time that I can change my mind about our need to include our gay and lesbian brothers and sisters, that other awareness makes me want to move carefully so as not to give unnecessary offence. It also prompts me to try even harder to articulate everything that we do in the "common language of the faith."

Train Ourselves to Hear Discernment
Often the initial responses to something we have articulated are rough and hard to take. It is easy to be defensive, and often we have to go through the stage of being defensive. However, it has been my continual experience that, just as I am deciding that I don't need to take account of some comment with which I disagree, suddenly I am hearing it differently and reformulating my position. Many of those comments have stayed with me and continue to prod my thinking. This process has been such a positive experience for me, that I now listen for comments I disagree with and try to live into them. Though this process is never easy, my experience tells me that, eventually, they will bear good fruit for the approach that we are trying to articulate.

Remind Ourselves of Our Eucharistic Identity
Difficult issues easily polarize us into warring camps. It can then be difficult to remember that we are members of the same table-fellowship, and that the whole purpose of the dialogue is to protect and deepen that fellowship. So we find it helpful to find ways of explicitly maintaining that awareness. Of course we begin all meetings of the Dialogue Group with prayer. One of our conservative members has begun the practice of celebrating the eucharist with Integrity, the organization that advocates for gay and lesbian Anglicans, and has continued this over many years. We also make a point of having dinner as a group. The fruit of this is reflected in the comment, made many times by different people, that the table around which we customarily meet is a eucharistic table. In other words, we experience each other as fellow believers, in spite of other disagreements we may have.

Find Other Ways to Connect

When we are deeply engaged in thrashing out a certain issue, it can be easy to let that single issue dominate our perceptions of each other. We have found it helpful to connect with each other around outreach, or liturgy, or other areas of shared Christian concern. The ties that bind Christians are many, and they can help us to put any one disagreement into proper perspective.

Take Time to Live into the Dialogue

Quality dialogue takes a lot of time and energy. When we first began the Dialogue Group, we were very guarded with each other. As we began to say what we really thought about something, we risked giving offence. A very important moment came when we listed conditions under which we would or would not continue the conversation. One of the negative conditions was "drawing a line in the sand" and walking away. We all agreed to try not to do that. And, as we have begun to know each other, we have begun at times to speak of ourselves and of the things that shape our own perceptions and responses. Whenever that has happened, it has taken our dialogue to a new and more profound level.

It is not always easy, of course, to live with diversity. Anyone who lives in relationship with another person knows that sometimes the person you are closest to can seem like the Absolute Other. Bodies, though knit together in intricate ways, don't always move gracefully or in harmony. The grace and the awkwardness, the harmony and the conflict, are all part of our incarnational reality. Moreover, they are in complete continuity with the human lives and situations pictured in scripture. If we can help each other to stay with these difficult processes, perhaps we too can work our way ever deeper into God's will for us, and may bear the fruit of the Spirit as well as the wounds of Christ.

Works Cited

Dunn, James D. G. 1975. *Jesus and the Spirit*. London: SCM.

McNeill, John J. 1996. *Taking a Chance on God: Liberating Theology for Gays, Lesbians, and their Lovers, Families, and Friends*. Boston: Beacon.

Williams, Rowan. 1999. "On Making Moral Decisions." *Sewanee Theological Review* 42:2.

Wood, Charles M. 1993. *The Formation of Christian Understanding: Theological Hermeneutics*. Valley Forge, PA: Trinity Press International.

Stepping Stones
in Faith

A Parish Learns about Reconciliation

MARGARET MARQUARDT *has been parish priest at St. Margaret's Cedar Cottage Anglican Church in east Vancouver since 1985. Ordained for twenty-three years, she has served nationally for the Anglican Church on the Program Committee, on the Residential School's Working Group, and as chair of the EcoJustice Committee. Recently she chaired The Charter for Public Education Panel, which visited over forty communities in the province of British Columbia and heard from the public about the principles of public education. She is married to Jim Circo and they have a seven-year-old son, Thomas Marquardt-Circo.*

On 28 May 2003 Kelly Montfort and Michael Kalmuk had their relationship blessed at their home parish of St. Margaret's Cedar Cottage Anglican Church in Eastside Vancouver. For the first time in the history of the Anglican Communion, the union of a gay couple was blessed with support from the diocese, bishop, parish, and priest. This is the story of what led the parish to this place.

In 1980 the parish building was destroyed by fire. The parishioners joined a neighbouring parish for about a year. There they discussed what the future of St. Margaret's might be. With the archbishop's guidance, they were clear about not rebuilding a replica of the old church, something new had to emerge. Together with the Reverend Fred Thirkell, the priest-in-charge appointed by the archbishop, about twenty people from the original St. Margaret's congregation explored their future. They renovated the former clergy house across the street from the vacant land on which had stood their church building. They created a small chapel and meeting rooms and extra kitchen facilities in the house, which had become their church home. Their willingness to worship and gather in such humble "alternative" space showed their spirit of openness to something new.

In 1985, after I had been volunteering in the parish in neighbourhood outreach while engaged in other work, I was appointed as Incumbent. By this time the parish was maintaining the vacant land as a park for neighbourhood use while exploring options for its future. Meanwhile the parish was functioning fully like any other parish. As we gathered for the eucharist and in parish discussions, it became clear that the parishioners were open to the introduction of inclusive language and varied images of God in the liturgy, as well as to preaching that raised questions regarding the context of scripture. This indicated their willingness to try new directions in discerning their future. I remember well a conversation with one of our older parishioners, Connie Chisholm. She said that the issue of inclusive language was not important to her, but she knew it was to many younger women, and for that reason she was in support. This kind of openness and understanding made the parish welcoming to people who were exploring faith in new ways.

Dennis Lou-Hing, the treasurer, was part of the original group that had returned and begun anew in the house church. He was also a member of Integrity, the gay and lesbian organization in the diocese. His being gay was known but not openly discussed in the parish. He neither hid his sexual orientation nor made it an issue. He was a faithful member of the parish and was trusted by all. As the years went by, the original group was joined by new parishioners, some of whom were gay or lesbian. There was ease in the parish about the diversity of people. The people who came to the parish and stayed, tended to be those who appreciated diversity.

I think this is where leadership is key — leadership by the priest and also by the lay leaders, such as the church committee and wardens. When the leadership is open to asking questions and seeking new insight into faithful living for today, an atmosphere of openness is created and builds. Questioning was a part of Jesus' interaction and stories, and it caused people to think about their assumptions and about the reign of God.

It had become my custom to ask people in the parish to share their journey of faith during our annual focus on stewardship in the parish. They did this during sermon time. One year I asked Dennis Lou-Hing if he would tell his story of faith. I knew that he understood his ministry in the context of his being a gay man. Dennis talked about who God created him to be — a gay man — and how he sought to follow Christ in his daily life and with the parish.

Dennis's generosity in trusting other parishioners with his life and story was another stepping stone along the way for the parish. Not long after this, Dennis's story was featured prominently in *The Province*, a Vancouver newspaper. His willingness to be open in the parish and beyond was of particular help to some of the older parishioners. During one of our later parish discussions about including gay people in the life of the church, I remember one of the older members saying that she didn't know much about homosexuality, but she knew and loved Dennis. This is the value of people entering into real relationships with one another. In a small parish, where there is a commitment to being the church together, we do not have the luxury of dismissing someone because of one aspect of their life that we agree or disagree with or are puzzled about.

About the same time, the Working Group on Gays and Lesbians and the Church, of the Human Rights Unit of the Anglican Church of Canada, published *Our Stories/Your Story* in 1990. It was a thoughtful mix of stories, which a small group of parishioners read and which gave further insight to the parish.

As parish life continued we became involved in many areas of justice locally, nationally, and internationally. In our own neighbourhood, we looked at many options for the land where the former church building had stood. Finally, a partnership was solidified with Coast Housing, an organization that focuses on housing and programs for people with mental illness. We were able, with help from the provincial government, to build social housing as well as a new parish building. A new chapter began for us in 1995 with the move into the new building. Meanwhile, as gay or lesbian people joined the parish, they were for the most part open about their sexual orientation, in the natural way that people have in sharing important aspects of their lives with others. This contributed to the deepening of relationships and to the diversity of the parish. Gay and lesbian people were accepted like everyone else.

During this time, some members of the parish were asked to serve on Anglican national committees. One of these committees produced the study, *Hearing Diverse Voices, Seeking Common Ground*, which included the stories of Anglican gays and lesbians. Our parish took part in the study and gave an evaluation. In this way we gave leadership to the larger community and had the experience also of deepening our understanding of ourselves as a community. The parish was becoming clearer about its call in this particular area, as well as other areas of social and economic justice.

In 1996 an opportunity came for the parish to invite an openly gay priest (who was in a committed relationship) to become an honorary associate. The church committee decided to have a couple of meetings with the parish as a whole to discuss the idea. Dr. Donald Meen, a psychologist and a gay member of the church committee, was asked to facilitate the discussion because his leadership is open and invites participation. For some time we have been developing a style of discussion that invites people to say what they wish, or to ask questions, without any pressure to conformity. The basis for this style of discussions is respect in the midst of difference. The parish has learned that it is not only "outcome" that is vital in moving forward as a parish. Equally important is how we arrive at the outcome. Our community life is deepened and strengthened by the way we work on particular issues. The process we engaged in for the discussion allowed for differences. The church committee had specifically decided not to have a vote at the end because votes can result in a feeling of winners and losers. Instead, there would be an informal show of hands. There was concern that people should feel free not to raise their hand if they didn't want to.

At the first meeting, some gay and lesbian members spoke of the positive role model it would be for them to have an openly gay priest. Others asked questions about what this would mean for the parish: Could we still have other associates? Would we be labelled as a gay church? What would this mean for inclusivity and diversity? At the second meeting, after further discussion, parishioners were asked to give an informal show of hands on whether they wanted the church committee to pursue the request with the bishop. Some people were strongly in favour. Some were less so, but for the well-being of the parish and out of respect for gay and lesbian members of the parish, still gave their support. Some were not sure but felt free to not raise their hands. As it turned out, there was general support, and the church committee and I made the request to the bishop.

The bishop responded by explaining that he had to turn down the request because of the guidelines in place in the Anglican Church of Canada. The parish of course knew the guidelines but had wanted to indicate our hope for eventual change. Parishioners met with the bishop and expressed our sorrow and concern that it was still not possible for a parish that was ready to welcome an openly gay priest to have one. It was a difficult time for us. The experience of injustice toward homosexual people hurt the whole community.

During the time of our parish discussions, there was a "Day of Dialogue on Homosexuality" in the diocese. A small group from the parish attended. In some groups, counsellors were present. However, their role was unclear. Afterward, the church committee wrote to the diocesan council expressing our concerns about the role of the counsellors and their professional background. The diocesan council responded by setting up a process with leadership from professionals, including Dr. Donald Meen from our parish. This led to the establishment of ethical guidelines for the diocese regarding counselling.

Meanwhile, the parish church committee began to explore what we were being called to as a community on the matter of inclusion of gay and lesbian people and their relationships in the wider church. This was in accord with our normal practice of trying to discern through prayer and discussion what justice requires on any issue and what our role should be. Our experience has taught us that you take one step at a time and then assess where you are.

The issue of justice for homosexual people did not feel "out there" for our parishioners. In a small parish where there is a desire to know others, labels don't work. We are all Christians seeking to serve Christ in our own lives and together as a Christian community. Gay and lesbian parishioners were involved in the ministries of the parish as Christian brothers and sisters and members of the Body of Christ. They were serving on the altar guild, as teachers in the church school, as administrators of the eucharist, readers, prayer leaders, sidespeople, on the church committee, and as wardens.

The church committee continued discussing ways to indicate our commitment to the full inclusion of homosexual people in the life of the church. We thought about what was done in the United Church of Canada, where congregations named themselves "affirming" to indicate their commitment. By late 1997 the picture was becoming clearer about what our commitment might look like. We began to ask new questions. The church committee minutes on 21 January 1998 include the following questions:

What would it mean to be a "welcoming congregation"?
What do we need to do?
Who would we contact?
Would we want to be affiliated with anyone else?

That meeting recommended that there be some public acknowledgement of ourselves as a "reconciling" or "welcoming" congregation or "a congregation walking with integrity." But we wanted to be sure that the whole congregation was included in the discussion of this possibility. A small committee was asked to formulate a motion for the annual vestry of 1998, which would include a public description of ourselves as an affirming parish and some acknowledgement that our denomination does not allow us to act fully upon this affirmation. The small group proposed the

Methodist Church language of "reconciling" because it named the ongoing process of seeking justice that the parish would be undertaking in pressing for the full inclusion of gay and lesbian Christians in the life of the church. Calling ourselves a "Reconciling Community" indicated the work we needed to continue to do within our own parish and as members of the diocese, and within the larger Anglican Church. St. Margaret's Church Committee took the following motion to the annual vestry meeting, 15 February 1998, where it was supported with overwhelming enthusiasm:

> Mindful of our baptismal promise to strive for justice and peace among all people and respect for the dignity of every human being, the Parish of St. Margaret's, Cedar Cottage, commits itself to be a Reconciling Community.
>
> *A Reconciling Community:*
> *a.* affirms the full participation of all its members in the life of the church regardless of sexual orientation;
> *b.* commits itself to work for the realization of this affirmation in the practice of the church; and
> *c.* names itself publicly as a "Reconciling Community" to indicate its commitment.

A eucharist was held on 28 June 1998 at St. Margaret's to publicly name ourselves as a reconciling community. We had greetings from guests invited from many groups within the church and larger community. That day the sermon time was shared by gay, lesbian, and heterosexual lay leaders and priests. I ended my sermon that day with these words:

> Our becoming a Reconciling Community is a symbol of what we are seeking and hoping for the whole church ... that we would find ways of celebrating the uniqueness of each person in the integrity of their sexual orientation, supporting those in relationships, and receiving with delight the gifts of all among us.

The invocation offered at the beginning of the eucharist was prayed by all:

O God, we have rejoiced in the stories of your faithfulness. We pray that you will so increase the hearing of our ears, the perception of our eyes, the compassion of our hearts, and the willingness of our hands, that stories of our faithfulness might reach your ears, and you, too, might rejoice.

At the diocesan level, St. Margaret's worked with St. Paul's in the west end and with Christ Church Cathedral, beginning in 1998, to bring a motion favouring the blessing of same-gender unions before diocesan synod. The final vote of the New Westminister diocesan synod of June 2002 indicated a substantial majority of synod in favour. The bishop, the Right Reverend Michael Ingham, continuing his efforts to reconcile parishes and clergy who did not support the synod motion, waited until just before synod 2003 to give permission to six parishes that had indicated (through a special vestry called for this specifc purpose) their desire to conduct covenant services for gay and lesbian couples.

During the five-year period leading up to the final vote in 2002, there was ample opportunity for people in the diocese to engage in dialogue on the issue of homosexuality and specifically what constituted a blessing. The bishop, in consultation with a diverse body in the diocese (including the clergy from St. Paul's, Christ's Church Cathedral, and St. Margaret's), set up three commissions in the diocese: one to consider the theological issues involved, another to consider the canonical implications, and a third to hear and record the voices of lesbian and gay Christians. The bishop, with volunteer facilitators led by an able staff person, set up an eighteen-month process in the diocese in which parishes were twinned in order to encourage dialogue.

St. Margaret's participated in two ways: as a parish involved in the dialogue process, and by providing significant numbers of people to participate in the Gay and Lesbian Voices Commission. Dr.

Donald Meen and I were asked by Bishop Michael to be co-chairs of the Gay and Lesbian Voices Commission.

As well as gay and lesbian members, that commission included one person who described herself as ex-gay, two parents of gay children, and heterosexual people who were in support of the full inclusion of gay and lesbian people in the life of the church. All members of the Voices Commission were members of the diocese of New Westminster. The role of the participants was to attend the parish groupings and to tell their stories. It was a powerful and courageous gift that they gave the church. They laid their lives open to all. The other offering of the Voices Commission was a video which specifically focused on what the blesisng of a same-gender union would mean to gay and lesbian members of the church.

During the winter of 2001 to 2002 members of our parish, along with the president of Integrity/Vancouver, began to work on a liturgy for the blessing of a same-gender couple that we would offer to the bishop for consideration. The Reverend Dr. Richard Leggett of the Vancouver School of Theology was asked to be our liturgical resource and guide in the process. I facilitated the process, and about eight gay and lesbian people reflected on the meaning of covenant to them. Various people brought prayers. Dr. Leggett listened and put shape to the reflection. There was much thoughtful discussion on gay and lesbian people's experience of the struggle for recognition, on what liberation meant personally, both for a couple and to the community, and how this could be reflected in the liturgy of a covenant. The liturgy was eventually offered to the bishop, and with some change became the liturgical rite authorized for use in the diocese in the blessing of a same-gender union.

At the diocesan synod on 14 June 2002, a clear majority voted to offer a liturgy of covenant for homosexual couples. The motion at synod allowed a process by which those parishes and priests who wanted to have the permission of the bishop to offer the liturgy could receive it. It also made clear provision for those who were opposed to the motion. As well, a bishop under our diocesan bishop's authority was made available for pastoral purposes to those parishes who were finding difficulty with this motion and what it meant for the church. Bishop Michael spoke to synod on 15 June, the morning following the synod vote:

> The synod of the diocese of New Westminster has now made a clear decision about the pastoral care of Anglicans in this part of Canada.
>
> We have voted not to compel but to permit those parishes that wish to celebrate permanent, intimate, loving relationships between persons of the same sex to do so in recognition of the God-given goodness of their sacred mutual commitments; and to permit those parishes who stand in continuity with the historic practice of the church, and with biblical truth as they sincerely believe it, to do so without compulsion, with full protection of conscience, and with the pastoral support of episcopal ministry.
>
> We are not compromising the Christian faith nor relativising its moral teachings. We are extending to gay and lesbian Christians the same freedom that is enjoyed by others to commit their lives to Jesus Christ together, and the same obligation to grow in the costly demands of love.

After the synod's decision, St. Margaret's parish acted quickly, for pastoral reasons, in calling a special vestry meeting.

A lesbian couple at St. Margaret's wanted to have the blessing on Thanksgiving weekend of 2002. In order to be ready when the bishop gave permission for the blessings, we did the necessary preparation and held a special vestry on 14 July 2002. I chose to hold the discussion during the sermon time because I wanted it to be contained within a liturgical framework of thanksgiving and prayer. And indeed it was that! Members of the congregation spoke of a "kairos time" — a time for new beginnings for the church, a time of liberation, a time to allow for various ways in which the church could be the church. They spoke of the wisdom of the synod motion in allowing for different paths for different congregations.

Since it was a formal meeting of vestry, we needed to record a vote. Before the vote, we had a time of silent prayer. The motion was a follows:

> That the parish of St. Margaret's Cedar Cottage request that Bishop Michael Ingham authorize the use of a Rite for the Blessing of Same-Sex Unions in this parish.

The vote was unanimous! I expressed my support. Subsequently a letter was sent to the bishop requesting permission to offer a liturgy of blessing. We did not receive permission in time for the lesbian couple, and they had a service of blessing in a United Church on Thanksgiving weekend in 2001. Permission was given to our parish, and to five others that had requested it, on 26 May 2003.

In the previous December, a gay couple in the parish, Kelly Montfort and Michael Kalmuk, had celebrated their twenty-first anniversary with a parish eucharist followed by a reception attended by friends, church members, colleagues, and family. At the service I said we had hoped that the Rite of Blessing would have been available, but since it wasn't, we were glad to gather with Michael and Kelly, and to thank God on their anniversary, for their life together, and for their community of friends and family. I said how sorry I was for the church's treatment of homosexual people, and for the experience of shame that many gay and lesbian people have felt personally, and as couples, because their lives together had not been acknowledged. I also affirmed that God had already blessed their lives. We see the fruits of the Spirit when the Spirit is present.

The eucharist on that occasion in December 2001 did not include the exchange of vows or rings. For that we waited until permission was given by the bishop for the Rite of Blessing. When it came on 26 May 2003, we were ready. Two days later, on 28 May 2003, a smaller and more intimate circle of church members and members of Integrity gathered and, using the diocese of New Westminster *Liturgy for the Celebration of Gay and Lesbian Covenants*, we witnessed the vows exchanged between Michael Kalmuk and Kelly Montfort. It was an experience of liberation. It also felt like something that we already had known for a long time. We shared in the bread and wine as Michael Kalmuk sang "Broken for you." It was a joyous moment when these two, who have been partners for twenty-one years, were able in their own church to name their commitment to each other before God and the gathered community. Finally, we could participate as a church with God in bringing about justice and ending discrimination.

Our parish will continue to seek the Spirit's guidance on what it means to be a reconciling community in our society and our world. We hope to continue to discuss things and to follow through with action in ways that allow for diversity in the Body of Christ. Faithfulness is not about sameness. It is, I believe, about finding the will of God together in this beautiful but broken world that God has given us, a world in which Christ is present with us and in all of us.

The song "Now is the Time," a favourite of the congregation, speaks of our sense of this "kairos" moment — a moment of God's breaking in:

Refrain: Come to us, you who say, "I will not forget you."
Be with us, you who say, "Do not be afraid."
Take hold of us, our hearts, our minds, our whole being.
Make us your own, now is the time.

Spirit of love, crush the pain of hatred.
Spirit of hope, stand before our eyes.
Spirit of light, dance within our darkness.
Make us your own. Now is the time

[Copyright 1998, Tom Kendzia. Published by OCP Publications. Used with permission.]

Works Cited

Alexander, Scott W., ed. 1990. *The Welcoming Congregation: Resources for Affirming Gay, Lesbian, and Bisexual Persons.* Boston: The Unitarian Universalist Association.

Our Stories/Your Story. 1990. A Resource by the Working Group on Gays and Lesbians and the Church of the Human Rights Unit of the Anglican Church of Canada.

"Sowing Seeds of Inclusion." 1997. *Open Hands: Resources for Ministries Affirming Diversity of Human Sexuality.* Vol. 12, no. 7 (Winter).

ABC Publishing
ANGLICAN BOOK CENTRE

Also available from ABC Publishing:

The Homosexuality Debate
Faith Seeking Understanding
Catherine Sider Hamilton, editor
How do we understand homosexuality? This issue touches on the
foundations of Christian faith and the context in which it is lived.
The authors of these essays represent a wide range of views. All
express a passionate concern for the church in this time of crisis,
and offer a sign of hope in this divisive debate.
ISBN 1-55126-397-1 $24.95

Discerning the Word
The Bible and Homosexuality in Anglican Debate
Paul Gibson
Focusing on the 1998 Lambeth Conference resolutions on scripture and sexuality, Paul Gibson examines the way cultural norms
influence our understanding of biblical authority. He issues a challenge to the church, and proposes a way forward that honours
scripture, tradition, and our evolving culture.
1-155126-320-3 $16.95

An Honourable Estate
Marriage, Same-Sex Unions, and the Church
Christopher Cantlon and Pauline Thompson, editors
An informative resource for Christians concerned about non-
traditional relationships and homosexuality and the church's
response. Includes open-ended questions, suggested scripture passages, and case studies to assist thoughtful discussion.
1-55126-158-8 $16.95

Hearing Diverse Voices, Seeking Common Ground
Anglican Church of Canada
Attempts to take seriously the biblical record and current biblical scholarship; Anglican tradition; current scientific research and understanding; and the witness of gay and lesbian Anglicans.
1-55126-112-X $16.95

Visit our web site
www.abcpublishing.com

Available from your diocesan or local bookstore or
Anglican Book Centre
Email abc@national.anglican.ca or Phone 1-800-268-1168